IN THE PRESENCE OF GRIZZLIES

The Ancient Bond Between Men and Bears

DOUG AND ANDREA PEACOCK

T0346492

THE LYONS PRESS
GUILFORD, CONNECTICUT
AN IMPRINT OF THE GLOBE PEQUOT PRESS

For ELK

The Lyons Press is an imprint of The Globe Pequot Press.

Text design by Nancy Freeborn
Layout by Ann F. Courcy
Project manager: John Burbidge

This book was previously published as *The Essential Grizzly: The Mingled Fates of Men and Bears* (2006)

Library of Congress Cataloging-in-Publication Data
Peacock, Doug.
   In the presence of grizzlies : sharing our world with the great bear / Doug and Andrea Peacock. -- Rev. and updated.
      p. cm.
   Rev. ed. of The essential grizzly. c2006.
   ISBN 978-1-59921-490-0
   1. Grizzly bear. I. Peacock, Andrea. II. Peacock, Doug. Essential grizzly. III. Title.
   QL737.C27P3657 2009
   599.784--dc22

                                                                                2008045953

Printed in the United States of America

10 9 8 7 6 5 4 3 2 1

CONTENTS

INTRODUCTION

■■ Since the dawn of human consciousness, great beasts have prowled the shadows of our primal campfires. They stalked us as prey on the African savanna, lingered near the mouths of our caves in Pleistocene Europe, and traveled with us across Beringia into the New World. They were our talismans, our monsters, and our mentors. The creatures hunted us, as we hunted them. They were there at the origins of hominid religious practice, and we scratched their images on the innermost walls of the first human art galleries. They were lions, crocodiles, and tigers. But mostly they were bears.

Of all the animals who challenged (and on occasion hunted) the upright ape, bears are the most humanlike. They share many physical characteristics with people: the rear paw track that looks like our own bare footprint, the upright stance, dexterous forepaws, and binocular vision. A skinned bear carries an eerie resemblance to a human corpse.

Bears are as big or bigger than humans and are called *same-size predators*. Because bears and men shared a similar omnivore diet, they lived in the same places. Neanderthals occupied the rock shelters of cave bears (*Ursus spelaeus*), and sometimes the bones of men and bears were interred together, mingled in the same graves. Everywhere in the Northern Hemisphere that early humans ventured, they found the tracks of brown bears (*Ursus arctos*). Pleistocene people followed these trails to northeastern Asia, and when human beings crossed over into North America, they walked in the footprints of bears.

The concurrent colonization of North America by brown bears and humans is a remarkable story. Both men and grizzlies came out of Siberia at about the same time, crossed over the land bridge to Pleistocene Alaska (the ice-free area of the Bering Strait and adjacent lands were known as Beringia), lived together for thousands of years, and perhaps traveled the same route south to the continental United States. Genetic evidence indicates a single invasion for both grizzlies and humans, with brown bears coming over the Bering Strait fifty or sixty thousand years ago and the first humans arriving some twenty thousand years later.

In Alaska the brown bear encountered an arctic-steppe environment, much like Siberia. Unlike Siberia, gigantic short-faced bears prowled the tundra along with other transcontinental carnivores. Adapting over time to this open periglacial habitat, the Asian-European brown bear evolved into a North American subspecies, *Ursus arctos horribilis,* also known as the grizzly bear. The changes to the bear were more behavioral than physical. In this treeless land, it is theorized, mother grizzlies had to protect their cubs against lions, wolves, other bears, and several now-extinct predators. Consequently they became more aggressive. The best defense was a good offense: Grizzlies often charged and, when they needed to, attacked threats to their young.

Whereas humans may have used three different routes to arrive in the contiguous states from Alaska, grizzlies came down the Rockies to Alberta before the ice sheets coalesced. A single brown bear cranial fragment from a gravel quarry outside Edmonton, Alberta, radiocarbon-dated to about twenty-six thousand years ago. Genetic analysis indicates the bear was related to a lineage living in eastern Beringia thirty-five thousand years ago. Grizzlies from Alaska never made it down the Northwest coast fifteen thousand years ago nor down the ice-free corridor that opened between the ice sheets some two thousand years later.

Thus the grizzly arrived in the contiguous states at least twenty-six thousand years ago and by historic times ranged everywhere in the West; as far south as Durango, Mexico; and east across the Great Plains to the Mississippi River. The only animal more adaptive—the two-legged primate—spread all the way to the far edges of North and South America. The timing and shape of these journeys are controversial.

The one uncontestable fact, however, is that within this vast range and across a time span of at least twelve thousand years, grizzlies and humans have been together. Until the appearance of European firearms, man and grizzly coexisted in North America, living in the same places and eating the same foods. People have always known bears. They have been out there since the beginning, just beyond the light of the fire. On a continent with no other primates, they are our closest wild companions.

■■ Prior to European contact, as many as one hundred thousand grizzly bears are estimated to have roamed portions of the lower forty-eight states. They were on the brink of crossing the Mississippi River into the eastern states; on the southern tip, the Mexican brown bear was poised to pioneer the jungle habitats of Central America and eventually colonize the Andes. European firearms put an end to this ursine expansion.

As a highly flexible omnivore capable of complex learning behavior, the grizzly occupied virtually every bioregion within this huge range except the lowest, hottest areas of the Mojave and Sonoran Deserts. Perhaps the highest densities of grizzlies lived in what is now California, especially the foothills of the Sierras and the great chaparrals where there were rumored to be ten thousand bears. Present-day archaeologists are discovering that these areas also supported the greatest numbers of native Californians; hence we know that grizzlies and early people lived in close proximity. The settlement pattern of Indians occupying the same river bottoms favored by the American brown bear was generally true throughout the West.

Spaniards were the first Europeans to encounter grizzlies in California. But it was the Lewis and Clark expedition that set the standard for subsequent human-grizzly encounters: They killed some forty-three bears, mostly for sport, and shot and wounded many more. Since then, the great bears have pretty much been shot on sight by settlers, poisoned on the range, and trapped and hounded out until the 1920s and 1930s, by which time they were eliminated from most of their territory. This extermination was facilitated by bounties paid out by ranchers and government agencies. By the time the same agencies questioned whether we should keep any around, the grizzly bear was on his way out: The last grizzlies of record in California were killed in 1922; Oregon, in 1931; Arizona, in 1935; and so on. A few pockets of survivors persisted; I found old grizzly sign in Chihuahua, Mexico, in 1985 and observed, with others, a likely grizzly track in the Chalk Mountains of southwestern Colorado in 1991. Those last bears are probably gone now.

Today, grizzlies survive in 1 percent of their former range in the continental United States, occupy most of their historic territory in Canada, and roam throughout Alaska. About a thousand now live south of Canada, although that number could be a few hundred more or less. Nearly all these grizzlies live in two ecosystems, the cores of which are Yellowstone and Glacier National Parks. A handful of animals hang on, perilously close to extinction, in three or four other ecosystems near the Canadian border. Another forty to sixty thousand brown bears may live in Canada (mostly in British Columbia) and Alaska.

A comment about grizzly bear numbers: All are estimates, usually based on extrapolations of smaller population units by people doing their best to come up with a reasonable and educated guess. Conservationists usually tend to find fewer bears, while the highest estimates of grizzly populations come from provincial and state game departments responsible for selling bear-hunting licenses.

A similar note about the written historic record of grizzlies: It is incomplete and selective. Often early pioneers, mountain men, trappers, and settlers left no documentation. Hence maps of the historic range of grizzlies may indicate areas where no written record of grizzlies exists, but ethnology and prehistoric rock art show the great bear indeed roamed the scene. The Owens Valley of California and portions of the Colorado Plateau are examples where the written record is absent but native traditions abound.

The grizzly is a thing of beauty and grace, a magnificent beast in his own right who is capable of stirring deep reverence and humility in humans. The awe-inspiring bear is, however, married to danger. For thirteen thousand years (following the demise of the megafauna), grizzly bears occupied the top of the food pyramid in North America, their dominance barely contested until the nineteenth century. This is the one animal who challenged human impulses to extend our dominion over all lands and creatures, informing us that we still live close to but not quite at the top of that pyramid. In that, they take us back to the dawn of hominid consciousness: They are a reminder of the ancient fear of falling prey to a wild beast. This primal awareness has helped direct the evolution of human intelligence throughout all time.

Of course, a walk through grizzly country these days is safer than a stroll down most any city street in America. The contemporary fact that we don't live day by day among same-size predators anymore, and that predation by grizzlies upon people is virtually unknown, does not banish this hardwired organic trepidation from our brains. It's still in there.

Other continents are yet prowled and cruised by an assortment of creatures that are reminiscent of that original dread, the so-called "man-eaters": lions, tigers, sharks, leopards, crocodiles, a few big snakes, the Komodo dragon. On our continent, we have bears.

The relatively harmless black bear (*Ursus americanus*) actually kills and occasionally eats people. The predatory polar bear hunts down pretty much whatever it can catch, including a rare and unfortunate ecotourist, oil worker, or Inuit. But it is the grizzly who is the most dangerous to man. By far, they account for the most injuries to humans, including a few deaths. This isn't much: On average, grizzlies kill fewer than one person a year. But it happens.

Worldwide, mosquitoes kill the most people. Bees, snakes, and scorpions also get a few human victims—a lot more than bears do. A couple of American hunters or photographers fall to stampeding moose or bison each year or so. On the other hand, the grizzly is a big, smart, humanlike omnivore who inspires in man a psychological reaction dissimilar to our response to these accidental killers. Here is one animal who still has the power to radically alter our perception of the world around us. An encounter with our most dangerous of land mammals offers the quintessential American wildlife experience. This is the one adventure still guaranteed to focus all our modern attention on the present.

It is a presumption, although a reasonable one, to suggest grizzlies made meat of man during the last twenty-some thousand years of their coexistence in North America. Predation by bears upon humans was no doubt a rare occurrence, although a familiar fear in that such attacks constitute the stuff of myth and storytelling. The spiritual power of these legends survives in the ethnographic record of Western tribes.

That record suggests Native Americans deliberately courted confrontations with bears, and those who weathered the encounters came away complete in soul and utterly alive. Traditional relationships with wild animals were contractual and based on reciprocity. You ferreted out the bear to get something, and if you survived, you gained wisdom and power. Now, at the beginning of the twenty-first century, the possibility of engaging the grizzly still lurks in the shadows of our diminishing wildlands. What value does this ancient enactment hold for modern humans?

■■ It is the thesis of this book that preserving the possibility of such an experience is of considerable value. Indeed, we suspect that the conservation of wild, sometimes dangerous animals is essential to rational thought, even the survival of our own species. The emotional mind-set behind reason is humility, a condition almost automatically guaranteed by a walk in grizzly country. The simple observation that the great bear is still out there is in itself a counterbalance to human arrogance and greed—the attitudes that have led us to the highest rate of species extinction in history, to overpopulation, and to damage to the health and viability of the biosphere. These are big claims that warrant scrutiny.

Grizzlies are rightly touted as indicators of ecological balance, as an umbrella species whose protection embraces the entire ecosystem. They are a native species with as much right to exist as we do. We should fight to preserve them for all these reasons.

It might also be a good idea for us to keep a few around for selfish purposes. A half century ago, wildlife ecologist Aldo Leopold pointed out that when we see a harmony in nature that works, "something we like but don't understand, then who but a fool would discard seemingly useless parts? To keep every cog or wheel is the first precaution of intelligent tinkering."

That entity we so tout as setting us apart from all other animals, our consciousness—the human mind itself—evolved within a continuing habitat, one shared by creatures like bears. In North America, we refer to the remnants of this habitat as *wilderness*. That which evolves seldom persists without sustaining the conditions of its genesis. Human awareness was shaped by the elephants we hunted and by the great cats and bears who sometimes hunted us. So as the wolf sculpts caribou evolution, what today hones our organic intelligence that was born of hunting?

▪▪ My wife, Andrea, and I had been interested in working on a project together for some time, melding her experience as a skilled interviewer and accomplished journalist with my background as a writer, activist, and observer of bears. Grizzlies have become a major focus in our daily lives, and we decided to combine our voices, attempting to use a reasonable division of labor to tell our story. Hence Andrea is the primary voice when it comes to talking with wildlife photographers, biologists, hunters, zookeepers, and the like. Wrapped around all this material are my stories of individual grizzlies. I also wrote "Fear of Bears" and the epilogue, "Practical Considerations in Grizzly Country." I added the latter material because I consider it of value, even though these informal notes lie outside the structure of this book.

We intend to use a broad spectrum of modern human–grizzly bear relationships to demonstrate how the great bear prowls the landscape of the contemporary mind. They remind us of where we have been, the value of that which is untamed, and of our natural place in the world. We spoke with all kinds of people who live and work intimately with grizzly bears: ranchers, photographers, animal trainers, biologists, wildlife managers, those who don't want bears around, and those who fight to keep grizzlies on the land. Through these conversations, we explore the passionate, complex, and cantankerous world of grizzly politics.

Even among modern conservationists dedicated to saving the grizzly, people argue about how bears should be represented to the wider world, about how dangerous grizzlies really are. On one edge of the debate is the message that bears are fundamentally safe to be around, loveable, on occasion even cuddly. This contention, as far as it goes, is often true and is necessary to offset the glut of overexploited killer-bear stories. Today we have a small library of such ursine snuff books. The shocking titillation misrepresents fact and, no doubt, creates unreasonable fear of wild animals.

Another approach is to take an unflinching look at that minuscule element of risk, the small but very real amount of danger in walking grizzly country, and argue that preserving the opportunity to experience face-to-face encounters with large carnivores, even those who on rare occasions size up *Homo sapiens* as chow, is important. Accordingly, we investigate the stories of people who had the misfortune to have been mauled by bears and examine tales of grizzly bear hunters who seek them out as the most dangerous and valued trophy on the continent. These ancient contracts yet prowl the wild landscape; as long as the bear persists, the possibilities endure.

So, what of the bear itself? It's one thing to hear what people have to say about grizzlies, even to read the information and data gathered by biologists; but the real animal out there on the mountain lives in a complete world only partially revealed by our science. As perhaps the most adaptable, flexible, and intelligent four-legged mammal on the continent, the grizzly must make daily decisions about food, travel, and survival. Grizzlies are constantly navigating a dangerous human landscape. They appear to have a map in their head and are the masters of seasonality. In all these activities, they seem to be thinking, and we can only guess at what.

I have written three bear portraits. These fictional stories are composites of grizzlies I observed and came to know; time and real events are often compressed into the experience of a single bear. Nonetheless, the tales are cast against a factual background of geographical and biological accuracy. The portraits span the past three decades: a dominant male grizzly who lived in Glacier National Park throughout the 1980s; a female bear who witnessed the great fires of 1988 and the mid-1990s reintroduction of the wolf in Yellowstone; and, the most recent, a contemporary sketch of a young male grizzly exploring the Montana-Idaho borderland in an attempt to escape the geographical island that is the Yellowstone ecosystem. Although the intention here is to suggest and illustrate the inner grizzly, many scenes are informed guesses. The portraits' origins are the bedtime stories I made up to entertain my children and lull them to sleep. Over time, they were embellished and expanded with the advantage of real experience. Biologist Lance Craighead was asked to read the portraits; he, too, slept well and registered no large complaint with the plausibility of the stories.

We have retained the traditional usage of *boar* and *sow* to denote adult male and female bears, as if they were a domestic animal, which they emphatically are not. My old friend and mentor, the great American thinker Paul Shepard, pointed out to me that the terms were probably used for bears first, and the word *boar* may be traced to the same origin as *bear*. Shepard, writing with his colleague Barry Sanders, noted, "[The bear] is a kind of ideogram of man in the wilderness, as though telling of what we were and perhaps what we have lost; wily, smart, strong, fast, agile, independent in ways that we humans left behind when we took up residence in the city."

■■ The future of the American grizzly depends upon what value we urban-dwelling people place in keeping viable populations of grizzlies on the continent. The duality of the independence and intelligence of grizzlies combined with their low reproductive rate and vulnerability to humans means we must grant them vast areas of roadless habitat to live in. They are not animals that we can bend easily to our human agendas or manage as we do whitetail deer. Grizzlies require large wilderness areas. In the areas south of Canada, this is a problem: All grizzly bear ecosystems in the lower forty-eight are being gnawed away at the edges and fragmented by industrial and commercial development. They are becoming islands of genetic and geographic isolation. Saving the grizzly will therefore require great human restraint and tolerance.

And why should we save them at all? Larger problems loom over the planet: In many places the air is poisoned, the oceans are overfished, and climate change threatens both men and bears. We are commonly besieged, and all the progress and economic growth on Earth isn't worth the sacrifice of those natural systems that keep both grizzlies and us alive. Is it possible our species no longer correctly perceives what lies in our own self-interest for longtime survival? The difficult answer to that question will entail prodigious strength and wisdom. From what inspiration might the requisite human resistance emerge? We could look to the bear. If we can't save grizzlies out of altruism, we must save them for the not-so-simple fact that we cannot live without them. Our fates—the clever modern human and our ancient companion in the fur coat—remain as mingled as the bones in the cave.

THE BLACK GRIZZLY

▦▦ The big bear moves through the shadows cast by wedges of spruce boughs now fading against the darkening sky. He travels a familiar trail. The grizzly sniffs the ground, detecting the stale scent of man. Hikers sometimes use the same path several times a week during the summer. But not now. It is nearly dark and the knee-high bracken fern carry the sweet reek of the first September frost. The human season is over.

The dark grizzly is traveling to a small mountain range fifteen miles away, where huckleberries abound. He has made this late-summer journey every year since he was a five-year-old. In the sunlight, his coat is dark brown with silver guard hairs when backlit, but here in the evening shadows he looks black. Now, having slumbered through seventeen Rocky Mountain winters, the grizzly glories in his prime years. At nearly six hundred pounds, he is about as big as grizzlies grow on wild foods in Glacier National Park. He would measure nearly four feet at the shoulder if anyone had had the opportunity to gauge him with a tape, which they have not.

The trail dumps out of the timber and down into a small clearing. The huge grizzly pauses momentarily, reaching up with his great barrel of a snout to smell the evening air, then snorts and hops, bounding down the path, sliding stiff legged on the loose alluvium, swinging his head wildly from side to side, his mouth open and relaxed, as if in joyful anticipation of this season of abundance. Across the valley, up in the high scrub fields, the berries will be ready.

The Black Grizzly stops at a muddy wallow on the edge of the small meadow. In the mud are the prints of four other bears: a female grizzly traveling with her yearling cub, a black bear registering his smaller, rounded track, and another younger grizzly. His own tracks outsize the others twofold, and one of his eleven-inch rear prints reveals a skewed outer claw and a faint line across the pad. He sniffs the tracks, identifying the fetor of the four animals, especially the sow. He knows this female. There is the slightest bristling of fur on the back of his neck.

Within the immense olfactory universe of the bear, there are secret connections hidden from the outside world. All grizzlies in a region seem to know one another and, within a given area or population, where they stand in terms of a dominance hierarchy. Grizzlies range widely; here on the edge of Glacier Park, the Black Grizzly's range covers more than four hundred square miles. A mother bear's home range might be less than a hundred. Within the overlapping ranges, there are pockets rich in seasonal foods, sources used by many different grizzlies at the same time. Should a moose or elk die or get killed this time of year, a dozen bears might vie for the protein-rich carcass. Competition creates the hierarchy, usually with a big male as the alpha animal. Other large males, sows with cubs, solitary adults, and subadults (bears who have separated from their mothers but have not reached reproductive maturity, generally two to four years old) occupy the lower end of the scale.

Competition also occurs among the bigger boars during the mating season in late May and June. Fights break out. Older males often carry deep facial scars that speak of these battles

Our biology has only glimpsed the tip of the grizzly's capacity for sociability. A single sniff of cool air, however, provides a grizzly with all the information he needs to know if the other animal is a bear to avoid, seek out, or dominate.

The dark grizzly is the alpha bear of this entire watershed. The land is fat. In this time of ripeness, he fears nothing.

■■ Life wasn't always easy for the bear. He was born far away, near the edge of Glacier's southern boundary, in the land above the river where the steel rail and paved road run. On the second of February, his mother gave birth to three cubs in a dark hole dug at 6,600 feet elevation into the side of a mountain under the roots of a huge fir tree. The den wasn't much bigger than she was. The male cub had two sisters, each weighing a little more than a pound at birth. The two females had blond Siamese-like colors, ink-dipped paws, and dark spots on their little humps; the male was brown all over. The three suckled blind for twenty days until their eyes opened.

In mid-April, the three cubs looked out into radiant light from the mouth of the den toward Brave Dog Mountain. The high country still wore a cloak of heavy snow. After a week and a half of short forays using the den as a base, the grizzly family shook off the lethargy of winter and left the high country for the valley below.

Spring food was scarce. The mother nibbled the early nubs of cow parsnip in the creek bottom, then moved south, crossing the invisible line marking the park boundary. She carefully skirted a block of salt that elk poachers had illegally placed to lure animals outside of Glacier Park where they could be shot. The valley of the Middle Fork was a dangerous place for bears. Any place with humans was.

The mother grizzly found an elk leg abandoned last fall by hunters. She scavenged the bones then grazed on a patch of early sedge. The bear found a small spot of spring sunlight, rolled over on her back, and offered her teats to her hungry offspring. The three cubs nursed, then wrestled and nursed again, vying for position. The little male dominated most of the play, though one of his sisters, the larger one, occasionally pinned him on his back.

Late April and May were starving months for bears. The sow grizzly knew this. There was a spot nearby where she could find food with certainty. But it was dangerous. Along the iron tracks lay vast deposits of grain and corn from countless railroad derailments. She had fed there many times and knew the risks were serious. The mother grizzly had seen other bears reeling drunk after digging up and eating fermented corn; sometimes they stumbled to their deaths under the thundering wheels of the iron monster. But she was now losing weight fast; her cubs could starve.

Two days later, toward the end of a long day in May, the grizzly family rose from their day bed under a thicket of subalpine fir trees on a mountain ridge and started the long descent to the valley bottom. They followed the elk and bear trail that ran along the ridgetop, then contoured below through the timber, and finally dumped out on a long bench paralleling the river below.

Here the railroad ran. They followed it, once darting into the trees while a train with many cars passed by. Ahead, on the tracks, stood a large black bear. The three small cubs cowered behind their mother. The smaller female cub tried to climb up on the sow's back. The mother grizzly continued toward the big black bear, her nose to the ground, as if he didn't exist. They closed to fifty feet. The sow stopped and looked directly at the black bear. She flicked her ears. The large black bear suddenly pivoted on his rear paws and exploded off the track, running through the brush until he reached the relative safety of the lodgepole forest.

The grizzly family registered no visible response and continued down the track to the grain spill. The mother started digging on the slope below the tracks. She fed into the night, twice pausing to let the cubs nurse. She chomped on the rancid grains until daylight, when she once again led the cubs down the tracks.

Off to the east, a whistle blew. The bears were caught on a narrow defile of track running below a sheer rock cliff. The sow broke into a run. The approaching train was moving fast on its downhill route. At the last moment, the female grizzly jumped the track and darted into the alder just off the grade. The iron monster swept by. The sow realized one cub was missing and returned to the railroad grade. The shrieking wheels flew by so fast they appeared invisible. She could clearly see the smaller female cub on the opposite side of the track. Peering under the train, she could see that the little bear was bawling, her plaintive cries drowned out by the thundering wheels.

In her terror, the bear cub could feel the ground shake and hear the deafening roar. She saw her mother, though slightly blurred, only ten feet away. The little grizzly was trapped between the cliff and the speeding train. She made a panicked rush for freedom and the safety of her mother. The grizzly watched her cub vanish in a wash of blood and steel. Chunks of bear cub flesh lay strewn along the tracks for a hundred feet. The train passed.

The sow grizzly and her two surviving cubs avoided the grain spill for the remainder of the spring and summer. They followed the melting snow up into the high country of Glacier, feeding on spring sedge, grass, and fleshy plants in the wet areas. Though the cubs nursed, they were gradually learning the seasonal plants—which grew in memorable places—upon which their mother fed. The country was still deep in snow, remote, unvisited by humans and populated by only a few other bears. One day in early June, the female bear scented a big boar grizzly moving toward them along Park Creek. She snorted the air, exhaled with a loud whoosh, and gnashed her teeth in agitation. Her cubs gathered around her. The big male was dangerous to the cubs, maybe even more dangerous than humans, especially now during the grizzly breeding season. She collected the two cubs and retreated rapidly, climbing to a high ledge above a vertical cliff. The boar looked up but continued down the drainage, passing below the family.

In July the bear family moved northwest through a narrow snowy pass into another glacial valley. Here, at the heads of four major drainages in Glacier National Park, the country opened up into some of the loveliest and richest subalpine grizzly habitat south of Canada. Stands of stunted fir framed flowering meadows. It was grizzly Eden.

The three bears passed the summer here, feeding on grass, sedge fields, and lilies emerging from below the melting snowbanks. The mother used her four-inch claws to dig up the bulbs and corms of spring beauty and glacier lily—little nuggets of carbohydrate. She excavated along the traces of rodent runs and the roots of bistort and biscuit root. The cubs sat back, watched, played, and nursed whenever they were given the opportunity. The sow and her cubs were gaining weight now.

The green of summer passed into the season of fruiting berries, the most important and caloric of wild foods here. The bear family dropped down into the lower creek bottom to browse the zone of berries back up the mountain as they progressively ripened with the season at increasing elevation.

A hiking trail ran along the creek, and nearly every day in August small groups of noisy humans came up the trail shouting and blowing whistles. In every instance, the mother grizzly either took her family into the thick brush or they remained hidden on day beds (the dish-shaped depressions bears claw out of the sod, usually next to trees, to sleep out the heat of the day). The people never knew the bears were there. The female grizzly behaved as if humans posed a serious threat to her family; she went to great lengths to avoid the two-legged creatures.

But they also had to eat. The abundance of the brief grizzly summer belies a biological urgency that says winter is coming. Biologists call this metabolic stage *hyperphagia*, which means to eat excessively. Here the huckleberries would last until well into September. For the next six weeks, the mother would juggle the necessity to consume at least thirty thousand calories a day with her need to avoid people. Without sufficient fat reserves, bears may starve to death during the long sleep of winter.

The hard frosts held off until the middle of September, when an early blizzard blew in from the coast and froze the berries off the bushes. Perhaps sensing the barometric low of the approaching storm, the grizzly family beelined back through the snow-filled passes south, arriving on a high slope not far from where the cubs had been born. The cubs bedded in the lee of a great rock while their mother dug away at the thirty-five-degree hillside, excavating tons of rock and earth from under the roots of a sturdy tree only a few hundred yards from their den of the previous winter. The sow scraped out a five-foot chamber with an elevated sleeping platform at the rear, which she lined with bark and grass.

Two days later, they left the prepared den and roamed for a month. The family hit the high country, where the adult female dug for roots and corms and occasionally browsed bunches of red mountain ash berries that still hung on the tall bushes. They spent two weeks on the river bottom, vigilantly skirting humans and their settlements, feeding as best they could. When they heard rifle shots, their mother carefully investigated those locations, knowing from experience this could mean a food source; twice they came upon a gut-pile left behind by elk hunters. During the safety of darkness, the bear family cleaned up the remains of the elk kill. Sated with berries and meat, they avoided the grain spill.

Then it was November, and an early storm triggered some instinct in the female. In a single evening they moved twenty miles southeast along the Middle Fork of the Flathead, crossed the river below Scalplock, and continued up Ole Creek until they stood under the mountain into which their den was dug. Near the mouth of the den, they wound down their metabolic clocks and dozed through the days. The mother had prepared a flattened porch at the entrance, and they bedded, sleepily looking out at the heavy clouds, and awaiting the snow that would seal them within their winter home.

▪▪ Spring came late to the Northern Rockies the next year, and it was almost May when the sow and her two yearling cubs emerged from the den to greet the season that was to forever shatter their family life. They dropped through the deeper snows of the high country down to the creek bottom, picking up a snow-covered trail heading northwest. They stopped for three days to feed on a winter-killed bull elk in Coal Creek and then continued until they arrived on a large flat along the Middle Fork River that marked the boundary of the national park.

Food, as was true every spring, was hard to come by. They prowled the bottomlands, sniffing out carrion and nibbling the first green-up in the wetlands. The south-facing ridges had melted out, and the mother grizzly led them up the slope where she tugged at the loose soil covering the rocky ledges, digging roots.

One morning the bear family looked down from the ridge across the river on the sparsely settled flat. A tall man, well-known in the two-legged community as a bear poacher, came out of a building and stalked through the cottonwoods to the riverbank, only three hundred yards away from the grizzlies. The morning sun glinted off his rifle. The man pointed his rifle's scope at the ridge. A shot rang out. The yearling cubs saw their mother fall back heavily on her side. For a few seconds there was no movement. Then the sow sprang up and ran off over the ridge into the brush with her cubs close behind. She staggered and fell on the down slope, her right front leg folding underneath her. The female rolled twice, then lay on the hillside for several minutes. The cubs nuzzled her and tried to lick the blood off the bullet wound high on her shoulder.

Their mother rose and limped east down into the creek bottom. With hardly a glance at her cubs, she crawled into a willow thicket and bedded. The sow didn't stir until the next morning, when she dropped into the shallow creek and drank. The cubs sidled up to nurse and drew a growl from their mother. During the next four days, the yearlings fol-lowed the wounded bear slowly up the drainage, traveling less than a mile a day. The sow slept on day beds twenty hours a day. By then, the cubs couldn't even touch the sow; she growled and cuffed and lunged whenever they approached. Bewildered, they nibbled green vegetation and stayed within sight of their belligerent mother.

But they were starving. One day the cubs dropped back to the river bottom, where they knew they could find food in the wetlands.

███ Now it was just the grizzly brother and sister. Even though the sister would remain to raise several litters of her own cubs in this same area, neither cub would ever see their mother again. Maybe she crawled back into the brush and died or starved to death in her winter den. In any case, the yearlings were on their own.

The brother bear was larger by a head than his sister. Neither weighed a hundred pounds. His coat was darkish brown while his sister retained blond patches on her face and back. They traveled together, fed together, played and bedded together. The brother and sister grizzlies avoided other bears and all signs of man. Finding food was the hard part. Fortunately, the yearlings retrieved every scrap of memory, every lesson they had learned while traveling that first year with their mother. They revisited hidden niches and secret springs, finding grass, bugs, and rodents. Just before the solstice, they came closest to starving; yet by trial and error and a bit of luck, they found just enough food to survive, turning the corner into summer.

Both yearlings were developing distinctive personalities. The male grizzly displayed more aggression in play and was clearly dominant (except when his play grew too rough, and his sister would retaliate and toss him, holding him by the scruff of his neck with her teeth). By now they knew that their solidarity as a unit gave them an additional advantage around other bears, especially black bears and subadult grizzlies. They still kept their distance from the big boars.

A heavy crop of berries solved the yearlings' nutritional crisis. The two grizzlies browsed the high scrub fields throughout August and

September. In this open country they encountered other grizzlies, tested the opportunities, and ferreted out their own place within the bear community's social hierarchy. All bears were relatively tolerant of each other—and sometimes humans—when there was plenty of food.

The two yearlings had passed a severe test: They had survived the season without a mother. Now they needed to sleep. Could they construct a winter home? They had only the experience of watching their mother dig a den out of the hillside under the big tree and, of course, their own instincts.

The siblings returned to the area north of Elk Mountain, in which they had spent the two previous winters. The old dens had collapsed, but this was typical. The brother and sister grizzlies poked about the mountainside, looking for a suitable site. They found a small cave and bedded in it for the day, but it was too exposed to the wind to serve as a den. Finally, the male yearling started digging, again under the roots of a giant fir. The little bear kicked out clouds of dust and gravel, working well into the night. The next morning, the smaller female had her blond head in the hole, clawing out medium-size rocks and boulders.

Within the week, a short, curved tunnel had been carved under the tree. A slightly enlarged sleeping chamber lay at the back of the excavation. Without the root system, the earthen den might have collapsed on the inexperienced bears during the winter. It was a good choice.

The brother and sister bear lingered around the mouth of the den, sleeping on the unearthed loam, watching the darkening sky for the big snow that would embrace them in the utter stillness of winter.

By the time serious snow arrived in late November, the siblings were so sleepy they could not keep their eyes open. They finally crawled into the rear of the den, curled up in the nest of dried bear grass, and wrapped their paws around each other for their long sleep.

The winter sleep prefigured the coming year in which they would separate from each other and begin to step into the light of their own being, eventually becoming the stuff of legend in the two-legged world of the Northern Rockies.

But that was still at least four years in the future, the time when the sister was to be widely regarded by men as the fiercest mother grizzly in the park, while her dark brother would be growing into the most powerful creature the region had seen in decades.

The inevitable separation of the two-year-old grizzlies came in late May, a time when big male bears begin to roam widely in search of females coming into estrus. The subadult siblings ran into grizzly trouble that spring. Big boars had threatened the pair on four occasions.

One day, on a broad stretch of river bottom, the brother and sister spotted a medium-size chocolate brown grizzly digging vetch roots out of the alluvium. In a second, the adult male bear's ears flicked back as he scented the air. The boar exploded into a full-blown charge, turning the siblings on their heels. The smaller bears ran for their lives. The sister darted into a thicket of small cottonwoods. The chocolate grizzly ignored her and tore after her brother, who raced at full speed up the steep bench and into the lodgepole forest above. The big grizzly closed in until he was only a bear-length behind the smaller male. The two bears hit another alluvial terrace, and halfway up the bench the big bear struck, grabbing the little grizzly's rear foot with his jaws. The smaller bear flipped over on his back and kept rolling, the flesh of his paw ripping free of the huge carnivore's teeth. The young male bear rolled to the foot of the slope and hit the ground running, paralleling the contours, racing through the sparse pine forest until he disappeared into a brush-filled gorge draining the country to the north. Never slowing, he headed upstream for five more minutes.

When the young grizzly finally stopped, only the breeze and faint tinkle of running water broke the silence; there was no sound from his pursuer. He had escaped. The bigger boar would probably have killed and eaten him.

He licked the raw flesh of his right rear paw. The wound would heal, but from that day forward, the mangled outer claw and long scar across the top of the heel of the rear pad would register in soft mud—a track that distinguished him from other grizzlies.

Now the dark brown, two-and-a-half-year-old grizzly moved on alone, the first time without his sibling. He hobbled northwest across the low ridges of the Lewis and Clark Range. At the crest, he paused and looked back at the Middle Fork country in which his sister would set up her own home range, close to where the two cubs had been raised.

■■ The male bear wouldn't return for four years, the same year his sister, then a full-grown mother with three of her own yearling cubs from her first litter, would have a fatal encounter with a photographer who pressed and harassed the grizzly family on a spring afternoon near Elk Mountain.

It had happened like this: The man with the camera just kept pressing forward, too close to the female sibling and her yearlings. The young sow finally stood and faced the man, popping her jaw and gnashing her teeth. The human ignored all her warning gestures and kept closing the distance for a better shot. When he drew within fifty yards, the mother bear charged the intruder. The bear was inclined to stop her charge short of contact, but the man turned, raced to a conifer tree, and scampered up the lower boughs. This frantic movement triggered the most protective of the mother grizzly's instincts, and she pursued the man eighteen feet up the tree, grabbed him by the leg, and dragged him down to the ground. He turned toward the bear and fought. She delivered a single blow to his head. The man lay still, the .45 caliber pistol inside his jacket, untouched.

The bear stood with her paw resting on the man's shoulder for a minute. Sensing no further danger to her young, she turned and gathered her cubs, then bounded away down the hillside. During the night, the man bled to death. The bear family never returned to investigate; the man was of no importance to them beyond his threat to the cubs.

He was not the only human to be mauled by the sister who was then recognized by humans as one of the most dangerously protective mother grizzlies anyone had laid eyes on. That same summer, a man with a rock hammer spotted the grizzly family on a ledge below him a few miles northeast of Elk Mountain. For some reason, this man shouted at the bears. The shrill vocalization provoked an immediate charge from the mother, who raced straight up the mountain, knocked the human intruder to the ground, and bit him. The man rolled face down and offered no resistance. The bear inflicted no additional injuries. She returned to her cubs and left the area. Later that year, people in the area noticed that the mother was missing a cub. They thought that maybe the little bear was killed by a train at the grain spill where dozens of bears have died.

■■ Meanwhile, brother grizzly moved north, bypassing a town site, to the land of the North Fork and into the heart of his bear life. He survived his subadult years by honing his attentiveness around other grizzlies and by using some of the most remote habitat of Glacier Park. His range was enormous; he emerged from his den high on the northeast side of Heaven's Peak in April or, in his later years, March, and dropped down to spend May along the bottom of the North Fork on the western border of the park. In June he was seen at the head of the Quartz Creek drainage in north-central Glacier. The dark grizzly summered high up in the Livingston Range, roaming all the way north to Canada. Then, around late August, he migrated to huckleberry habitat in the Apgar Mountains on the southwest border of Glacier Park.

Unlike his sister, the male bear grew in size and weight every year (adult female grizzlies channel their surplus nutrition into cub reproduction and nurturing). As a 350-pound young adult grizzly, he still had to defer to larger male bears. When he reached 400 pounds, however, he would become a contender. He challenged other bears for prime feeding areas and, in June, fought other boars for the attention of receptive females.

Once the grizzly left his den, his journeys and movements were largely dictated by what food was available. The exception, however, was the mating season, a period of six or seven weeks in late spring. It was during this season that the dark grizzly roamed the farthest corners of his range: the low meadows of the North Fork bottomlands; the upper reaches of Camas, Dutch, and Logging drainages; and south to the land where he and his sister had been raised. He encountered many other bruins along the way. All other bears had to take stock of this brawny newcomer. His favorite place, which was totally devoid of humans, was upper Quartz Creek. In fact, his first successful breeding unfolded under the great walls of the Cerulean Cirque. He could remember the acrid smell of crushed cow parsnip where he had bedded along the snowfield. The big bear's nose would recall that June day: the young blonde female, her coyness, his own swagger, how he had finally mounted her, grasping her flanks with his front legs, a copulation that went on for twenty minutes.

During his ninth year, the Black Grizzly underwent a growth spurt. By the time he reached ten years of age and a weight of well over a quarter of a ton, the bear had become the dominant male in the region, prowling the mountain and forest trails with regal disdain, his coat now coal black in the timbered shadows. His fierceness had become legendary. He tolerated no challengers, no other bears, and no humans.

▪▪ The Black Grizzly now pads across the open meadow under the cover of darkness. He detects the musky scent of a bull elk near the end of his rut. Bull elk are vulnerable to grizzly predation when their alertness is consumed with tending to their harems of cows. The big bear killed one near here on Quartz Creek two years ago, catching the elk from behind with a burst of speed and collapsing the bull's hind legs with his weight; he then shook the enormous ungulate by the neck with his teeth, like a house cat with a vole, breaking its spine.

The bear silently measures the effort of taking down another elk. He moves on. This year, the Black Grizzly is anxious to return to the high berry fields of the Apgar Mountains. His body wants the calories the sugar of fruit provides. He needs at least forty thousand calories per day for most of a month to get ready for hibernation.

The boar enters the timber again, still following the trace of a hiking trail. There is a dirt road just ahead, which the bear has crossed many times and on which no traffic should run after dark. Still, it is a road, and the boar is cautious.

Alongside the trail, near its junction with the dirt road, maintenance workers have dislodged a three-foot section of culvert from a drainage ditch. It wasn't here the last time the Black Grizzly passed by. The bear now makes his first significant detour of the night, circling the metal tube at a safe distance. The grizzly knows culverts are sometimes used to bait and trap wild bears. He has seen many traps and has always managed to avoid human capture. The culvert means danger.

The bear crosses the dirt road without incident and turns south following a wet meadow for several miles. There is another road, a paved one, and he darts across it in the dark. Now the coast is clear for a run up the mountain where the huckleberries grow. There should be no human sign in these little mountains; there are no hiking trails in the forty-some square miles of prime grizzly habitat. In all his years up here, the Black Grizzly has run into a human or his sign only five times. It was always the same man.

The boar reaches a small creek and looks for a spot to bed. Amid dried stalks of cow parsnip, devil's club, and alder, he claws out a large washbasin-size depression with his enormous daggerlike claws. The moonless sky sparkles with the constellations of the northern sky. It is about midnight. The bear sleeps.

At first light, the bear moves out. The creek-side vegetation is trampled by the passage of numerous animals, many of them grizzlies. He swaggers up the creek with the absolute confidence of his primacy in this gathering of bears. The Black Grizzly takes a brief side trip up an avalanche chute to browse on *Vaccinium* berries. The boar feeds voraciously but briefly; he is anxious to complete his journey, to return—as he has for the last twelve years—to his favorite spot in these mountains, a tiny tarn perched in a high basin. He is almost there.

The little creek tumbles along. Here and there, muddy pockets record the traffic: two moose, a dozen elk, and many, many bears; perhaps twenty have ambled through here in the past two weeks since the last hard rain. Only three sets of tracks belong to black bear; the remainder are grizzly. The bear pauses, his nose to the mud, and in moments sorts out the complicated pattern of sign. The latent scent retained in the tracks provides the big boar with a universe of bear information: Several other adult males are on the scene but none large enough to vie with the Black Grizzly. The same sow with the single yearling is here, and again she troubles him, with something reflexive and painful imbedded in memory. Three other family groups have passed by. He doesn't recognize one of the grizzly mothers with her two little cubs. But another sow and her two yearlings he recalls instantly. He mated with this female two years ago. The Black Grizzly raises his head, as if fondly recalling that spring day when he drove off a huge brown grizzly for her favors.

The olfaction of memory is powerful: Does the boar sense his own offspring in those yearling paw prints? Why does the other sow with the single yearling vex the Black Grizzly? How does he reflect on his old paramour?

Now he picks up another scent, which lingers on the Vibram pattern of a size-twelve boot print. It is the man.

He lifts a low growl into the faint breeze. The Black Grizzly is cranky. The idea of that sow and yearling up here irritates him. The thin tolerance he displayed toward other bears in August will vanish. From now on, the berry crop will be limited to the high country. Frost will come and the fruit will fail. He will drive all competitors out of the mountains.

The man, especially, exacerbates his sour mood. During previous seasons, the Black Grizzly had given this human plenty of warning.

The man carried a camera mounted on long sticks. One day when the man wasn't around, the bear knocked the tripod to the ground with a violent cuff and took a bite out of the camera. Another September, he found the man's camping equipment tied high in a ten-foot tree; the Black Grizzly tore the cache apart, batted the tent and camera lenses to one side, and then proceeded to chew apart the man's sleeping bag and T-shirt—everything that smelled strongly of the human. Once, the man approached too closely to the day bed occupied by the huge boar, who emitted a growl so low and deep that the man felt it resonate on his forehead before his ears picked up the warning. In all cases, the man left the mountain immediately after his run-ins with the Black Grizzly. Still, it seemed the man had yet to learn his lesson.

A small clearing marks the junction with a tiny tributary that will end in a subalpine basin—the grizzly's destination. The bear strips berries off the branches with his teeth as he passes through. A sudden rush of air and feathers—heart-gripping to an inexperienced human—catches the boar's attention. He looks up as a golden eagle breaks its near-vertical swoop with outstretched wings, stopping ten feet above the bear as if having mistook the huge carnivore for a giant marmot.

The morning has warmed. The Black Grizzly moves directly up the drainage, through thickets of fir, alder, and mountain ash. He emerges into another opening; a miniature, shallow pond fills a small amphitheater. The plentiful sign of other grizzlies marks the basin, but the Black Grizzly is unperturbed. Seemingly oblivious, he eases into the pool, his nose furrowing the brown surface. His head drives wavelets before him. He curls into the dark waters and emerges dripping on the shoreline. He shakes, a rainbow of droplets. It's time for a nap.

The bear wakes in the shadows. He reenters the dark tarn for another quick swim, then shakes off and goes into the thick understory of *Menziesia* and *Vaccinium* bushes to browse on the sweet purple globes. He starts to work his way southwest, up the steep slope, feeding as he moves up toward the ridge, which is now in deep shade.

The north side of the steep-sided ridge is timbered with spruce, fir, and larch; the south-facing ridge side is more open and drops into another basin. Moose-high brush grows under the trees. The ridgetop lies eight hundred feet above the basins; it runs flat for a quarter mile west into a deep notch, and then continues on up to the summit.

As the Black Grizzly browses his way up, the grizzly mother with the single yearling is working her way up the same slope toward the saddle. Neither bear is aware of the other, though they are only two hundred feet apart. The big boar, however, is moving faster, rapidly closing the distance between them.

Undetected by either the boar or the grizzly family, a man is watching the bears from the top of the ridge. He can see the Black Grizzly closing in and knows that he is about to witness a potentially violent interaction between the male and the sow with the yearling. The man carries a camera mounted to a five-foot tripod, but is uninterested in taking pictures. Instead, he fears for his safety. The bearded human knows this big Black Grizzly. He knows his distinctive track, and he knows the animal's thorny disposition. He has seen the boar charge and run off other grizzlies. The man took to heart the message sent by the bear when the beast ate his sleeping bag and T-shirt. The human has a camp far up the ridge, beyond the notch, which is just a hundred yards away. The female with her yearling cub now approaches that notch. The Black Grizzly is just behind her. Both animals stand between the man and his tent. It is getting dark.

The Black Grizzly catches a sign. Suddenly, he knows he is not alone on the hillside, which immediately becomes unacceptably incommodious. He recognizes the sow's scent. Something about this animal grates on the big bear.

A primal roar breaks the silence, followed by huffing and the sound of animals running through the brush. The sow breaks onto the open ridge and races across the saddle. The tiny cub struggles through the brush, running at her heels. Unseen, a hundred feet downwind, the man watches and hears the intake and exhalation of each bear breath with every stride. The sow and her yearling contour along the rock outcrop below the ridge, running for their lives before the Black Grizzly, who tears up the slope and bursts over the ridgetop. He gallops with the speed of a racehorse. The sow and cub fly below the small cliff. The cub falls a couple of yards behind, and the man hears a high-pitched coughing, a panicky sound as if the little bear knows it has but seconds left to live. The Black Grizzly gains ground until his jaws are within a yard of the cub's hindquarters.

At the last second the sow spins on her heels, allowing the cub to slip under her as she braces, with a chilling roar, for the crush of the huge grizzly. The boar bellows back, and they lock jaws, rising on their hind legs. The Black Grizzly slashes with his teeth. The sow parries and wards off the attacking jaws of the bigger bear. The cub retreats to a rock thirty feet above and stands there, bawling. The boar leaps forward and knocks the sow off balance, forcing her to expose her vulnerable flank. He lunges and seizes her by the neck. She yelps in pain, throwing her head against the bigger bear, and breaks the grip of his jaws. The sow quickly recovers.

The two bears alternately slash and parry, then stand nose to nose roaring amplified growls, the likes of which the man has never heard in nature. The Black Grizzly slows his attack. Abruptly he changes tactics and lunges once again for the throat of the sow. She leans into the attack; they lock jaws and rise to their hind feet like circling wrestlers. They break and drop to all fours, bellowing into each other's snouts.

The face-off stabilizes as the Black Grizzly gives up trying to kill the sow. The last roars rumble throughout the valley. The boar slowly turns, exposing his flank—the sign he is done with the fight. The sow rejoins her yearling cub on the cliff above and disappears into the brush. The Black Grizzly returns to the ridge. He stands just above the saddle.

The bearded man with the camera is in a predicament. Miles from nowhere, he is perched on a knife-edged ridge with steep, impassable brush on either side. It is almost dark. The only way out is up the ridge past the saddle to his camp near the summit, a place he calls the Grizzly Hilton. Between him and the Hilton stands the biggest, most cantankerous bear in the mountains at his ugliest after an inconclusive fight.

The Black Grizzly has not yet seen the man, who is now a hundred feet down the ridge. The great bear is startled when the mountain stillness is broken by the conversational tone of a human voice: "Hey grizzer bear, it's only me, good old Arapaho. Sure hate to bother you."

The grizzly rears and spins, directly facing the man, who is dressed in black clothing and is holding his arms outstretched. The Black Grizzly takes a huge breath, exhales like a sounding whale, then drops to all fours. The grizzly clicks and gnashes his teeth and advances stiff legged toward the man who stands fifty feet away. The ruff on the bear's neck is up. His ears are flat back. The Black Grizzly advances to within thirty feet of the man in the near darkness. Suddenly, the huge bear lunges, hop-charging half the distance to the human in a single angry leap.

The man is strangely calm, as if resigned to his fate.

FEAR OF BEARS

■ ■ I was the bearded man on the mountain ridge facing the Black Grizzly. Alone, in the fading light with the bear between my camp and myself, I had to make a move on the most dangerous animal I knew on earth. I decided to let my instincts loose, knowing a failure of confidence could be fatal. I felt I had no other choice.

Holding black garbage bags in my outstretched hands, I inched up the ridge and spoke: "Hey grizzer bear, it's only me . . ." The words were irrelevant, but the tone and posture everything. I turned my head to the side, but the big boar faced me straight on; the rough of his neck was up, his ears flat back. Although all these bear signs signaled imminent aggression, I sensed I still had a chance to get out of the confrontation unharmed.

At fifteen feet, the Black Grizzly stopped coming toward me. Without moving a muscle, I kept up the soft human jabber and stole a glance at his eyes: The stony aggression was gone, replaced by something more contemplative, a muscular pondering I still wonder about. Slowly, almost regretfully, the great bear turned his head off to the side and ambled into the huckleberry brush, leaving me alone on the ridge.

Taking no time to examine my extraordinary luck, I skidded past the spot where the grizzly had disappeared and scrambled up the ridge to my hilltop camp. The tiny pyramid-shaped mountain was dark by the time I arrived. Stunted trees and tall brush grew all the way up the steep slopes; only the summit was open. My tent was pitched in a small patch of moose-high spruce trees. Quickly, I gathered twigs and kindling. Normally, I built no fires in this place because I didn't want to disturb the bears. But this night I felt a fire might be my only defense in case the Black Grizzly came visiting.

I got a little blaze going a few feet away from my tent, wondering if I had seen the last of the big boar. Half an hour later, I stepped to the edge of the hill in the darkness to investigate a sound; a large animal was moving uphill through the thick brush. Hastily, I gathered bear grass plumes and made a torch. The bear grass burned poorly. I added dead branches and got the whole thing blazing. Something snapped in the undergrowth, and I stepped toward the noise. Waving the burning branches in front of me, I saw a shadow, then the head of a giant bear. Barking soft platitudes into the darkness, I talked to the bear for a couple minutes, telling him I was sorry for invading his domain and would leave the next morning. The grizzly was thirty feet away but came no closer. I caught the red-eye shine reflected in the night. This blinked off as the Black Grizzly turned and disappeared.

I returned to my fire and tried to stay awake. An hour later, I heard the bear coming again, up the other side of the pyramid-shaped hill. Again, I stepped away from the fire and confronted the bear, this time throwing a burning branch down the hill.

About midnight, the scene was reenacted for a third time. I was so tired I was ready to give up. I thought about the irony of meeting my end in the jaws of my favorite animal. What was he trying to do to me? I tried to fight off sleep, and then dozed, waking every twenty minutes to rekindle a small blaze until the light of dawn crept into the eastern sky.

I didn't know, and still don't today, what the Black Grizzly intended by terrorizing my camp that night. Maybe it was only cranky inquisitiveness or measured payback for allowing me to pass on his ridgetop. Still, I believe I glimpsed a discerning intelligence in those red eyes.

The Black Grizzly and I maintained a relationship for seventeen years; at least, it was a relationship to me. What I was to him I can only guess: probably a diminutive irritation of some kind. But we continued to have encounters, most of them back up in huckleberry habitat. Normally, it was eye contact: He'd stare directly at me with the full frontal body posture I associate with only the most dominant bears. Except for that hop-charge, which I took in part as bluff, he never came after me.

He did take a bite out of my camera. And he ate my dirty T-shirt and smelly sleeping bag, while ignoring the tent and all the other scentless items in my cache of gear. I took this, and virtually every other encounter with the Black Grizzly, as a clear message that I always heeded: to get the hell off his mountain.

I saw him elsewhere in Glacier Park on two other occasions: once with certainty at remote Cerulean Cirque, twenty-some miles to the north, and another time on the North Fork bottom. At least, I think it was the Black Grizzly; his track was often distinctive if not quite unique.

This great bear became central to my notion of a world in balance: As long as he was out there roaming the mountain vastness, the wilderness was intact and hope abided. This one animal defined for me the meaning of the wild—a wildness that still lives in us all and that I believe we cannot live fully without. Every year, I'd stalk the mountains to find him; I no longer snapped his picture or even let him know I was around, but I'd make sure the Black Grizzly was still there, alive and indomitable. He was my Moby Dick bear.

I also found in that red-eye shine the seed of a primal awareness, and I didn't know what it was at first. Back then, twenty-five years ago, I imagined myself without fear. But here was something new, an exhilarating encounter with an astonishing creature, a trepidation inextricable from reverence like nothing I'd ever experienced in war. It was a thing of great value to me, this fear of bears, and I wanted to explore it.

■ ■ The ageless essence of a bear encounter is a single human, shorn of the tools of modern technology, stalking through wild land inhabited by grizzlies. It begins with mutual awareness. This could happen up close, such as startling a sleeping bear on a day bed, or far across a meadow, when a person and a bruin first spot each other. Most of the time, but not always, the grizzly will run away.

Besides flight, the bear can demonstrate a spectrum of responses from curiosity to naked aggression. The actions of the human contribute significantly to the outcome of an encounter. Even while charging, a grizzly is deciding if he or she should conclude that charge. So what a person does is important.

Uncommonly, there is contact. Humans have been injured, even killed, by bears. On exceedingly rare occasions, people have been eaten. No other animal on the continent can so inspire that original dread: a creature so smart and big who may be hunting you.

Of course here, in discussing the possibility of people getting mauled by bears, we are turning probability on its head: Human injury of any kind by a grizzly is the least likely outcome of an encounter. Nonetheless, any basis for rational fear of bears resides in the uncontested chronicles of modern grizzly attacks.

An "attack" is when a bear makes contact with the person. In the professional literature, one invariably reads that there are two main types of bear attacks, defensive and predatory, and that you need to be able to tell the difference so you can respond appropriately to the situation. This truncated menu—defensive or predatory—is offered up at nearly every agency office and in most all of the field guides designed to tell you what to do in grizzly country. Nonetheless, the notion of grizzly bears deliberately seeking humans as prey is imbedded in a great deal of uncertainty and misinformation.

Predation means a grizzly hunting down a human with prior intent of making meat, as opposed to a bear finding itself with a dead person upon which the grizzly feeds—what the agencies call "opportunistic feeding." The distinction, which I imagine a matter of utter indifference to a bear, carries profound implications for human consciousness.

Polar bears do seek out people as food. A daytime pattern of black bear predation is also an observable phenomenon; there are a number of documented predatory attacks by black and polar bears. The same cannot be said for grizzlies. The data are simply not conclusive, nor should they be expected to be. Predation is not an area of inquiry that lends itself easily to the scientific method. The victim is dead, the grizzly can't be interviewed, and the evidence is accordingly circumstantial. This is not, however, to dismiss the possibility of a grizzly hunting a person.

A very rare but disturbing pattern of grizzly attacks involves bears who have had previous experience with humans and their garbage. Having associated people with food, they may come into camps at night. The transitions from investigatory behavior to attack and then scavenging can unfold with great rapidity; a grizzly might be attracted to a tent by food scents and then in a matter of minutes turn to opportunistic feeding on the human victim. These most exceptional attacks are indeed the stuff of nightmare. No doubt some are predatory.

But the bear that hikers meet in the light of day is different. Virtually all daytime grizzly attacks are defensive on the part of the animal, and most involve mothers with young. These accidental encounters usually result from surprising a bear, often on a day bed. The grizzly merely wants out, safely and, in the case of a mother, with her cubs secure. Surprising a grizzly on a carcass is a slightly more dangerous state of affairs. But all these situations are defensive and not in any sense predatory. There is a critical, practical side to this difference because there are consequences: How we react to bear encounters in large part determines the outcome. People have mistakenly believed a daytime attack to be predatory and then behaved too aggressively—by running, trying to climb trees, or, if attacked, fighting back—and have been badly injured by grizzlies who otherwise probably would have left them alone. In terms of sensible, safe travel in bear country, we could, as a matter of utility, dismiss the notion of grizzly predation almost entirely.

But not quite: Two recent attacks challenge this notion and, indeed, all our well-meaning attempts to stuff such tragedies into convenient pigeonholes.

■■ On June 25, 2005, Robert Thompson, an Inupiat from Kaktovik, a native village on the Beaufort Sea, was finishing a raft run down the Hulahula River, which flows through the Arctic National Wildlife Refuge of northeastern Alaska. He was guiding two clients, Kalin Grigg and Jennifer Stark, both from Colorado. The couple had scraped together enough money for a trip; they had a history of fighting to save wild places and knew they needed to see it firsthand to be effective advocates for the refuge.

Coming around a bend, the three rafters spotted a ransacked camp on the gravel bar. A grizzly bear lingered near the tent site. They beached the raft across the river and glassed the wrecked camp with binoculars. The bear was about four hundred yards away.

As they watched, Stark had a bad feeling and urged her companions to leave. They dragged the raft over several hundred yards of gravel beds, but Grigg was still interested in watching the bear—after all, this was what they had come for: to see the wildness in the refuge. Stark felt as though she was spoiling everyone's experience but couldn't shake the feeling that things weren't right. When the bear moved to cross the river, Stark scouted out the current in case they needed to move fast. Grigg snapped off one last picture before he realized they were in trouble. The grizzly crested a small dune and then charged.

"I knew when the bear crested the dune, before we got into the boat, that it was a bad situation," Grigg told us later from his home in Durango. "But I still thought that the bear might stop when he got to the river's edge."

The trio jumped into the raft and paddled for their lives. The grizzly raced along the riverbank, closing the distance between them. The rafters pulled into the current next to the bank with the grizzly running alongside. The animal jumped into the river and continued the pursuit, swimming after them with methodical persistence. He was within thirty feet when Stark spotted a rock in the river and called out to her companions to "shave" it. The bear didn't see the rock until the last moment, and the impact stunned him, ending the chase.

Both Grigg and Stark have spent lots of time around black bears and grizzlies, but they've never experienced anything like this. "I just remember when he turned and started running up that bank," Stark says, "it wasn't like I was dealing with an animal anymore. I was dealing with a thinking creature—a creature that was analyzing that this was possible. It put that bear in a very different place for me."

Thompson called the authorities. When Alaska Fish and Game officials responded, the bear was still at the campsite, acting aggressively, as if he were guarding the site. They shot the grizzly, and then found Richard and Katherine Huffman dead in the tent. The couple had been attacked in their sleeping bags. An unused firearm lay by their side. The bear was a healthy three-hundred-pound male grizzly. The *Anchorage Daily News* reported the attack (according to state, federal, and local authorities) as "a rare, unprovoked attack by a predatory grizzly bear." Fish and Game spokesman Bruce Bartley stated: "All the indications now are that it was a predatory attack." Later reports confirmed that the bear had fed on the couple.

The Huffmans, two skilled and conscientious wilderness travelers, did everything right. They were careful about their food storage, to the point of cooking in one place then floating downstream to make camp. Theirs were the first deaths by bear ever recorded in the refuge.

Normally, these refuge bears are extremely wary of humans and run off anytime a person gets within three hundred yards, sometimes fleeing at even greater distances from the two-legged predator. Grizzly hunting is legal here, despite the "refuge" designation. But this animal behaved differently. One observer speculated he might have had a grudge against people; indeed, the attack took place twelve miles from the community of Kaktovik, the only village within the refuge where the bear might have had bad experiences. In the history of grizzly maulings, the violence of this incident is staggering. The deadly vehemence of the attack seems deliberate and maliciously conscious, as if the animal were weighing a private vendetta against the price he would pay. We don't know, of course. What lingers is the misgiving that human voyagers must carry with them into the wilderness: the awareness that they share the landscape with a creature who appears to be thinking.

Grigg and Stark are clear about the value of their experience. "I think that one of the best gifts the animal gave me," says Stark, "is to confirm that I'm not in control. It's given me a different lens to move forward in what I think wilderness should be."

Grigg agrees, adding that the sometimes dangerous presence of grizzlies means "there's a completeness, an 'all-rightness' in spite of how everything else in the world sometimes seems all wrong. It isn't about us and our experience. Part of it is about those places, which are enormously special and have a history far beyond our own. The bears have every right to be there and deserve to be there without human intervention."

■■ A second fatal attack took place the same month in Canmore, Alberta. The circumstances could not have differed more from Stark and Grigg's encounter in the wild Arctic refuge. On June 5, 2005, a two-hundred-pound, four-year-old male grizzly killed a woman jogger in the Bow Valley of Alberta.

"No Warning Before Grizzly Struck," the *Toronto Globe and Mail* headline read. Early rumors surfaced that this was a possible predatory attack. "It behaved like it was guarding a kill," a male recreational biker, who came upon the scene just after the grizzly attack, told reporters.

Isabelle Dubé, a well-known and accomplished athlete, rounded a sharp corner on a popular trail with two jogging friends and, according to news reports, saw a grizzly only sixty-some feet away. Her two female companions slowly backed down the trail, while Dubé decided to try to climb a tree. The young grizzly apparently pulled her from the tree and fatally mauled her. The two women could hear Dubé shouting at the bear.

The women ran a half mile to a golf course clubhouse, where authorities were called. A wildlife officer responded and shot the grizzly dead.

One disturbing aspect of this tragedy is the juxtaposition of a grizzly attack in an urban landscape. This "wilderness trail" cuts through a "wildlife corridor," a strip of bear habitat awash in a sea of subdivisions and golf courses. The same grizzly was scared off the eighteenth green earlier that same morning. "We get them [bears] all the time," said the clubhouse manager.

The eminent Canadian wildlife biologist Brian Horejsi, writing in a commentary for the *Calgary Herald*, was not surprised by the event—it seemed a misfortune waiting to happen—and laid blame squarely on corporate land developers who were aided and abetted by provincial and local government. "Canmore's municipal council and mayor(s) have produced a habitat-consuming expansionist monster that has added 10,000 people in less than two decades," he said. "Numbed by decades of isolation from government process, a docile public stands dazed before the onslaught. So poorly informed is the public, they accept as measures of sincerity and concern token 'wildlife' corridors and gratuitous protests from the very people who promote the fact that progress cannot be slowed."

Horejsi's comments apply evenly to most all of the Rocky Mountains today. The habitat-eating elements of his "monster" currently thrive in the lower forty-eight: notably in the Bitterroot Valley of southwestern Montana, the Flathead Valley near Gleacier, and in the private land surrounding the Yellowstone grizzly bear ecosystem.

▓▓ Running into a grizzly on the eighteenth green, however, is quite atypical—or was until very recently. Up until the last twenty-five years, virtually all grizzly attacks occurred in what we call wilderness. The exceptions involved bears used to human food and garbage. Today, a new arena is emerging: As the march of progress chews away at the islands of wild bear habitat, we find ourselves wandering a curious landscape; the edges of the isolated grizzly ecosystems are carved into a tame and surreal countryside. Great bears prowl the edges of strip malls and the backyards of condos, marching past casinos and pizza parlors, perhaps looking for the shrinking wildlife corridor that might lead them to another island ecosystem and a better bear life.

Not literally, of course, at least not yet. But the apparent incongruence is still disturbing. Since I first stepped into grizzly country—it was just after my return from Vietnam—a recurring scenario has invaded my sleep. I dream of white bears. The white bears are grizzlies, not polar bears. They alternately fascinate and terrify me, and I spend much of my dreamtime breathless from fear, trying to scurry up trees and into rafters of cabins just out of reach of the marauding beasts. It's puzzling because the fearsome dream bear often threatens me on the fringes of civilization, in cabins, outbuildings—human structures oddly out of place in the wilderness. I was confused and shared this bearish dream with numerous ursine-wise friends and students and discovered that it is a common and emerging modern prototype.

Bears do kill people on the edges of industrial culture, the hazardous borderline between wildlife habitat and human development. During the summer of 1980, another bad year for bears and people, a grizzly killed the brother of one of my friends, along with a young woman, on the eastern border of Glacier National Park. The couple had camped on Divide Creek between the visitor center and a private dump at the town of St. Mary. It was a tragic choice of a campsite because the narrow, willow-choked creek constituted a natural travel route to the dump, where a fresh horse carcass irresistibly drew bears. The private dump was a quarter mile away. The late writer Edward Abbey and I investigated the site later that same summer.

The creek tumbled noisily through tunnels of willow and alder. It had been hot, and the couple was sleeping on top of the tent, which lay by the creek on a narrow bed of gravel. By the time the young grizzly noticed the people, they all must have been just a few feet apart. Abbey and I noted with a chill the claustrophobia of the place and imagined the terror of waking to a bear in the darkness. A cottonwood tree grew just across the creek. I can picture them trying to climb it.

The pattern of wounds on the young man's forearms suggested he fought the bear hard and courageously for both their lives. The grizzly, shot nearby, was identified by matching its bite to the victims' wounds and by the fact that the bear had human remains in his stomach. Later, I tried to explain to Abbey how I felt when I finally saw my friend, the dead man's brother (who had himself been mauled once by a grizzly): the flood of confused emotions—disbelief, injustice, and something approaching personal responsibility. And I myself a champion of grizzlies, I couldn't look him in the eye. Instead, I turned my anger on the criminality of the landowner who, for decades, refused the park's request to bear-proof or close the dump.

Later that summer, another marauding grizzly killed one man and injured three others during the course of a week in late August and early September. The 761-pound boar, huge by Rocky Mountain standards, attacked the four victims in thick vegetation less than a half mile from the town of Banff, Alberta. Authorities concluded that this giant bear probably frequented the area because of the available garbage at a nearby restaurant. After filling up on refuse, the grizzly would retreat into nearby thickets to bed. Unfortunately, this settled area was popular with tourists and fishermen, who probably surprised the bear at close range on his day bed. The aggressive boar responded with violent but short-lived attacks. If the grizzly had wanted to kill these men, they'd all be dead.

Other bear attacks out on the edge of development are, however, clearly predatory and closer to the dream, especially the depredations of polar bear. These ursine hunters probably evolved from an isolated population of brown bear in Siberia. The theory is that a couple of hundred thousand years ago, a brown bear wandered north on the ice and started hunting seals. The end product of this evolution is a highly efficient predator. Unlike the grizzly, who, like *Homo sapiens*, remains a generalist, the white bear is a specialist in ring seals, plucking them out of their breathing holes in the ice. Attacks on humans reflect this strategy, where people are snatched up during the dark of the Arctic winter at the isolated outposts of industrial culture—cold drill rigs, geological camps, scientific stations—or while camped on the ice, ecotourists sticking their seal-like heads out of tents in the morning.

Grizzlies are a different story; they have diets that tend toward the vegetarian side of the table. Yet, walking in grizzly country feels much like hiking the tundra of the high Arctic—at least it does to me. In the back of your mind, you know there's a big critter somewhere nearby who can kill and eat you anytime it wants to. Maybe the openness of the barren ground of the north or the treeless alpine grizzly habitat contributes to your sense of human vulnerability: You can, at times, like early humanoids living on Africa's savannas, feel like you are being hunted. I'm saying there is a level of organic fear appropriate for humans living in grizzly country, a landscape in which I am massively more comfortable than in Wyoming bars or the local Wal-Mart, and it may be biologically tied into our chromosomes.

This fearsome mixing of wild beasts and human settlement, as in the dream, could also be a mere metaphorical confusion of people who no longer maintain a bestiary apart from the barnyard or city zoo. The grizzly bear maulings in the Bow Valley and at the Banff town site seem more frightening than those set far apart in the wilderness. But this terror could also be a simple aberration of association, caused by the poverty of our minds and the fear of everything beyond concrete barriers.

■■ Living amid a culture for which the most ordinary of deaths often arrives as an unexpected shock, death by wild beast today strikes us as utterly bewildering, unbelievable, hitting us in the gut the way drive-bys never will.

When a grizzly kills, our reactions are no longer simply those of a grieving community. The tragedy is broadcast across nations, shared in the realm of imagination by urban and rural people alike. As the collective shudder is amplified by newspaper headlines, the nuances of the attack are lost. Official renderings, accepted as definitive, are seldom challenged.

Such was the case of one mother grizzly named Chocolate Legs. She was trapped, collared, and moved first in 1983 by Blackfeet tribal biologist Dan Carney, then trapped again in 1997 after being caught on the reservation licking a barbecue grill. Locals remember her as a good mother, a beautiful bear who ranged along the northern Rocky Mountain Front, straddling the boundary between Blackfeet tribal lands and Glacier National Park. The Humane Society chose her as the poster bear for its children's book, *Chocolate, A Glacier Grizzly*. But at age thirteen, with twin yearling cubs, Chocolate Legs would become in the world's eyes, "The Killer Grizzly." This "incident," as the park service would call it, became one of the most widely reported of modern grizzly stories.

On May 17, 1998, twenty-six-year-old Craig Dahl started up the popular Appistoki Creek trail in the scenic Two Medicine country on the east side of Glacier National Park. Dahl was a summer employee, but his friends say Dahl took to the country, and that "he got it." Given the chance, he might have stayed.

The weather that day deteriorated and Dahl's hiking partners cancelled on him, so he traveled alone. This was no big deal; the young man was fit, experienced, and used to solitary treks. Besides, there were other people on the mountain. A snowboarder and another pair of hikers who were interviewed later reported hearing what might have been a shout. But none could be sure. On an average day, one can hear stray human voices coming up from campgrounds and the well-used trails of the Two Medicine Valley. A wet, blowing snow settled in, and all visitors except Craig Dahl descended the mountain.

About 2:00 p.m. the next day, two young men hiked up the same trail toward Scenic Point. They saw tracks in the snow and then found a daypack. On the way back, they picked up the daypack and took it with them. They did not inform authorities of their findings until weeks later.

That night, four of Dahl's friends, concerned because he had not shown up at work, drove to the Scenic Point trailhead looking for him. They found his Buick: a sign that something was very wrong. One of the searchers was Marty Connelly, an East Glacier resident, skilled mountaineer, and experienced wilderness trekker in grizzly country. At 9:00 p.m. on May 18, Connelly notified park rangers that they had a missing hiker. Daylight faded while the search-and-rescue team met at the East

Glacier Lodge. As everyone was briefed, one ranger took Connelly aside and confidentially informed him that the search would not begin until the next morning. Connelly was furious and decided to act on his own.

"The bottom line is, when someone's hurt, the only thing that's going to keep a mountaineer alive out in the mountains is hope," he says. "So it does help if other people are out there." He and a group of locals set out to cover as much territory as they could, yelling all the while, with the goal of letting Dahl know there were people looking for him.

"We got real close to the area where they actually found him. We had headlamps, and we did have ropes in case we had to go underneath the snowfields. But it was very difficult to see," Connelly says. Rather than lose anyone to an accident born of exhaustion, they went home to get a few hours of sleep.

When the official search began the next morning, Connelly and his friends formed one of many rescue teams. As they combed their assigned turf, Connelly imagined the things that could have happened to his friend; none of the scenarios involved a grizzly bear. "In my mind what he did was go up the trail, miss the switchback. He slipped and fell and got hurt. That's the first thing I thought happened."

May 19 passed without authorities finding any clue to Dahl's disappearance. The teams quit with a few hours of daylight left. The next morning the search team found him. "Dahl's body was found near Appistoki Falls off the Scenic Point trail at an elevation of 6,000 feet," the park service reported. "Scavenging by bears or other animals had occurred, but the actual cause of death is still under investigation."

An experienced ranger discovered and examined Dahl's three-day-old tracks descending a little snow chute that was littered with Craig's belongings: broken eyeglasses, pieces of cloth, a hat. The ranger noted, "Several sets of tracks, which could have been made by humans or bears, were observed heading downhill in the area." He also reported that "The tracks leading down from the trail toward the site of the victim did not indicate a speedy descent."

Investigators collected bear scat and hair samples and sent them off for DNA analysis. With the aid of telemetry, officials pinpointed a radio-collared grizzly with twin two-year-old cubs in the vicinity of the fatality. It was the mother grizzly locally known as Chocolate Legs.

Meanwhile, Connelly and his friends had seen a number of things that last day of the search to make them suspicious of the final conclusion that Chocolate Legs was the killer. First, they stumbled across a set of diggings in the snow, probably a few hours old. From the tracks, they knew it was a mother grizzly with two cubs. But while grizzlies do dig for roots and for rodents, these marks seemed frenzied to the searchers, as though she were digging out of frustration rather than in search of food.

Furthermore, Dahl's body was not found on the part of the mountain where the tracks of the sow and her cubs were headed, and Connelly began to suspect that another bear, a big locally known grizzly boar named Melvin, might be involved. "Melvin was in the same area when Craig Dahl died," he says. "We saw him a couple days later. He rules that area, the big old griz. I've seen him pretty damn close." Melvin's involvement, he thought, could explain why the sow and her cubs weren't feeding on the man they had allegedly killed when Dahl was discovered.

"A sow and two cubs are not going to leave the remains of a carcass. The only thing that's going to scare them off is not going to be a helicopter; it's not going to be human beings. It's going to be a bigger bear," Connelly says. He reasons further that a three-bear family would have had a much harder time hiding from the helicopter—which had passed through the valley continuously during the search and rescue—than a solitary boar. But scat samples and subsequent DNA analysis proved Chocolate Legs and her cubs had fed on Dahl, and although no forensic evidence was produced to show she did the killing, this was ultimately proof enough for the park service. The bear family would die. Rangers tracked the radio-collared Chocolate Legs and the female cub, trapping the daughter on June 3. The next day, rangers shot and killed the mother at nearby No Name Lake. The male cub was still at large.

For the better part of a week, the park service kept the female yearling alive in a trap in the Two Medicine Valley, hoping, according to one ranger, that the young female's cries would bring in her brother. While her bawling echoed through the valley each day, brother bear stayed away. After four days, managers euthanized her.

The official decision to kill the grizzly family was sanctioned by an advisory panel. On June 25, rangers found the male cub on the north slope of Sinopah Mountain a day after he had bluff-charged a group of hikers. He, too, was shot and killed.

During the thirty-six-day interlude—between the time Dahl's body was found and the last member of the grizzly family exterminated—the national, regional, and local press made much of the story of Chocolate Legs. In dozens of articles, the specter of killer bear and marauding grizzly at large was paraded across the pages. Virtually every piece reported the fatality as grizzly predation, with Dahl "killed and mostly consumed by the three bears" or "killed and eaten by a thirteen-year-old sow."

Another missing hiker had vanished into the Two Medicine the year previously. It was widely implied that Chocolate Legs might be a serial-killer predator grizzly and responsible for the disappearance in early July 1997 of concession employee Matthew Truszkowski on Sinopah Mountain. Speculation that Chocolate Legs was a "man-eater" linked the stories of the two missing hikers. Sensationalism of this tragedy lingered in the press for years: The *New York Times* reported on the story in August 1998, and Roland Cheek subsequently wrote a book about it, *Chocolate Legs: Sweet Mother, Savage Killer?* The basic assumption in all these accounts was that Chocolate Legs and her cubs stalked, killed, and ate Craig Dahl.

Which might have been the case. But what is missing is a mitigating note balancing the race toward a predatory conclusion. Glacier Park might have noted that the only circumstantial evidence supporting the prey hypothesis was the scattering of the personal items on the snow and the tardy testimony of the two hikers from Missouri who, after reading of the fatality in the press, said that they saw the tracks of someone running downhill.

It was abundantly clear, however, that no one really knew what happened. Dahl might have taken a fall; he might have been caught in the storm and suffered from hypothermia. Another bear might have killed him. No one knows how he died, only that Chocolate Legs and her cubs were among those who fed on him afterwards. The park's uncertainty was expressed in coded language—the words "believed to have killed" or "growing circumstantial evidence indicated the bears killed Dahl" added almost as afterthoughts. The distinction was lost on much of the media, which reported that the park was out to trap killer bears.

Marty Connelly still grieves for his friend, Craig Dahl, and for the bear family as well. He knows grizzlies will eat anything dead and doesn't fault Chocolate Legs for eating Dahl. He believes the park service found a convenient scapegoat in the bear family and fell for the myth that eating human flesh turns a grizzly into a killer. But mostly, he finds it abhorrent that bureaucrats refuse to extend the considerations we give each other (innocent until proven guilty) to the bears he loves.

■■ The journalistic rendering of Chocolate Legs's story is a fair representation of a current media drift: The tendency of modern reporting to exaggerate the terror of a grizzly mauling mirrors our individual recoil at the thought of such a death. It's as if we are inappropriately trying to hang on to the residue of a primordial story whose origins we recently misplaced. The immense power of the bear and deep human respect for the animal still reside in the legends and stories (such as the genesis tale of the Bear Mother whose offspring are the ancestors of all the people) of early Americans and other traditional people of the North; there is a solid sense of the familiar throughout the ethnographic record. Is the modern migration toward the sensational a mere shift in the style of storytelling, from the awe and reverence of people who lived intimately with grizzlies to a "civilized" culture that wants to pretend it exists apart from nature?

The dream of fearsome bears may be the archetype that bridges culture, that transports modern bear stories back to the land of myth. What were the alpha predator dreams of natives living amid the richness of America before European contact? This awareness, which has traveled with us from our time at the mouth of the primal cave, could be changing, its vitality ebbing as wilderness is transformed into domestic landscape. The living bear keeps us tethered to our original home, a wilderness of place and mind that provides the psychological context in which human beings evolved. It has informed us how our own species, until very recently, perceived its natural place in the world.

Near the heart of that context, of course, lies the ancient fear of becoming prey. The consideration of this relationship is carved like a canyon into our evolution. No wonder the question of bear predation arises whenever a human is killed by a grizzly.

By the time naturalist Timothy Treadwell was killed and eaten by an Alaskan grizzly bear in October 2003, he had spent as much time in the company of wild bears as anyone. With almost no camping background, and zero experience with bears, Treadwell thrust himself into the Alaskan wilderness of Katmai National Park in 1991, a desperate act of a man plagued by alcohol and drugs. In his biography, *Among the Grizzlies*, Treadwell describes how his ill-prepared camping trip (he couldn't get his tent up, and his sleeping bag turned out to be child-sized) climaxed with the meeting of a grizzly bear:

> The thick brush behind me began to crackle and swish with the unmistakable sound of a large animal approaching. Startled, I jumped to attention, my eyes darting and straining to see the visitor. Thirty feet up the river, a golden-brown ball of fluff sprang from the bush and began moseying in my direction. . . . The bear was a vision, a perfect creation that appeared to have materialized from an artist's canvas. The shiny, golden, shaggy coat was flecked with blonder tips that glittered in the warm light. . . .Within twenty feet of me, the animal stopped and sat down, peering toward me. I was ecstatic! I wasn't afraid, only worried that my presence might spook the bear.

Treadwell sought me out after his early trips to the north country. He'd read my book *Grizzly Years* and wanted to ask my advice. In retrospect, I wonder if he was looking for approval.

We spoke mostly of the bears themselves, of the nuances of bear behavior that people can learn to recognize. We agreed on many points, even on the idea that it is often best to behave aggressively with younger grizzlies, who are testing the parameters of acceptable behavior. But when it came to older males, we lost our common ground. Treadwell told me he felt comfortable sidling up to big males, whose presence often kept other less-predictable grizzlies at a distance on the broad beaches of Alaska. Huge male grizzlies often have hideously scarred faces, I pointed out to Treadwell, presumably from fighting other bears. "They didn't get those scars by digging clams," I told him, adding that I consider two times of year to be the most dangerous: the mating season in June and late in the year before denning, when bears are hungry and food is scarce.

Treadwell didn't seem interested in hearing my advice on that count. He argued that he'd never had any trouble, even during mating season. But fights happen, as evidenced by the scars, and even the mildest pro-longed physical altercation between a grizzly and an unarmed human will result in a dead or seriously wounded person. Treadwell resisted this possibility. "I make my peaceful intention known," he told me, "and the bears recognize it." When I pushed him on the matter, Treadwell flashed anger. He insisted, "I've got to do it my way."

Treadwell's considerable experience, even at that time, made him hard to argue with, though I still worried about the young man. In the end, all this second-guessing of grizzly behavior comes down to a judgment call about what is running through the animal's bearish mind. Timothy's bears, and a few of my own, may have recognized us as individuals, as specific humans they could tolerate, but we were both speaking a foreign language to wild animals. In general, grizzlies do treat humans much like they would other bears. Most face-to-face confrontations are resolved by each party reading the signals and back-ing off, or with bluff-charges followed by withdrawal. I've been charged about thirty times by a dozen or so grizzlies, and only a handful of those times were serious threats; by the end of his life, Timothy had survived many more.

For thirteen years, Treadwell returned seasonally to the coast in a self-styled form of rehab. He gave up drugs and alcohol and threw himself into the task of advocating for grizzlies by publicizing their friendly side. He gave them names: Booble, Ginger, and Blondie. In time he had sponsors, movie star friends, and appearances on David Letterman and the Discovery Channel. During his long stretch of luck with grizzlies, Treadwell spoke to thousands of schoolchildren; he was by all accounts a charming and charismatic entertainer. Eventually he went high tech and began using a video camera to chronicle his adventures. He filmed himself hanging out with bears—on the beach, along salmon streams, sometimes close enough to touch them. Occasionally, he took friends and girlfriends along, though his footage was usually of a man alone on a mission.

Scientists were appalled by Treadwell's approach. Biologists and government officials who believed that Treadwell set a bad example for tourists belittled him. "At best he's misguided," Katmai Park Superintendent Deb Liggett told the *Anchorage Daily News* in 2001. "At worst he's dangerous. If Timothy models unsafe behavior, that ultimately puts bears and other visitors at risk."

Almost all his friends worried about him. At the least, they thought he should have bear pepper spray in his tent. Charlie Russell, a Canadian who has also made a reputation working closely with wild bears, chastised his friend Treadwell for choosing campsites at the confluence of bear trails and not using electric fences around his camp; yet, as Russell respectfully noted, "this so-called fool has spent about thirty-six thousand hours with brown bears in Katmai."

Therein lies some truth. Timothy Treadwell contributed considerably to the analysis of bear behavior. No one else pushed the envelope like Timothy. He routinely charged wild grizzlies, including huge males; even Demon, the bear he considered the most dangerous.

Once, Treadwell wrote, he thought Demon was going to kill him near the Grizzly Maze, a section of impenetrable alder thicket laced with tunnel-like bear trails. The bear followed him from the shoreline of a lake and then across a creek. "[A]s I backed up, he did not turn away. I simply worked my way up a steep grassy hill so that the dark male would have plenty of room and access to all the paths." But Demon did not turn away, and although Treadwell could not find any outward sign of distress in the bear's body language, he was concerned by the odd behavior. "Just as the dark male closed to within ten feet, his ears went back, and the most menacing, wicked eyes I'd ever seen turned to ice. The black male was coming for me. In a last, desperate moment, I lunged toward him, kicking and screaming. Confused, the dark male retreated slightly. I continued charging and growling, and he slowly backed off, those wicked eyes blinking."

Treadwell always claimed to be protecting the grizzlies from poachers (though this was dismissed as bullshit by Katmai officials; after all, it was a national park). People wondered why he kept going back; he certainly didn't need any more video material or pictures for his lectures. Yet, summer after summer he returned to the remote south coast. Dropped off by floatplane, he would camp alone on the rain-blasted shore. One can imagine him holed up in his leaky mountain tent, cowering in a damp, musky sleeping bag while the horizontal rain, driven by the shrieking wind, lashed the tent-fly and great bears repeatedly crashed through alder thickets only a few feet away. It was unimaginable boldness. He persisted, saying always that his work was unfinished, facing down giant male grizzlies again and again. It was as if Treadwell was seeking that final embrace.

On October 5, 2003, his mission ended. Treadwell and his girlfriend, Amie Huegenard (herself a seasoned backcountry camper from a family of conservationists), were killed by a grizzly bear. An audio recording made from a video camera with the lens cap on caught their final minutes on earth. From this we know a little: that in the early afternoon of October 5, a bear entered camp. It was raining, but Treadwell went outside to investigate. He got into trouble and called for help. Amie told him to play dead—a tactic that seemed to work as the bear then left (which also seems to indicate the initial attack was not predatory). But for some reason the bear returned, and the mauling resumed. Treadwell's last words were for Amie to save herself. Instead, she attacked the bear. The couple died trying to save each other's lives.

Park rangers investigating the scene killed a large male grizzly who was lingering near the couple, as well as a smaller bear who made them uncomfortable.

I heard of their deaths from a friend, but soon the news was all over North America. The recriminations were instant and hostile, with intense anger directed at Treadwell. Pundits sought to wedge blame into familiar cracks. Whether motivated by professional jealousy or an irresistible need to tell the dead man "I told you so," the human community immediately went to work trashing Treadwell's reputation.

U.S. Geological Service researcher Tom Smith, who spent time in the backcountry with Treadwell before his death, asserted to the *Los Angeles Times* that "[Timothy] was breaking every park rule that there was, in terms of distance to the bears, harassing wildlife and interfering with natural processes . . . Right off the bat, his personal mission was at odds with the park service. He had been warned repeatedly. It's a tragic thing, but it's not unpredictable."

A memo from the Alaska Department of Fish and Game was more blunt: "A person could not have designed a more dangerous place to set up a camp," wrote Larry Van Daele, the biologist dispatched by the department to investigate what it believes to be the first deadly bear attack in Katmai history. Not incidentally, pilot Willy Fulton, an experienced woodsman and the first person on the scene, disagreed with Van Daele, noting that the camp was situated on the highest knoll in the area with a commanding view of the surroundings. Frankly, in Kaflia Bay and similar coastal bear-feeding areas, there is no good place to camp; any open ground is a bear trail or feeding zone.

Treadwell's supporters were also at a loss to draw any larger wisdom from the tragedy in the days following his death. Biologist Dave Mattson searched his own soul for answers. "I fear ego was a factor (in the mauling), as it sometimes is for all of us," he told me. "I know that feeling of adrenaline rush in wanting to get close to grizzlies; respect means for me giving them their space."

Another grizzly biologist, Barrie Gilbert, a friend of both mine and Treadwell's, who was himself badly mauled by a bear in 1977, urged caution in an editorial piece for the *Los Angeles Times*. Gilbert says that human-bear relationships are far too complex to make easy judgments about the role Treadwell may have played in his own demise. "[M]aking sense of all this also requires that we recognize that humans and bears have coexisted for millennia and still do," he writes. "Just as there are aberrant, aggressive people, so too are there bears driven by hunger, disease or age that will kill and eat us."

Treadwell would be most vilified for causing the death of the two bears. The Katmai superintendent had told him that none of her staff "would ever forgive him if they had to kill a bear because of him." This criticism should be examined; it is a bit misleading. In that it is considered axiomatic by many bureaucrats that a bear must die whenever implicated in a fatal human mauling, she is correct. But some fatal bear attacks are defensive or the fault of the people who get killed. Park service personnel have more discretion than they generally exercise; in Katmai they didn't use it. Likewise, the facile assumption that once a bear tastes human flesh it becomes an insatiable killer is false: No evidence has been found to support this folk belief. A carcass becomes the province of the most dominant bear in a given area, no matter the true identity of the killer. And it's that dominant bear who takes the bullet.

But bear management personnel have not been known for their restraint when it comes to shooting any or all bears at a human death site. So while Timothy didn't kill those bears, we all know the government's customary retribution to be an expected consequence, and we are accordingly personally responsible.

Tragically, Treadwell's great legacy of education was likely undermined, with each of those schoolchildren now acutely aware that the nice man with his cute bears was killed and eaten by a grizzly. Treadwell sought the wild, and the experience was the gift of a new life. He tried to repay this debt by working to save grizzlies from poachers—though his antipoaching stance was largely a romantic pretense for just being there and living a wild life scarcely imaginable today. He wanted to show the wider world that bears are not the monsters of our Pleistocene nightmares.

In his last letter, written to friend and benefactor Roland Dixon, he shared his hope: "My transformation is complete—a fully accepted wild animal—brother to these bears. I run free among them—with absolute love and respect for all the animals. I am kind and viciously tough."

This is what Treadwell missed. Wild creatures accept us only according to their own dictates, impervious to the agenda of human expectations. Any encounter can turn dicey. I concur with Treadwell, though perhaps not for the same reasons, that you can talk yourself out of injurious situations with most all grizzlies by acting appropriately. Treadwell did it many times, often leaving his tent when he heard a bear in the vicinity, prudently confronting it rather than letting the animal come in too close. But a grizzly with a bellyful of salmon is a different animal from the hungry bear that came around on October 5. In the end, a bear will always be tougher.

Above all, what is the importance of preserving the opportunity to experience face-to-face encounters with large carnivores who on rare occasions may regard humans as food? Treadwell's work and life in part answer this question. Only a landscape so primal and vital, teeming with great flesh-eating bears could have sufficed to tame the urban demons he brought with him to Alaska. Could his unique experience of working close to wild brown bears be considered indulgent? It certainly could; the best thing for the bear is to leave it alone. I also received a similar gift by hanging out with grizzlies in the Northern Rockies after my return from Vietnam, but like Kalin Grigg (who had the encounter on the Hulahula River), I don't think the wilderness exists for the benefit of whackos.

In our charge to domesticate this continent, we missed a few pockets of wildness where that risk still dwells. A hundred thousand years of evolution bind our genome spiritually and psychologically to these ferocious beasts. We could live without these creatures, though something in the imagination would stray aimlessly. The anchor of wild risk keeps us tethered.

Despite the proclamations of innumerable grizzly experts, the cradle of the Treadwell tragedy is unknowable. The fact is no one will ever know who the killer bear was or if the unfortunate loss of human and bear life was triggered by a predatory attack. These two knowledgeable people were well aware of the risks, and it was their right to experience the wild as they chose. We might honor their courage.

▩▩ A lingering question arises from these tragedies and encounters: If our fear of bears survives as a natural and useful element in the contemporary mind, and the source of that fear endures because of the very small yet real risk of bear attack, why is human predation by bear unacceptable to our wildlife managers (who presumably represent a larger public)? Why do agencies and institutions insist that all such bears must be killed?

Back in 1980, my boss at Glacier found the skeletal remains of a Texas man who was probably, though not certainly, killed and eaten by a particular male grizzly. The park wanted this bear taken out. "The last thing we want out there," said Glacier's acting superintendent, "is the legend of a killer grizzly." Similarly in 1998, when officials made the decision to kill Chocolate Legs and her family, the U.S. Fish and Wildlife grizzly bear recovery coordinator, Chris Servheen, was quoted in a June 18 newspaper article summarizing his agency's position: "So we have chasing, killing, and consumption. That is not classified as natural aggression. We do not tolerate predatory grizzly bears. Period."

Despite the previously discussed uncertainty about the predatory nature of Chocolate Legs or the fact that the charge of grizzly predation is seldom an airtight case, the message is clear: Such bear behavior is deemed unacceptable and classified as unnatural. Of course, these are the official positions of agencies that may need to cover all the legal bases in case of lawsuits. But this contemporary hard line toward killer bears, I think, also represents a generic human misgiving: We like the idea of having wild grizzlies around but would prefer them on our own terms.

Here is a modern dilemma: Humans, with their brainy technology, are drawn to problem solving and management. Animals like grizzlies (and the wilderness habitats they require) exist because we have chosen to let them run wild and live beyond our control. But we also seem to regard them as modern-day renegades holed up in their last stronghold;

if they wander out or get too bold, we want to treat them as rogues. We see the value in their independence, but it makes us nervous.

We probably can't have it both ways. Within the spectrum of natural grizzly behavior lies the remote possibility they may attack or slay the occasional human. On the other hand, managers don't want "the legend of a killer grizzly" out there in the flesh, roaming the remote mountains.

All the same, I can picture journeying to the valley of the killer grizzly: I doubt I'd travel confidently or sleep very soundly, but, with discovery pouring off every blade of grass and a sensuous caution riding on the wind, I can't imagine either a wilder place or feeling more alive.

Perhaps "fear" is not the correct word here; it doesn't entirely encapsulate this pulsating vitality, which comes wrapped in both danger and mystery. In my life, only a visit to the wild Tribe of Grizzly has afforded such an experience. This approach is certainly not for everyone. Today, people seldom find the opportunity to visit grizzly country. That doesn't make it any less important in individual lives. The most urban of people are drawn by image and symbol into the world of the bear. This contemporary magnetism underscores an ancient bond. Somewhere buried in the modern psyche, we crave contact.

THE
PHOTOGRAPHERS

■■ The war correspondent in photojournalist Bill Campbell's soul sends him to the mouth of the cave, tempting the beast within. In his case, the cave is an island of trees in the middle of Yellowstone National Park's Hayden Valley, and the beast is a large male grizzly bear who sometimes lives there. From the road the island appears deceptively small; a discrete and unremarkable patch of trees not worth the notice of the steady stream of summer tourists who prefer their wildlife encounters out in the open and from the familiar confines of their Winnebagos. Watching from the east end of the island, the traffic is likewise inconsequential, the splash of sunlight on windshields stretches like shiny droplets of water along the road next to the Yellowstone River. Here, it is dark and cool. Pine marten lope across elk and bison trails that weave along the fringe of trees before plunging into the depths of a mature lodgepole pine forest, crossing dead-falls deeper into woods that seem to go on much farther than they should from outward appearances. There is wolf scat on the trail and a small herd of buffalo to be surprised in a hidden gully. Skirting even the edges, one's breath quickens, tense and alert. This is grizzly country.

Campbell comes here to evoke and purge his past. He spent nearly two decades covering combat in Africa and the Middle East for *Time* magazine, and his resulting demons would probably amount to a compensable disability were he a veteran of the military. Instead he comes to places like this to scare himself a little. "I have to admit that the reason I do work around grizzly bears is because they give me some of that adrenaline rush. The grizzly bear is the closest thing that I can find around here to a land mine or a sniper or a rocket."

My husband, Doug, and I met Campbell and his wife, Maryanne Vollers, when they left the East Coast in 1997, moving to Montana in part to turn his career in a new direction. Campbell began The Yellowstone Project to explore the relationship between humans and wildlife in the modern American West. He's fascinated by wildfire; this transfers metaphorically to the rest of his work, which is characterized by his search for the elements that fuel the passion and anger evoked by our struggle for control over the land. A few years back, Campbell made the switch to video and has since shot footage for CNN, ABC News–Nightline, and NBC, among many others on his resumé; he's made two feature films for Animal Planet: *Season of the Grizzly* and *Sole Survivors—The Yellowstone Bison*.

Campbell first saw his bear near this tree island. He'd been hiking a trail just to the north at the base of a ridge, following a small creek with feeder springs that made for a wet hike and good tracking mud. A few flat miles into the country, he stopped. "I was looking for bear tracks; I wasn't really looking for bears," he says. "Something had happened out there. There were a lot of wolf tracks." So he pulled out his binoculars and had a look around. Next he saw the ravens, which meant a carcass, which probably meant a bear. He was downwind, able to watch as a coyote took nervous bites. "Then it would run away, and a wolf would come eat off it. But the wolves were as freaked out as the coyote. I thought, there's gotta be a grizzly bear."

Campbell settled in to watch. It's an idyllic setting, meadowland bisected by a creek warmed from hot springs; a good place to see buffalo and elk. He'd been sitting for a couple of hours when suddenly, a feeding wolf ran off. "A grizzly bear came out. It was a beautiful bear." The bear—he was sure it was a male—couldn't see Campbell hunkered down in the sagebrush on the hillside, but the wind swirled, carrying his scent to the animal. At one point, the bear waded across the creek, but the breeze shifted again and Campbell remained hidden.

"That's my favorite bear because it's a big bear, it's powerful, it hasn't been trapped, it doesn't have any ear tags, it doesn't have a collar. It's living in great bear habitat. Sometimes, if I have the balls, I go in and cut through that island. You go in there and it's spooky. You see all these day beds, cached skulls all stacked up around, bones and pieces of elk, big piles of bear shit. You just know that there's something in there. I never go too far in, but sometimes you just want to see what's there."

This is the way Campbell likes to see bears—on their terms. He's got little patience for crowds of people and prefers to hike alone into places with good bear potential and wait. He finds this approach well suited to his purpose: taking photos of bears that convey the political and social context within which they live. His pictures and footage accompany stories about oil and gas development, wildfires, and the changing social landscape of the West. "One of the things I learned when I came here is that land has a personality, the people who live on it have personalities, and the animals all have personalities," he says. "I'm not a strict nature photographer. I work with issues. In dealing with those issues, I often put myself where these issues take place. In doing that, I tend to not go out specifically looking for a grizzly bear picture. I go and spend time in the habitat."

The profession of nature photography is fraught with physical and spiritual peril, Campbell says, especially when you throw grizzly bears into the mix. There are bitter debates over whether it's proper to use bait or captive animals. The National Association of Nature Photographers has sidestepped that issue, advising only that staged shots with trained animals should be labeled as such. The lines between right and wrong are not entirely clear, even to Campbell, who spends a lot of time considering the consequences of his actions and calls game-farm photography "animal porn." One year, he had a lot of close calls with animals "throwing" themselves in front of his old Chevy Suburban. Campbell knew something nonlinear was going on. My husband and I took him and Maryanne to one of Doug's shrines, a ghost herd of buffalo and bear skulls, seashells, eagle feathers, and turquoise beads. The idea was for Campbell to take pictures of a new hot spring Doug was writing about. Instead, he quietly left his roll of film with the cache, later claiming the pictures were no good. Whatever the cause, the animals' suicide attempts ceased.

■■ It was nearly Christmas 1998 when Montana Fish and Game officer Tim Manley picked up a copy of the latest *National Wildlife* magazine. He flipped to the cover story on grizzly bears, and what he saw on page 26 infuriated him: a full-frame shot of two bears—a mother and cub—climbing on "an abandoned bird feeder" near Glacier National Park. In fact, the feeder was on private property, next to the home of an accomplished wildlife photographer named Stephen Krasemann. Manley alleged to the state's newspapers that Krasemann had lured those bears with food, and that several months later the cub had been killed by a human. The tragedy, he asserted, was Krasemann's fault.

When I spoke with Manley in the spring of 1999, he said he'd been working with Krasemann for several years to clean up his property. "Back in '96, I got notified by a number of people—his neighbors—that he might be attracting bears to get photos, but I couldn't substantiate that," Manley said. "Then in the spring of '97, I got a call from the Forest Service, and they had been laying survey lines in there and kept running into grizzly bears. I went out and found scat with grain in it all over the place. I talked to Krasemann, and he said he had been feeding elk and deer with corn, oats, and barley.

"This spring we were radio tracking a bear, and it took us right to his place. There were sunflower seeds and corn in the bear scat. When I went and asked him, he said he was feeding the ducks. But there was old bear scat out there; he knew what was going on." Manley says he and a colleague helped Krasemann clean up his yard. "I was in Utah and saw those photos in the National Wildlife Federation magazine, and I recognized the bears before I even saw who took the picture . . . The cub ended up being killed, illegally, near an airstrip along the Flathead. That bear had been habituated, food conditioned. It had been searching cabins and was not wary of people. He had a belly full of birdseed when he was killed."

After talking with Manley I call Krasemann, who invites me to his home. Like many wildlife photographers, he migrates seasonally. In addition to his work for publications ranging from *Rolling Stone* and *Sesame Street* to *Audubon* and *National Geographic*, he wrote and illustrated a book called *True North*, a journal about a year spent in the forests and mountains of Canada and the northern United States. I catch him just before he leaves for the summer.

Krasemann's cabin is nestled in the relatively thick brush northwest of Polebridge, Montana, up the North Fork of the Flathead River nearly to Canada. Few of Glacier's tourists brave the twenty-two miles of potholed, washboarded road, and those who do find few amenities in Polebridge. There are cabins for rent, a hostel, a saloon, and a general store with fresh-baked goods. A 1988 fire turned the surrounding trees into ghostly remnants of a forest. After spending the night at the hostel before my interview with Krasemann, I wake early enough to drive north into the park. It's special country for me and Doug. I take the road toward the lake where a friend and I scattered the ashes of a college buddy who died of cancer several years previously. This is where Doug retreated for a night of solitude the day after we first met. He howled for wolves, and eventually one howled back.

Back south and across the North Fork, a winding dirt road leads to Krasemann's cabin. When I arrive, I am greeted by his companion, a friendly woman who, before the day is out, offers me lunch and a jar of her homemade preserves. Krasemann is painting birds in his study. "You wanted to watch me work? This is what I'm doing," he says. I start right off asking him about Manley's accusations. He points out to the yard, about twenty-five feet from the house, to the spot where the controversial bird feeder once sat. It has been dismantled, a sauna built in its place. He disputes nearly all of Manley's charges. The feeder, he says, was empty. He never intentionally baited bears. Manley's dead cub, he insists, was not the one in his picture.

"I didn't put out meat or dog food to attract and hold a bear. They wander through, that's it. I will cop to this: The first winter, I put out feed on land instead of on the pond," where it would sink in the spring as the ice melted. After Manley first confronted him about feeding animals, Krasemann put up an electric fence. And as for the misleading caption in *National Wildlife,* he claims no responsibility for that either. "Those captions are written by people in New York. I don't market my own photos. The feeder was abandoned—there was no food on it. I was sitting with friends in the kitchen drinking coffee when [the bears] showed up. That little bear was a real climber. He climbed all the trees. He got up on that feeder and got stuck."

Krasemann puts himself somewhere in the middle of the continuum of photography ethics. He'd rather bait animals than bother them in the wild but looks down on those who use captive subjects. "How different is it to put out birdseed to bring birds to a feeder then take a picture through the window here, than to go into the wild and scare a bird from branch to branch all over the forest? Where's the stress on that bird?" While Campbell might argue that Krasemann loses the context of that bird's existence by luring it to a bird feeder, and Doug believes a photographer should either be a good enough woodsman to avoid harassing his subjects or should leave the animals alone, I let these points slide. In the wake of the controversy over his methods, Krasemann says no other journalist has bothered to call him for his side of the story. He is feeling a bit defensive.

Although Krasemann once taught classes at a game farm in exchange for shooting some pictures there, he says he won't do that again. "I don't like the flavor of it. You're in a little compound and the animals are led out of a cage. They put food in a stump or on a rock, and you take pictures. It's a zoo. When I started out in the field, someone suggested I take wedding photos for supplemental income. I said that if I've got to take wedding photos, I don't want to be a photographer. If I've got to use wildlife models, I don't want to be a photographer."

It's more difficult to earn a living his way, he adds. "These are unspoken demands: no mud, no matted fur, nice settings. Editors get conditioned to those kinds of photos. That's why Daniel Cox is making a living at this. His animals have no mud, no matted fur. They [the magazines] publish pictures of these perfect animals that are wild models. No one wants to see photos of scruffy-looking wolves, of scruffy-looking anything."

■■ Daniel Cox responds warmly when I call him on the phone. The Bozeman-area photographer's work is everywhere, from sporting magazines (*Outdoor Life, Sports Afield, Field and Stream*) to conservation media (*National Geographic, Audubon, National Wildlife, Sierra, Wildlife Conservation*). He's published seven books of photography and professes the need to make conservation part of his work ethic. "I got into this work because I love being in the outdoors and I love photography," he told a writer for NikonNet. "Equally strong is my interest in natural history and wildlife and my concern about our environment. I want my photos to be used in a way that's consistent with my feelings about the animals I photograph."

Cox tells me he'd like to be more involved in the local conservation community. "I just travel so much, I haven't had the time." And he is a cautious man. He prefers Alaska's well-fed coastal bears to Yellowstone's grizzlies, saying the latter are "highly stressed" and "grumpy." Likewise, he is hesitant to talk with me. A native Minnesotan, he got burned early on as a youthful hunter when a journalist took out of context a quote of his about baiting animals. "It nearly ruined my career." After hesitantly agreeing with me to meet to talk things over, and then failing to show, Cox e-mails me saying he won't be interviewed. "Unfortunately, after careful consideration and some additional research as to the direction of this project, I have come to the conclusion that I would rather pass on being involved."

Cox has some reason to be reluctant: He's earned the enmity of photographers like Krasemann and Campbell by building much of his career taking pictures of captive animals. Bill Campbell first turned me on to Cox's work with a snapshot Campbell had taken of a grizzly bear named Cocoa. The bear is in a small cage that fills the back of a pickup truck, and it is set against a backdrop of the snowy Gallatin mountain range near Bozeman, Montana. Two feet away stand a man and two children holding balloons. A sign on the truck's windshield reads ANIMALS OF MONTANA.

Animals of Montana is a modern game farm, a place where wild animals are shot with cameras rather than guns. When I first punched up its website in 1999, Cox's pictures were all over the place. At the time, no one from Animals would return my phone calls. Five years later, however, trainer Troy Hyde, Animal's proprietor, surprises me by agreeing to meet.

■■ Winter arrives late to Montana in 2004, but by mid-December the road to Animals of Montana requires four-wheel drive. Set on a south-facing slope in the southern Bridger Mountains, Hyde's complex of cages and outbuildings straddles the transition between the slow-paced, relatively undeveloped Shields River valley to the east and the trendy trophy homes on the road from Bozeman to the Bridger Bowl ski resort to the west. I arrive on time, but no one is around. A trailer truck advertises Hyde's other love, race-car driving, but the only sign of recent activity is icy tire tracks next to a garage. After knocking on all possible doors, I stroll down the driveway for a look at the animals. The gate to the complex is open, but I stand outside: A Bengal tiger has its eye on me. Caught in the viselike grip of its stare, I catch the silhouette of a bear out of the corner of my eye. I know there are wolves and smaller animals here. But only the tiger seems to care about me, and I sense its interest is gastronomic.

Two more roads lead farther up the hill, and from the tracks I can tell one hasn't been used in a while. So I start hiking up the other. At the top, I knock on the door of an upscale log home. A woman I take to be Hyde's wife directs me back down to where I started. Hyde had to make a run to town; he'll be back any minute.

No one has had much good to say about Hyde's operation: Photographers who abhor captive-animal pictures believe he contributes nothing to our understanding of the wild; animal advocates say Hyde meets only the minimal requirements of rather lax laws; a former employee questions his motives. But the man I meet when I get back to the bottom of the hill is pleasant enough. He's of medium build and carries himself with the presence of a man who's comfortable communicating with tigers and bears through his body language. He starts out by introducing me to the bears. There are two grizzlies sharing a cage—four-year-old Adam and sixteen-year-old Cocoa. Each cage has an enclosed area where the animals can get out of the weather. Cocoa appears sluggish; she wants to hibernate, Hyde tells me. Nearby are two small black bear cubs—born the previous winter, not yet a year old, and each about the size of a full-grown border collie—undergoing treatment for mites. In a third cage is a huge, solitary black bear.

"[He] just kind of wants to go to bed," Hyde says of the older black bear, as he clangs open the door to his cage. "Hi buddy, come on, come here. Can I come see you? What are you doing, you going to sleep? Thinking about it?"

Hyde invites me into the cage, and I slip just inside the door. "He's seven years old, weighs 625 pounds. He's trying to go to bed, but he's still coming out and eating a little bit now and then." The black bear ignores me.

Sensing the bear's indifference and probably my own discomfort, Hyde doesn't linger. We step back out into the glare of the sun, warm despite the snow, so he can tell me how a kid from the Midwest ended up in this business. His father worked for a Wisconsin fish hatchery, and Hyde had little interest in school but an attraction to animals. "I was young. I was seventeen and naïve. When you're that young, you always think you can do everything. I just thought, 'Well, I'll train animals for movies.' Not knowing anybody really ever did it." He started out with a mountain lion, moved to Montana in 1989, and eventually got into bears.

"The first grizzly was good. I had the right ideas and was very uneducated. Got very educated by him," he says. "He wasn't a bad bear, but he wasn't a great bear because I wasn't a great trainer. See what I'm saying? I learned from him." Cocoa came into Hyde's life when she was two, and the two of them have been working together ever since.

Though people willing to drive way off the highway are welcome to pay $10 and tour the place, Hyde's animals are trained for the movies. His animals have starred in *The Long Road Home*, *A Dog's Tale*, and *Wind Dancer*. They've appeared in an IMAX movie about bears, in a documentary about wolverines, and have been featured on the Discovery Channel. "Our grizzlies love to perform, whether for still photography or video," his website advertises. "They will amaze you by running toward the camera, standing on command, snarling viciously, or posing cute for the camera." The price tops out at $500 an hour for single-species sessions with the big-game animals: African lions, grizzlies, snow leopards, and tigers. Black bears, badgers, mountain lions, and such rate $200 an hour, while raccoons, coatis, and skunks rent out for $150.

Hyde organizes wildlife photo safaris, placing mountain lions, tigers, and grizzlies on location in the red rock country of southern Utah; gray timber and arctic wolves in northern Minnesota and frozen Lake Superior; and snow leopards, African lions, and lynx "in the Wild West of Montana." These expeditions cost anywhere from $1,900 to $3,000. But the grizzly bears, he says, are his real passion.

"You cannot lie, you cannot deceive, you cannot do anything with a grizzly bear that you might be able to do with a person. They understand," he says. "You have to build a trust, where the animal trusts you and vice versa. You trust them. *I know what he thinks; I know what makes him think what he thinks.* We communicate without saying anything."

Hyde is impatient with his critics. He sneers at "purists" who take pictures from roads. "Wild to me is like if you see a grizzly bear tearing across that meadow right there, and you ain't gonna get within a hundred yards of him without getting killed. That's wild. The bears in the park are habituated [accustomed] to people. It's not really wild there," he says. "There were mountain lions down in Jackson Hole, Wyoming, a couple years ago, you know, and everyone went and took pictures of these wild lions. They got thirty-five guys there taking pictures. And, of course, the mountain lion cubs got destroyed." The lions got used to people, Hyde says, and began frequenting backyards. "So that was somebody wanting to get photographs so bad that it didn't matter to them what happened to the animal, as long as they got the photographs."

Hyde credits his work with one documentary film crew for changing the state of Montana's policy toward wolverines. He used eighteen trained wolverines for that movie, and says the result—an end to Montana's open season on wolverines—justifies the fact that those animals spent their lives in a cage. "It's worth it; I believe it. If you have wolverines in a cage for no other reason, I think that's wrong. I don't consider these guys pets. I consider them trained. I consider them my friends. They are colleagues of mine," he says. "The wolverines now, in Montana, you can't shoot them anymore. You can trap them, but there's a season. You can't just see one on the road and get out and shoot it."

Daniel Cox, who shot his share of photos at Animals of Montana, also justifies his work with an appeal to environmental principles. In an essay on his website, Cox attributes the Yellowstone wolf reintroduction project in large part to captive wolf photography. "Many of the published wolf photos of the last decade were of captive animals . . . [T]hese photographs and films helped people get to know the gray wolf, providing the public with a better understanding of the animal, its life, and its needs," he writes. "With that understanding came the political and financial support necessary for its reintroduction to Yellowstone and other parts of the West."

But Cox's peers say the man has done real damage to the animals he purports to help. Among those is Tom Mangelsen, arguably North America's premier nature photographer. Mangelsen, who is based in Jackson Hole, Wyoming, has worked all over the world. Though he photographs near his home in Yellowstone Park, his most well-known grizzly shots were taken along the salmon streams of Alaska. He's partial to mountain lions and was displeased in the extreme to see the cover of a new book about the big cats. "There's this latest book by David Baron about cougars in Colorado. The title of the book tells it all—*Beast in the Garden*—evoking this fear, and then on the cover of the book is a picture of a cougar up in the left-hand corner overlooking a scene of an aerial view of Boulder, Colorado, where I used to live.

"Well, the cover's a picture from a game farm taken by Dan Cox, Animals of Montana, up there by you. But it's a totally contrived image, so you evoke this fear in people and you sell a shitload of books. But the animal is in a cage: It's been placed in a setting and digitally manipulated into a view of what appears is this cougar lusting after the poor . . ."

". . . metropolis of Boulder?" I offer.

"Yeah, and so you look at this and think, wow, cougars are bad. So that's the kind of shit people want to perpetuate, whether it be bears or cougars or wolves. Not only is it inhumane and immoral to keep animals in cages, but you are then telling a lie about who these animals are. You're creating in many ways hate for an animal that doesn't deserve it. So there's a cougar on the front cover of *Wildlife Conservation* magazine, growling, and I know that this was again the same photographer. And I know just right or left of the cat was somebody poking it with a stick. Pissing it off enough to growl so it would give this very threatened gesture that would sell magazines. Sure, cougars will growl, especially if they're being treed by dogs. Bears will growl on command if you feed them chocolate-covered cherries."

New Jersey photographer Leonard Lee Rue III finds people like Campbell and Mangelsen to be elitist. "I have noticed that many of the 'purists' who decry the photographing of captive animals are either not professionals or else have money enough from other sources that they don't need the photographs of all the species possible because they are not dependent on their photos' sales for their livelihood," he writes for the online magazine, *Vivid Light Photography*. Some animals, Rue tells me on the phone, are just too hard to find. Rue, whose biography bursts with superlatives (he says he is the most published wildlife photographer in North America, with eighteen hundred magazine covers to his credit), has trouble with cats. Despite his extensive portfolio, mountain lion, lynx, and bobcat have eluded him. "Now when you are competing with everybody else in the country, if you don't have the photographs when an editor calls you, and says 'Geez, I need a cougar picture,' because you're a competitor, that's a bad thing," he says. "So if you want a cougar, if you want a lynx or a bobcat, I say go down to your local rent-a-cougar shop and you rent them."

But to Bill Campbell's way of thinking, what the public learns from a picture of a grizzly bear has to do with how that animal lives in its environment. "If you just go and rent a bear the way you would a model, you don't have any connection to where that bear came from, why that bear is there, what that bear is doing. If you're imposing the client's wishes or what you think is going to sell, it's not even a real bear anymore."

The National Geographic Society used to provide photographers with an ethical reference point, Campbell says. If you wanted to get published there, you couldn't use captive animals. That ended in 2001, when Geographic ran a cover photo of a snarling, captive bear to illustrate a conservation-minded piece by Montana writer Doug Chadwick. "You need a benchmark," Campbell says, "and it used to be a place like Geographic. If you ever wanted to work for Geographic, you would never, ever work with captive animals. Now it's like, they don't give a shit because they want to sell magazines on the newsstand. If you have a grizzly bear sitting in a meadow of wildflowers digging yampa root, you know, you're probably not going to pull it off the stands. Chances are that the type of bear pictures that you would get in the wild, where the bear is not aggressive, . . . would not satisfy the demands of the market."

Campbell believes that if photographers would simply stand their ground, magazine editors would make better decisions. "What bothers me is when the photographers and the documentary filmmakers were all willing to say, 'No, you're not going to have that. A bear doesn't do that.' Like I did a bear show for Discovery, and, of course, they wanted all kinds of stuff. I said no. I mean, you're not going to get that behavior from a grizzly; you just have to let me follow something for a year.

"You know, I'm older and I've been in the business and I can do that, whereas most [photographers] will go, 'What do you want?' And that could be a lot of what drove the Treadwell stuff. I don't know. Would Timothy Treadwell have been so successful at his endeavor if so much of it wasn't done for TV? I mean, nobody will ever know. What drove the cart in that case? Was it his own quest to live by these bears or that he happened to have been by these bears and got really close interacting with them, and happened to have tape of it at the same time. And then the TV people went 'Oh man, that's wild. Can you do a whole show like that?'

"And then that drives him to do a whole show, and then he starts justifying it: *Well, it's really for education. So if I show some of this stuff that I really shouldn't be showing in the name of education, then that neutralizes or that justifies what I'm doing with bears in order to be on cable channels.*"

■■ Our hunger for and fascination with these pictures indicates a deeper and real need for wild grizzlies, and arguments about the nature of these institutions are signs of the passion these animals generate. At its core, this demand for posed bear pictures—and the willing involvement of those who supply it—pushes us further from an understanding of the wild, when what we really crave is to be closer to it. A grizzly encounter becomes less like Bill Campbell's tentative walks through a haunted woods and more like the pranks of children filmed for modern "reality" television shows.

It's the product of a culture that mixes Goldilocks and Yogi Bear with the Discovery Channel, Tom Murphy theorizes. Murphy is another Yellowstone photographer, and he has made the study of this place his life's work. This soft-spoken rail of a man sets out on journeys that would kill most people, like winter ski trips across the park with gear that gets no more high tech than wool gloves. One two-week solo trip resulted in the stark, frigid photos illustrating his first book, *Silence and Solitude: Yellowstone's Winter Wilderness*. In this sense, Murphy is the antithesis of Rue. He's devoted decades to learning about Yellowstone's wildlife so that he can make a living taking pictures *in situ* without harassing the animals. "Say I wanted to get an environmental shot of a grizzly bear. At this point, if I had three or four days, I could do that. But for most people coming in here from Chicago, they'd have to spend the next three years to get a decent shot of a grizzly bear. They wouldn't be able to do it."

And so Murphy supplements his income by guiding people on photography expeditions. What they want, he says, are two shots: wolves and bears. "Bears can serve in our culture to provide a connection to wildness," he says. "People can make a connection because if they know there are grizzly bears in Yellowstone Park, then they can say Yellowstone really is a wild place. To know that that wildness exists, I think that's important to the American psyche." Murphy is precise in his language: Yellowstone is his sacred ground. "If I'm in bear country, I know I'm in a special place. I'm in a cathedral basically. My hearing improves; I pay more attention. I can smell things that I don't normally pay attention to. I'm more alive because of that. Not because I'm afraid of seeing [bears]. I want to see them. Because they're beautiful and they belong there, and I want to belong there, too."

▪▪ To describe Michio Hoshino by calling him a wildlife photographer is a bit like knowing the full moon only by its reflection. His work stands out in the small world of grizzly bear photographers as elegant and complicated, full of context. In his absence, there are only clues to the nature of the man, echoes of a remarkable life left in his photos, writings, and friendships. In one of the opening shots of his book *Grizzly*, a sow and three cubs cross a valley floor in the Alaska Range, four small dark blotches casting shadows on the snow, dwarfed in an immense landscape. "He had a very heuristic way of demonstrating that sort of symbolism to the world, instead of just putting it in so many words, you know. Which I think is really the genius of his work, particularly with bears," says Hoshino's friend, Juneau-based guide Lynn Schooler. "The other piece of his genius was just being able to show as much about the animal by showing you where it exists [rather] than getting in there for that portrait that so many people seem to think constitutes a good photo."

Hoshino first traveled to Alaska from his native Japan at age nineteen when, after seeing a picture of a remote Inuit village, he wrote the mayors of six arctic villages. One, the mayor of Shishmaref, responded and offered Hoshino a place to stay. He went for one month and stayed for three. Back at home, Hoshino earned a degree in economics, but he found after he had experienced Alaska that he was no longer part of his old world. Though he traveled back to Japan annually, he had found his home in North America and never really left it.

"One thing I'd encourage you to think about is unlike in America, I mean, he was absolutely completely famous in Japan," says Wyoming filmmaker Shane Moore, another of Hoshino's many friends and a traveling companion. "The wildlife photographers there are something like rock stars. I remember once in Alaska we were in Denali, and this busload, two busloads actually, of Japanese tourists disembarked, and you'd have thought they'd found Mick Jagger."

People who knew him agree that Hoshino made everyone feel like his best friend; but one gets a sense from Schooler that his relationship with Michio was a particularly special one for both men. In his book about their friendship, *The Blue Bear*, Schooler describes himself as a person damaged by a variety of life's circumstances, including the horrific murder of a woman he was coming to love. He met Hoshino under professional conditions—taking the photographer and his crew out to get pictures of humpback whales—and that trip became an annual voyage, six seasons strung together to form a single story. "Having few words between us required precise, explicit choices and allowed little of the aimless chitchat that often supplies an easy path around the difficulties of true communication," Schooler writes. Near the end of one trip, Hoshino asks in his broken English if Schooler has ever seen a glacier bear, a rare black bear with bluish-tinted fur colloquially referred to as a blue bear. "'Well, it's not really the sort of thing you can expect to see, Michio,' I said. Michio's laugh took me by surprise. His shoulders shook, and an unrestrained jiggling spread to his belly. I started laughing along, too. 'What? What's so funny?' I asked. Michio resettled his hat on his head, gave one more laugh, and then rearranged the tripod in his arms before answering. 'Well, maybe . . . you have to *[l]ook*.'"

I piece together what others say about Hoshino, looking for the essence of this man I will never meet. He was a good cook. He longed for a family. He was patient, willing to wait a month camping in frigid weather to photograph the northern lights. "I want to value these moments that flow by, without producing anything at all," he wrote in a Japanese-published book entitled *The Traveling Tree*, translated by his friend Karen Colligan-Taylor. "I always want to know in my heart that there is another kind of time flowing by in parallel with the hectic conduct of man's daily life."

Hoshino was generous with other photographers, sharing advice among people who generally hoard knowledge. He was trusting in a way that affected the world around him. "He really did have an aura that made animals behave differently. Both ways. I've seen animals act aggressively toward Michio when they weren't aggressive toward anyone else, and I have seen bears literally walk up and lay down by us and take a nap," Schooler says. "I don't want to try to deify him or sanctify him or anything, he was just a hell of a nice guy with a childish approach to the world that, in turn, somehow created a very trusting and childlike response from the world."

And, Schooler adds, Hoshino never let his fear of bears stop him from sleeping outdoors in his tent. It was an indulgence that killed him.

Kamchatka's brown bears are the closest relatives of North America's grizzlies. They are separated by only about ten or eleven thousand years (when the land bridging the Bering Strait drowned in the rising ocean, cutting off the route between the Asian and North American continents). Hoshino found himself intrigued by the grizzly's cousin and planned a trip to the peninsula for August 1996.

The single cabin at Kurilskoy Lake in Kamchatka was full for the two weeks of Hoshino's trip: A Japanese film crew claimed one bunk and filled the other with their camera gear. A brown bear had broken into the cabin several days earlier—leaving claw marks on the outside walls—but the crew simply boarded over the window and moved in. Other visitors were forced to sleep outside. Alaskan photographer Curtis Hight claimed a nearby bear-viewing tower for his bed; Hoshino put up a tent.

Russian biologist Igor Revenko and his brother Andrei were working for the Japanese crew, which was filming a documentary about Hoshino's work. A short, solid man with a piercing gaze, Revenko has since immigrated to Canada and now lives near Vancouver, British Columbia. Though he was raised in the relatively urban world of the Ukraine, he jumped at the chance to take the ranger/biologist job at the newly created South Kamchatka Sanctuary after graduating in 1985.

The camp at Kurilskoy Lake was not a place for someone seeking solitude. People came and went constantly in the days before the tragedy. In addition to the Russian and Japanese TV people were American and Russian biologists Bill Leacock and the Revenko brothers, naturalist Charlie Russell, a CBS correspondent, and tourists sponsored by Friends of the Earth.

Revenko tells me that when Hoshino arrived, a male bear had been frequenting the camp at Kurilskoy Lake. "He was a little bit interested in what was going on around the camp because maybe he tried some human food or something, maybe some garbage," he says. It had so far been a poor salmon year, but Revenko says there was nothing physically wrong with this brown bear to indicate that it might be dangerous.

As Hoshino was in the habit of sleeping in his tent, he continued to do so. Charlie Russell spent one night sharing Michio's tent, an experience he recalls with fondness. "I remember we talked a little bit about why he wanted to sleep in the tent, because there was no question that this was an unusual bear. I mean everyone, including Michio, knew it. Igor knew it. It was an unusual situation because of the total disrespect [shown by the bear] toward the humans. And it was spooky, I thought. Several times during the night I checked my plane to make sure it was all right.

"That night there was a bunch of people, a bunch of tents all around, you know, so we were like a school of fish. You knew that a barracuda was going to get one of you, but you felt secure because it probably wouldn't be you."

Revenko says he asked Hoshino each evening to please sleep inside the cabin. "Maybe because it's too cold, maybe because of mosquitoes, 'Just go and sleep inside. You will feel more comfortable, we will feel more comfortable. Just to be more comfortable.'

"But Hoshino always refused, saying, 'No, no, I'm fine. I don't like people snoring, I like fresh air' and so on, so on.

"But it's easy to be smart afterwards, you know? I had two groups of Americans for two years stay there for a week or so, look at these grizzly bears right before Michio, put up tents around. Nobody get any sense that this is too dangerous in terms of bears."

That sense of security ended on August 8, 1996.

Revenko, Hoshino, and company had gone to bed late after spending the evening in a sauna. So Revenko had a hard time waking when the cameraman starting shouting: "Bear! Bear! Michio! Bear!" Igor, his brother, and the three crew members grabbed their flashlights and ran out of the cabin.

They saw the remnants of Hoshino's tent flattened. "I remember there was tall grass around. You couldn't see much of what was happening on the ground, but the bear's head was down, so we heard Michio scream," Revenko says. Hoping to spook the bear, Igor grabbed a metal bucket and a shovel and began banging them together. "I think I did crazy things because I was like maybe three meters from the bear doing this. I was almost naked and it was dark, with four scared people behind me just really watching all this." The bear did not shy away. "When I became too noisy, he just picked up Michio and went in the darkness. Everybody saw it. Michio was so small compared to this bear; he was carrying Michio, who didn't touch the ground because it was like a dog carrying a small toy in terms of size and strength.

"You felt like you were helpless, and you have no rifle or anything. It was a horrible moment. He carried Michio in the dark; as much as our flashlights work, we followed him. And so he carried him and disappeared behind the bushes."

Revenko says he had pepper spray in camp, probably in the cabin, but in his panic did not think to look for it. Nor, in hindsight, does he believe it would have been of any use.

I press Revenko several times during our conversation for things he would rather not talk about. "Was there any chance Michio was still alive when the bear dragged him off into the bush?" I ask.

"I remember his face was frozen, maybe because of shock. It's hard to say. He didn't make any move when bear carried him off. I don't know. Who needs these details?" Revenko is disturbed by the memory I have asked him to dredge up. Perhaps he suspects I am too interested in the sensational aspects of the attack. But I am thinking of another story, a woman who lay dying all night after a grizzly attack in Glacier National Park in 1968, when park rangers forbade other campers—including a doctor—from leaving the shelter of a chalet to venture out several hundred yards into the dark to rescue her.

I elaborate. "Just if someone had a gun, could he have been saved?"

"Yeah, if I would have a gun, I thought about it a thousand times. If I would have gun, I would stick gun in neck and shoot it. Yeah.

"It's strange to understand for an American, that in this area, sometime you are not allowed to carry gun. It's up to you. You have to be cautious, you have to be careful. Nobody discusses with you; it's your personal responsibility."

The question of the pepper spray lingers, but I cannot second-guess Revenko. Naked and armed with only a bucket and shovel, he rushed a grizzly bear that was eating his friend. This father of two children risked his life. He replays the scene in his head, searching for a way he might have confronted the beast in the night and won. The scenario never works itself out right. In the end, someone is always dead.

At the time of his death, Michio Hoshino had fulfilled his deepest longing: He'd fallen in love, married, and fathered a son. His work was taking a logical new direction for a man who saw the world as an intricate collection of relationships. He'd been spending time among the caribou-hunting people of the far north, where oil companies have long hungered to tap into the Arctic National Wildlife Refuge. Hoshino's photos were not taken in a vacuum, and he knew this. Hoshino wrote: "One summer afternoon the few caribou I saw as small dots in the distance, suddenly multiplied, becoming tens, then hundreds, then thousands of caribou, filling the horizon. They were heading straight toward me. Soon I found myself in the center of tens of thousands of caribou. I felt taken back to an earlier page in the history of the Earth. As I watched the river of animals disappear over the horizon, I was not only profoundly moved, but strangely saddened, as if I had just witnessed the passing of an age."

"His intention in photography was shifting more and more toward the human," Schooler says. "Before he died he was starting to work as much toward presenting humans in a natural setting as he was wildlife. He was really becoming interested in the place of humanity in nature. And bears were part of that. How people live around bears was important to him."

■■ Nearly all photographers who work with wild bears find themselves abruptly facing their own mortality. It is, as Shane Moore says, the essence of the value of the animal. "Frankly, if they didn't have the ability to do exactly what they did to Michio, they wouldn't have quite the power over us that they do."

There's Bill Campbell's self-styled therapy, tempting the boar on its home turf. Tom Murphy once surprised a mother with three cubs on a buffalo carcass. "She was standing on her hind legs, huffing and puffing and throwing dirt on this carcass. The three cubs wake up, and I think, 'oh shit, this is going to hurt.'" He and his companion stood up simultaneously, together resembling one large animal, and the sow turned and ran. Tom Mangelsen's closest call came when a bear walked up on him in Alaska while he bathed in a stream appropriately named Igloo Creek. In retrospect, he says, "what I realized had happened was the bear thought I was an injured animal because most animals that are injured, like caribou, moose, you know, go to the waters when they're attacked by wolves or something. It's an instinctive behavior. I'm sure that the bear heard the thrashing and yelling and then saw me, this object—I'm sure it had never seen a naked human before—thrashing in the water and thought, that looks like a tasty little meal there." Mangelsen says he forgot about the cold, drew himself up as large as he could, and readied to throw a rock. Once the bear realized Mangelsen was a human, it turned and moved away.

Those experiences are far beyond the ken of most roadside and game-farm photographers. At best, the spiritual death of a caged animal conveys nothing; the physical death of the wild teaches. Hoshino wrote: "We all die and go back to nature eventually. When we are in the city we tend to forget—we don't really think about it. But nature reminds us . . . It's not a sad thing. It gives us energy. Nature has a kind of power to encourage you to live because Nature teaches—you are going to die."

BEAR KEEPERS

■■ Probably it started with a track. Or a ghost trail of footprints in the moss, as though an invisible tribe haunted the forest. No wonder when people first saw the great beast making those tracks so much like our own, they looked for the human beneath the fur.

Among people who lived with them, the most enduring myth was one of kinship, of the woman who marries the grizzly and bears his children, half man, half beast. Paul Shepard, in his seminal book *The Sacred Paw*, calls the story of the bear wife "the most persistent and widely told tale ever devised to entertain and educate." In subsequent stories, her sons teach men hunting ceremonies; how to seek out the bear in his den and ask him to sacrifice himself to them. The final feast is a sacrament of respect with proof of relationship revealed in the skinned carcass, a strikingly human form.

On continents with no wild primates, bears are our mirrors. In addition to our shared physical traits, bears snore when they sleep and cuff their youngsters when the cubs misbehave. Grizzlies possess a cognitive complexity: Aware of their own track-making, they may travel to denning sites only during a storm so the heavy snow will cover the sign of their passing, walk backwards carefully in their own tracks then suddenly leap off a trail onto a rock or behind a bush, veer from their path to avoid leaving their paw prints in muddy areas. They've been known to set ambushes. These resemblances spawned stories and rituals everywhere bears and people shared a homeland. So far as we know, bears were never merely food.

In Asia and to a lesser extent in America, tribal people developed elaborate ceremonies—still practiced today by the Ainu of Japan, for instance—described by Paul Shepard, in which a captive bear was feted, honored, and then killed. Shepard speculates that these were some sort of transitional cultures and finds not only the seeds of demise of the revered bear in the rise of agriculture (about ten thousand years ago in temperate climates) but the hunter's role diminished in importance as well: the shift from a co-occupied wilderness to a human-controlled landscape. The magic of a mother bear giving birth in the den during the winter death of hibernation was first controlled by shamans, then reshaped by priests. "[T]he sacrifice of a captive rather than a free-living bear shifts the psychology of the relationship between man and bear—and the natural world—in profound ways," Shepard writes. We used these rituals to take the bears' power for ourselves until only hints remain today: the grizzly transformed into a groundhog to predict the end of winter; the real rebirth of a bear each spring now owned by Christians as the mythical resurrection of a savior.

But these really are only recent developments; a few thousand years worth of civilization balanced against the eons we considered brown bears our cousins. Despite the interruption of progress, we still seek out the remnants of these ties. They persist in children's stories (Yogi, Pooh, and Goldilocks); we gape at lethargic zoo bears, and we shiver like our ancestors when movie grizzlies play monsters.

Some special few feel these bonds more strongly than any other force in their lives, and we still develop myths from their stories. There's the one about a grizzly joining Alberta naturalist Charlie Russell around a campfire, to sit and stare at the flames for a while. "Don't worry," Russell reportedly told his human companions. "I know him." Or Timothy Treadwell, who believed his grizzlies were capable of intuiting his intentions. And of photographer Michio Hoshino's calming effect on wild animals. Of the three, only Russell is still alive, the others killed in nightmarish scenarios that force us to reconsider our forgotten fear of four-legged beasts in the night.

Then there is Doug Seus.

■ ■   Grizzly trainers and handlers refer to Seus as the Moses of the business, the "best bear trainer in the world," one man asserts. Before Seus raised Bart the Bear, no one knew what was possible. "He has inside of him things that only he knows," says Casey Anderson, of the Montana Grizzly Encounter.

The compound Doug and Lynne Seus share with three grizzly bears and a pack of timber wolves near Heber City, Utah, appears from the road to be nothing more than a quaint old homestead. It's bordered by a small trout stream at the back, an irrigation ditch in front, and neighbors to either side; to Lynne's relief, a steep hill at the back of their property keeps development at bay.

My husband and the Seus family are old friends. Doug took Seus to see his first wild grizzly at one of Doug's most holy places in the universe, a basin in the high country of Glacier National Park where bears congregate every fall to eat huckleberries. Seus once asked him to join Wasatch Wildlife as a bear handler for the Jean-Jacques Annaud movie *The Bear*, but after consideration, Doug turned him down.

"Mostly it was a matter of dealing with wild animals in a controlled way that contradicted all my half-baked theories on why these animals were important to begin with. You have to discipline. You have to take a cub and whack him [the bear], like Seus does," Doug says. "What I realized was I'd end up knowing more about grizzly bear behavior than anybody would, but I'd pay a huge price for that; it would diminish the value of wildness for me."

We convince Seus to sit down with the tape recorder. Doug joins in, and what evolves then is less an interview than a conversation between men who each know intimately a side of a grizzly—one in captivity and the other in wilderness.

"I was born in Pennsylvania," Seus says. "They had a lot of vernal ponds, wetlands that dry up in the summer. But I used to have frogs in the basement. I was really enamored with reptiles and amphibians. It was a big, rural farm area. I spent my summer days sketching butterflies. That type of stuff. It resurfaced, that great childhood, fishing down on the creek, later. I think this line of work was just an extension of the happiest part of my childhood." Seus started out training wolves. He says this as though it's a logical starting point: Some people have cats, some people have goldfish. He had wolves, and when the Mutual of Omaha filmmakers came to town, they paid him to film his wolves.

Seus's first bear, Bart, was a captive Kodiak (a brown bear from the island of the same name, often classified as a subspecies of the grizzly), born in a zoo on January 10, 1977. Seus got him when Bart was about two months old. "I bottle-raised him, and we just went forward. Trial and error.

"At that time, zoos—it's sort of a disgusting thing—they used to keep cubs. They used to propagate the offspring of a lot of animals, and they wanted them for the tourist season, for Memorial to Labor Day weekend, then they would euthanize them," Seus says. "Come Labor Day, now they're bigger, they're not the charming little attraction. And this zoo recognized that they were going to have to do this. They stepped up and placed him [Bart] with me."

Lynne elaborates: She and Doug had just gotten licensed to have a brown bear and were looking for a "little Kodiak" when Bart became available. "Bart was basically an unplanned pregnancy; I think his parents were teenagers," she says. "The zoo didn't have funding for an additional brown bear display. As they say, the universe lined up for us."

Before he died in 2000, Bart became perhaps the most famous Hollywood animal actor next to Lassie. He starred in more than a dozen feature movies, including *Legends of the Fall, The Edge, The Bear, Wind-walker, White Fang*, and *Clan of the Cave Bear* as well as several dozen television appearances, including the 1998 Academy Awards.

No one knows how many grizzly bears—dozens, hundreds—live in captivity in North America. State records are incomplete at best, and no one appears to be keeping track of the big picture. Their homes are zoos, roadside menageries, educational parks, and, in many cases, small cages in backyards. Some, like Bart, are trained for film or still photography; most simply live out their lives as curiosities and exhibits.

To call them "grizzly bears" breeds a little confusion. The grizzly is the American brown bear, a subspecies of *Ursus arctos*, which is to say that while all grizzlies are brown bears, brown bears living on other continents are not considered grizzlies. Though there are often marked behavioral differences due to their different environments, grizzlies and brown bears can interbreed and are considered the same species. Some brown bears live on the coast, eat salmon, and grow very large; some live in forests and others on plains and steppes, and they range far and wide foraging for food. Because the grizzlies in the contiguous United States have been considered a threatened species since 1975, it's illegal to have a wild-born *Ursus arctos horribilis* from the lower forty-eight states in captivity. (With exceptions: The federal Fish and Wildlife Service will sometimes first try to place a "problem" grizzly or orphaned cub in some sort of facility rather than kill the bear.)

Dealing in grizzly bears takes a whole lot of paperwork to satisfy the requirements of the Convention on International Trade in Endangered Species, the applicable international law. So many hobbyists stick to mixed breeds: brown bears with lineages traced to Siberia, Syria, Romania, and so forth. The differences between wild American grizzlies and their captive cousins end up being largely semantic, the results of lines on a map, traceable only by DNA analysis. So for convenience sake, the captive brown bears here are all referred to as grizzlies.

The grizzlies Seus has worked with learn to trust him first with their food and eventually with their lives. In exchange, he says he trusts them and that ideally there are no limits. Well, he qualifies this: As cubs, they learn parameters. "They can't bite you and attack you and usurp your position from you. Bite me and I'm going to knock the shit out of you. I mean, I will. Fair, quick, just, over. Okay? You have to be in control. Control is a bad word; it's not a vogue or appropriate word. It puts up the alarms. But control is absolutely necessary when you're working with a big carnivore."

Seus's power is not about physical control—a human can never win a fight with a grizzly bear—but evolves from a meticulously constructed relationship. Things like stun guns destroy that rapport, Seus says. For instance, standard operating procedure among wild animal trainers involves always having backup, someone who can step in if something goes wrong. Trust, he says, means going without it.

"If you're going to clean up poop [in the cage], oh my wife should come out and you know, attend the door and stuff like that. That's the wise thing to do. But there's a part of me that I don't feel threatened, and I go without a backup. I believe the bears interpret it as I totally trust them," he says, adding that the situation is a catch-22. "You should never do that, but on the other hand, if you never do that, where's the trust?"

"So you think the animals pick up on that?" I ask.

"Oh, I know they do," he says. Seus admits to spending hours alone with the bears with no one watching. "But I feel that confidence because of the foundation. Because that's what it's about. That's the crux of it."

I suggest to Seus that in his case, his bears are willingly relinquishing control and could take it back at any time.

"That's the same thing. That's the beauty of them. They're these uncontrollable forces. They're the epitome of wildness and magic and wilderness. But what I'm talking about is, if you're going to be a bear, you have to be the bear that's in control," he says. "That's building a relationship, right? It only happens after you've weathered these plateaus. To get where this bear thinks you're cool."

Working with the bears, Seus says, gives him a break from the frustrations of the human world. Grizzlies have no hidden agendas, a fact he finds enormously satisfying.

"You've got this communication with a primal beast that you don't have with your own species because you go to your normal job, and you may have to smile and say good morning to your boss, or any situation where you have an obligation. Civilized communication. That is removed from working with these animals, and that's what's satisfying, that's what's relaxing for me. That's the honesty in the communication that I appreciate because there are no façades. The bears give me freedom to discuss and to act on a primal basis. No façade, no bullshit, everything is right up front. They react instantaneously to each other."

These bear guys are likewise prone to describe each other in ursine terms. My husband, Doug, is like a bear, Seus says, because he gets grumpy when certain resources are scarce; because he makes snap judgments; because of his intolerance for what Seus calls "civilized communication." Seus functions on the same levels.

"See, there's bear people, and there are other people. I really believe that," Seus says.

"You're probably a lot more patient with the bears than with people," I venture.

"Yeah, and see, that's bad. I mean I recognize that. When I'm let down by somebody's word, Lynne can say, 'Well, something must have happened,' and I know that's true." But Seus finds people's excuses hard to accept and says bears are equally impatient.

I am ready to turn off the tape, but Doug has more questions of his own: What about fear? What goes wrong when trainers get mauled? Does Seus see any parallel between Timothy Treadwell's relationship with wild bears and his own?

"Timothy Treadwell was not in control," Seus answers. "In all candor I respected his independence and liked him, and I don't like using the term *naïveté* because I think that's a negative term. But he was not in control. And here's the problem. A good, effusive bear on a bad day could be trouble. Or a serene bear on a good day can be great. But to go amongst and reach out tactilely, touching those bears without being in control of the situation, in control of the wild dynamics, is naïve. It's because he wanted them to accept him as them. And they did perhaps, but they ultimately took their positions."

Finally, Seus takes us out to see his bears. The weather in northern Utah in 2004 is pretty mild for late December. His three grizzlies are not eating much, though no one has gone to sleep for the winter. Wild grizzlies usually go into their dens just before the first big snow of winter, though on a mild year, if there's food available, some have been known to come out midwinter, or even stay out all year. So while captive bears can get groggy—and some even hibernate—the steady supply of food may help keep them awake. Tank, a ten-year-old male born in captivity, is half-grizzly, half-European brown bear. "I heard that his mother was a Yellowstone grizzly problem bear and that the father was a captive cross between a northern European, Norwegian *Ursus arctos arctos*, and a North American interior grizzly. Tank's got the European size but the North American look," Seus says. Tank sits serenely, watching us discuss his lineage, resting his chin on his two front feet, which he's stuck in a bucket. Seus says he believes Tank would get along fine with his other male grizzly, Little Bart, but that the female, Honey Bump, would probably try to kill him. And while Little Bart and Honey Bump love to be together, they play too rough. So each bear has his or her own cage, each with an enclosed area filled with straw. Tank keeps taking his straw out of the den, while Little Bart grabs hold of Seus's arm to drag him inside. "He wants me to hibernate with him," Seus says.

Little Bart and Honey Bump are twins. Their mother was a wild Alaskan interior grizzly who was shot by a poacher. "[Alaska Fish and Game] had been watching this guy who was a poacher for a couple years. And they followed him, and the undercover cop pulled in the parking lot and this poacher's coveralls were there with lactation on them," he says. "So they knew that it was a female grizzly that he had poached, who had cubs. So what they did was they went by helicopter, and these cubs were running around, and they had been four days without their mother. They were going to euthanize the cubs, and someone from Alaska Fish and Game called. This was when Bart was dying, and I was very emotionally distraught."

Little Bart is now rather large—about 600 pounds. Seus and Doug hypothesize that he'll keep growing for the rest of his life. Honey Bump has slowed down at around 350. Seus takes a few minutes with each of the twins; Bart wrestles with him, while Bump likes to touch feet. Seus talks to the bears, lots of "good boy!" and "good girl!" but a lot of their communication involves touching. He says much of the information he gets resides in the tactile part of their relationship, and he believes that trainers who avoid touching do so at their peril.

"I've actually seen some European trainers with cubs. The first thing they do is put on a muzzle. Then you know what they do? They pick them up by their ears. It's an old, culturally archaic process. What a lack of common sense, what a lack of passion," he says. "Oh, here's another thing. I've seen them with welders' gloves. Now what is that? That's not teaching any parameters. They don't want to be bitten, which nobody does. But you really can't feel emotionally where you're at."

■■ After our visit with the Seus household, Doug and I head north to visit with another bear guy. This man has a darker story to tell, and in the interests of the bear involved, names and places have been changed to protect their identities.

"Larry" had a problem in the form of a female grizzly bear named "Curly." Larry had acquired Curly as a young cub under rather dubious circumstances. But as an experienced keeper of wild animals, Larry knew that Curly was going to start growing very soon and would no longer be content to, say, continue living in Larry's living room.

The problem is, Curly was on the lam. She'd been born in a zoolike facility in the winter of 2000. Curly, however, owed her existence to her former owner's desire to make money: Cubs attract tourists. Her owner—let's call him "Moe"—had hit on the idea of breeding his bears—blacks and grizzlies—to produce cubs, which people visiting the nearby wild bear habitat could then pay to bottle-feed. The logistics were less cuddly. "Every year all these black bears, the big males, would impregnate all the females, and we'd have six females have litters of three, so we'd have like twenty cubs," Larry, a former employee of the facility, explains. "Well, the first spring we have to take the cubs out of the den before all the bears emerge because the males will eat the cubs.

"But we had to have the cubs because people want to see the cubs when they come here, you know? And for X amount of dollars, they can feed them with a bottle, too. So the more cubs the better, because the more bottles you can stick in their mouths, the more money you make. This is going on for some time. Then when those cubs get older, they start going back in with the rest of the bears. Well, then the population was starting to get a little too big. So there was going to be a need for some kind of birth control or something going on. That was my idea: We're going to have to start spaying females, neutering males, doing something." Moe balked, according to Larry. "So basically what happened at that point was the cubs were used until the end of the summer, and then they were euthanized."

The next spring, the park's grizzlies produced four cubs. Larry says Moe justified this part of the breeding "program" by saying he was bolstering the population of a threatened species. "He'd try to put it in the same category as the panda, like where the world wildlife population is really endangered and captive breeding is really helping a little." Moe's operation, however, bore little resemblance to an official captive breeding program of the sort prescribed by U.S. federal law. The official Policy Regarding Controlled Propagation of Species Listed Under the Endangered Species Act, for instance, calls for "controlled propagation" to be used only as a last resort, and then as a coordinated effort spelled out specifically in a given animals' recovery plan. Such a program has to take genetics into account, and "intercrossing" is forbidden. A short list of considerations includes "analysis of geomorphological similarities of habitat, genetic similarity, phenotype characteristics, stock histories, habitat use, and other ecological, biological, and behavioral indicators."

In the United States, places like Moe's are governed by a patchwork of state laws. In Montana, captive wild animals must be neutered or spayed. Breeding is allowed in Idaho. "As bizarre as it sounds, they're private property. Just like you can shoot your car, you can do anything you want with them," Idaho Fish and Game biologist Steve Nadeau says of his state's regulations. In Texas, practically anything goes.

From a purely intellectual standpoint, Larry found the situation at Moe's park during the season of the grizzly cubs fascinating to watch. "The best way I have to describe it in layman's terms is that I think grizzly bears are more emotional than black bears," Larry says. "When these little grizzly cubs got older, they'd get in moods. So when the people would go to bottle-feed them, sometimes they'd almost get their hand ripped off, you know? All of a sudden, Moe didn't want grizzly cubs there any more. It was too much of a liability."

While Larry had been upset about the demise of Moe's black bear cubs, he reached his breaking point when Moe insisted on killing the grizzly cubs. "The bears were going to be put down or he'd find someone else to manage the place. I knew that was the day that I was done playing everyone else's stupid game for a job." Larry found homes for three of the cubs. The fourth he hijacked. "This is illegal and not that I'm proud of it, but I basically told the guy that Curly was coming with me or everybody—the newspaper—was going to start hearing about this stuff. It was blackmail. So he agreed." Moe declined to comment for this story, so we only have Larry's version of the events.

While Larry could have gone to jail for his grizzly-napping, ironically there is nothing illegal about Moe's final solution to his overpopulation troubles. In the jurisdiction where Curly was born, bears can be bred; bears can also be killed. One wildlife manager raises a disturbing scenario: Could the grizzly cubs have been shot as part of a canned hunt at a nearby game farm? He has no evidence that any such event took place. He just points out that it's both legal and possible. "It just seems logical that the next step would be to charge some guy to shoot some bear," he says. "But I haven't actually heard of that happening."

After working for a decade at other people's facilities, Larry came to believe he could do things better. No cages. No breeding. No overpopulation. He wanted to open his own bear park, and given the fact that

Curly was a growing girl, he had to do it soon. "She was on the run. I didn't have any permits, I didn't have all these things, you know? But I had to take her," Larry says. Curly traveled the countryside, hiding out at other licensed bear facilities. "It wasn't always the right way legally, but we got a little help here and there, even from people above us who would bend the rules."

While Larry got unofficial help from official people who saw he was trying to do the right thing by his cub, he still fears Curly could be taken away from him, killed, or stuck in a cage.

■■ When Casey Anderson and his two business partners first applied for a roadside menagerie permit from the state of Montana, they included a laundry list of potential uses for their bear exhibit. One of these was so bizarre, they were nearly laughed out of the county: It was a grizzly motel.

The plan was to build a set of cabins, each sharing a one-way glass wall with the bears' dens, so people staying there could see into the lairs from their rooms. Now, locals opposed Anderson's permit for every conceivable reason—from fears over declining property values to concerns for the animals' welfare—but the sheer weirdness of the bear motel eclipsed everything else. On assignment for Writers on the Range (a regional syndication service), I called up Anderson in the summer of 2003 and made arrangements to meet for an interview. When he stood me up and did not return my subsequent calls, I wrote a satirical column at his expense.

About a year later the phone rings and Anderson introduces himself when I answer it. "Your husband's one of my heroes," he says, referring to Doug. "I have to say, you kind of hurt my feelings." He invites us out to see Montana Grizzly Encounter, now open for business (albeit as a roadside exhibit—the motel idea long abandoned). Admiring his courage and feeling a little guilty, I take him up on the offer.

When I first go to meet him, the parking lot is deserted in mid-December. Anderson talks fast, ignoring the cold, gale-force wind gusting in our faces. He is one of those people who can interview himself; with the tape recorder on, he barely pauses for the questions.

Now, Anderson claims the bear motel was not a serious proposal, and he fiercely guards the bears' dens as "their private space."

"That one was an idea that we wrote down on paper because we had to write down every possible thing that we could ever think about doing; knowing that we probably never would do that," he says. "So when we went public, of all the things people grabbed onto, they grabbed onto that one. And it was so far away from what we were really trying to do. It was a controversial thing, you know. That was our first impression. It really sucked, it really did. Everyone made fun of it, even you."

At the time of my visit, there are three grizzlies and no cages at the Montana Grizzly Encounter. Squeezed between the frontage road just south of Interstate 90 and the Northern Pacific rail line on the south, the facility is situated to siphon off tourist traffic that invades the Northern Rockies each summer. The two-year-old male, Brutus, was saved from what Anderson calls "a living hell." Two female twins, Christie and Sheena, who spent the first eighteen years of their lives—twenty-four hours a day, seven days a week—locked in a four-by-eight cage and an old windowless trailer, respectively, were destined for a hunting ranch when Anderson rescued them from the sweltering heat of Texas. "They're in surprisingly, relatively okay shape for being where they were," Anderson says. "But their muscles were atrophied, they had very strange development in their rear ends especially." At the facility, just east of Bozeman, the bears live on a one-acre plot landscaped with a couple of gentle hills, a waterfall, and pond. A cement wall, a twelve-foot-deep moat, and an electric fence (with backup generator) keep them from wandering out into the Gallatin National Forest. It's not much when one considers that a wild male grizzly can call up to one thousand square miles home, but it is certainly better than the alternative. At least that's what Anderson believes.

Anderson is a Helena boy, a fifth-generation Montanan on one side of his family, a California hippie on the other. "I'm a hypocrite in my blood," he says. While he can talk rancher with the best of them, his dark beard and scraggly hair suggest a strong influence from the other half of his heritage as well. He got into the captive bear business as a sideline during college at Montana State University, when he was studying wildlife biology. He was, he admits, idealistic about the profession.

"Now you know most biologists sit in an office and write down data, blah, blah, blah. In my mind, I was going to go save the grizzly bear, do something, save the wolverine," he says. Then he took a job at Troy Hyde's Animals of Montana. That facility, he says, was understaffed and overpopulated. "There were times they had sixty different animals, and the greatest number of people I remember being there was three. It doesn't lend itself to a very humane environment," he says. "The other thing was that every one of those animals has a dollar sign on their head. Here's this bear, maybe [Hyde] bottle-raised and gave a name to, who really looked at him as the only thing in its life, and if someone came in and said, 'Hey, I'll give you twenty grand for that hide,' that bear would be dead."

Hyde declined to respond to Anderson's criticism, but Casey's words were echoed by David Pauli, director of the Northern Rockies Humane Society. "Animals of Montana appears to me to be a purely commercial enterprise," he says. "I have no knowledge of them being involved in any conservation movement here or abroad. The few contacts I have had, the organization's interest seemed to be in getting rid of animals [in any way including gunshot] that were not profitable and acquiring animals that could potentially be profitable."

A series of similar jobs both repelled Anderson (he left nearly all on bad terms) and bound him to grizzly bears and the profession of keeping them. He grew particularly close to a cub named Teton and began to believe there was something special possible with a grizzly bear; a relationship of sorts. The bears were open if he could be, too.

"I always loved bears in the wild. But being right there in the Tetons over by Driggs, and having Teton, the little bear, and going out hiking around, that's when I started molding myself into something instead of just being whatever I was—a shit-shoveler."

We talk while standing out in the wind for a while, watching the bears. Christie is hibernating. Brutus and Sheena are out poking around, playing with each other. Anderson says he hides smelly things out there for the bears to find—his low-budget effort to keep their boredom at bay. He knows it's minimal, as are the bare concrete walls and treeless acre. Anderson continues, "'Are they tame?' people ask me. No. The thing is, those girls are so pissed off at the world, they have something that a wild bear usually doesn't that is even more dangerous, and that is the lack of fear of people. You go out hiking, walking, you walk across a bear on the trail. Most of the time that bear wants nothing to do with you and takes off. These bears in the fight-or-flight mode don't have that flight option. So what they choose to do is kick your ass."

Anderson should know. Though he's still a young man at twenty-nine, he's worked with captive bears all over the Yellowstone ecosystem, including a drive-through park, where keepers have to deal with upwards of thirty free-ranging bears at a time.

When he decided to open his own place, he went to the guru of captive grizzlies, Doug Seus, for advice. "I was talking to Seus about this the other day. I realized that in this little bear society, I had become an expert at bear body language. When I'm out there—say I'm feeding and here come these twenty bears running at me—every right, sane thing in me says be scared shitless.

"So you have to—and Doug Seus and me laughed our asses off about this—you have to convince yourself that you're tougher than these bears are, that you're the dominant dude. And then you hope that in your stupidity your body will react and show that to the bears."

Anderson suggests we go inside out of the wind. He had joked earlier about sharing a den with the bears, but I soon realize he wasn't kidding. He's squeezed a bedroom, kitchen, and office into one end of the metal shed that also houses the three grizzlies. We hear Christie banging around behind the wall. Anderson says he and his partners agreed to new rules for themselves last month. "Basically I'm the only one who goes back in the den to clean it. I keep it dark in there. Anytime she gets bothered, she gets pretty grumpy."

Upon arriving in Montana, the twins spent the first week in their man-made dens. When Anderson let Sheena out for the first time, she climbed to the top of a hill to look around. "They'd never experienced Big Sky country before; you can see here where she lived." He's incorporated a picture of Sheena's Texas cage into his exhibit. "It was brushy, bayou country. She looked around and it scared the crap out of her, so she ran right back inside.

"The next day, she wouldn't come out. But the day after that, Sheena came back out, climbed the hill, and spent a couple hours just staring around. Then she walked down to the pond to take a swim and was just splashing, playing, throwing her head around. It was one of the greatest days; it made me cry." Anderson says Christie did the same thing the next day. After swimming she got out of the water, and "I don't know how to describe it except to say she bucked like a bronco."

Anderson has erected educational placards, advising people about everything from the grizzlies' eating habits and the annual rhythm of their lives to proper behavior in grizzly country. He knows some of this is overkill: Visitors to Glacier National Park in particular have been coached to shout at the top of their lungs, running off wildlife for miles around. While he thinks his advice probably helps some visitors who plan to hike or camp in the backcountry, the real lessons happen with locals, with ranchers' kids who live with grizzlies and will largely be responsible for their survival if the bears are removed from the endangered species list, a move announced by the U.S. Fish and Wildlife Service in March 2007, but now being challenged in federal court by the Bozeman office of Earthjustice. "We get the average Joe who doesn't know anything about bears but is going to go hiking or camping in grizzly country. They drive by here, they come in, and leave a little less ignorant," he says. "But the other thing is, we're on the cusp of bears being delisted. People who live around here are the ones who are going to be involved."

Anderson says the park is open free to local schools, in part so kids can get a firsthand look "at these awesome bears that Dad told them are the devil."

Anderson recalls one rancher who visited during the facility's first season, a man who'd been dragged in by his wife. "He initially comes up to me and says, 'Where are you from?' I know what he's thinking: Here's this guy trying to move in here and capitalize on Montana. I tell him, 'I'm a fifth generation Montanan, and my family's cattle ranchers over in Helena.' Well, he looks at me differently; in his mind he gets a respect for me. So he sat down. The bears were being very playful that day, jumping around. I could see him; he was really fighting enjoying it. Then he started asking questions about the bears and started telling stories about how his dad used to see grizzly bears all the time, and the conversation got real light.

"When he left here, he looked at me, shook my hand, and he said, 'You're doing a pretty good thing. I see another side of it now. I hope you can do that for other people.' I made an impression on somebody who, at that point, you couldn't make an impression on."

For all his talk about the bears not being tame, Anderson admits to a special relationship with Brutus. He'd never admit it to his paying guests, but he and Brutus are buddies. They touch. They lie together in the grass. They once shared a soak in a hot tub. It's a fulfillment of the possibility Anderson first saw in the grizzly cub Teton. But when I ask Humane Society director David Pauli about the Montana Grizzly Encounter, he sees a sad future.

"The bread and butter of captive wildlife facilities are the oohs and ahhs of babies. If you don't have babies, you don't have that big a draw. As that grizzly bear gets to be older and there's no new baby brought in, the local traffic will stop bringing in people, and it becomes an insufficient enterprise," he predicts. It's easy to imagine he is right, and I picture the image of an aging Anderson and old bear Brutus lying in the grass together, as traffic on the nearby interstate passes them by, drawn instead by the prospect of bottle-feeding cubs at places like the one where Curly was born.

There will be more chances for cubs at the Montana Grizzly Encounter. In late 2007, the facility took in two more young bears, Jake and Maggie. The older twins, while in relatively good shape given their former living conditions, are unlikely to live past the age of thirty. Then Anderson can adopt more orphaned cubs or surplus bears from a breeding park. But to what end? Even a bear born in captivity must smell the wild on the wind, and in his heart he knows what he is missing. Meanwhile, captive grizzlies produce countless cubs for us to cuddle with. We then relegate them to cages in places like Texas, or to zoos for the prime years of their lives, and in the end send them off to hunting ranches where yahoos who can't afford to kill a wild grizzly in Alaska or British Columbia or Kamchatka can shoot a bear in a pen. Captive grizzlies who get to live out their lives like Brutus and Christie and Sheena are scarce.

Conservationists, the animals' advocates, are prone to seeing the issue in black and white. Wild animals: good. Captive animals: bad. Yet the so-called "problem bears" are our own creation; we've squeezed the wilderness so tight—from Yellowstone country to Glacier Park and up north through Alberta, Canada—there aren't many places for wild grizzlies to simply live their lives in peace.

Anderson finds himself a bit schizophrenic as to his role in the whole debate. He sees the Montana Grizzly Encounter as a refuge for bears with bad lives. Yet he—albeit sometimes reluctantly—cultivates the carnival atmosphere of a for-profit venture (which the Montana Grizzly Encounter is), erecting billboards that announce SEE GRIZZLY BEARS . . . NO CAGES . . . EXIT NOW! He's waded deep into a murky swamp of American culture, human culture really, that most people prefer to ignore and now is trying to keep his head above the water for the sake of his bears.

"A lot of people would argue that those bears are better off dead. I don't know. I don't believe that. They're out there playing right now. It's hard to believe they're better off dead. Brutus has been in our lives since he was this big. He doesn't know any better. This is his life. He never could have known any better; it wasn't a possibility.

"On the flip side, the argument is, is this a big enough area for these bears? Well, I'd love to put a fence around the whole damn mountain, but I can't afford that. Then what am I doing to the area I put the fence around? I'm a hypocrite in some ways. I love the wild bears and everything, but I cram this poor little bear down on this acre and a half out there. But the truth is, in this acre and a half, I try to make it bear paradise. He doesn't go around working for food every day, he doesn't walk a hundred miles to try to get ten thousand calories and end up short anyway. He's served with a silver platter, he has the people he loves, he has a warm, secure place to sleep. In the bear world, that's a lot."

■■ A few months later, Doug and I drop by the Seus household again. Seus is out in the backyard, rope in hand, with his back to the cage where Little Bart paces in anticipation. Seus is waiting for the bear to settle down so he can work with him out on an adjacent patch of spring green grass. We sit in lawn chairs, separated from Seus and his assistant by a calf-high electric fence. He explains that Little Bart (the name now incongruous with the adult grizzly before us) wants out, but needs to learn to wait, to find patience, before they can work together safely. We sit listening to the creek where Seus has dug a swimming hole for the bears and wait for Little Bart to relax. Eventually, Seus enters the cage and loops a loose length of rope around the bear's neck.

They exit the cage without incident, Seus talking to the bear all the while, and everything seems fine when suddenly Little Bart roars and crouches, ears back. Seus's reaction is instantaneous: He simultaneously drops the rope, goes into his own crouch, reaches for the cutoff baseball bat in his back pocket, and roars back, "No! Don't you do that!"

There is a pause; the moment is frozen. Then each side senses an ease of tension in the other. Seus's hand leaves the bat in his pocket. Bart relaxes his crouch and flicks his ears in a conciliatory gesture. Seus breathes a deep sigh of relief and removes the rope from Little Bart's neck.

Seus's assistant figures it out first. "The rope caught on his ear," he says. That was the problem: the rope. When Little Bart and Honey Bump were captured by Alaska Fish and Game, they were tranquilized for the helicopter ride. Little Bart woke during the trip—his feet tied up—and freaked out. When Seus began to remove the rope leash this time, it caught ever so slightly on Little Bart's ear. "He remembers that trauma," Seus says. "And you saw the reaction: It was instantaneous."

Lynne rushes out of the house. "I hate that sound," she says. "I have to come out and make sure my husband's still alive." The rest of the training session goes without incident. Seus puts Little Bart through his paces with frequent rewards of a frying pan full of whipping cream. After about half an hour of practicing tricks of the sort he might perform on camera—sitting up, waving, growling—Seus lets Bart relax in the pool. "I'll let him stay out for a few hours," he says.

Seus feels the need to explain the cutoff bat in his back pocket. He calls it "the equalizer" and says that he can't just take it out and whack the bear whenever he feels threatened. It's part of a carefully constructed system of escalating cause and effect, which he teaches to the bears when they are cubs. There are situations—like when a cub is learning that Seus can pet him while the bear eats—when Seus feels it is not appropriate to react to aggression. If a cub bites him in such circumstances, Seus just takes the stitches in stride.

But in other cases, Seus says, his reaction must be proportional to the bear's offense. He starts with a verbal reprimand: "uh-uh," then "easy." The ultimate, emphatic "no!" means "you're on the edge of volatility," Seus says. The bears learn what Seus considers to be inappropriate behavior and take their cues from his verbal response. "You give the bear the opportunity to make the right choice," he explains.

Unlike the talkative Anderson, Seus gropes and fumbles for the perfect words to express the things he's been thinking about for the last thirty years. The result is thoughtful and precise, if a little jumbled. "There's a prehistoric connection, and it captures your spirit," he explains. "I think that we have similar personalities," he says, referring to the bears, himself, and my husband, Doug. "Subsurface, instantaneous reactions. Which in the human world isn't the greatest of attributes. Changes in a bear evolve instantaneously, in microseconds. I attribute that to the Pleistocene evolvement of the bear. In other words, they evolved to survive on the barren grounds: They make their living, they breed, they gather their food, they protect their young. So there's survival in instantaneous gratification. Because the demand and the need are immediate, I enjoy curbing and working with that.

"I think there are certain elements that are conducive to working with them passionately and professionally. I am by nature persistent, tunnel-visioned. I enjoy rapport. And rapport involves hours, and rapport evolves through learning that they can receive their dignity from you."

Lynne is a woman inclined to find the mystical connection between events; she sees purpose in the fact that the twins were born as Bart was leaving them. In the spring of 2000, Bart was dying of cancer. Lynne shows me a six-page list of all the vitamins and drugs they gave him, a regimen that took hours every day to administer and that extended his life for eight mostly good months. Eventually, Seus and Lynne knew it was time to let him die. Bart spent the final days of his life lying on a pile of hay next to the creek he used to swim in. Tears stream down Seus's face when he talks about Bart's death. "I came from a humble background, and he took me around the world," Seus says. "He was my livelihood, he was my friend. He was my life. Our life."

As Seus mourns for his lost friend four years after Bart's death, I think of Troy Hyde at Animals of Montana. While Hyde talks of the importance of his relationship to the bears in terms of his ability to get them to do what he wants on camera, I've also seen the paperwork he files with the state. In 2002 and 2003, Hyde euthanized an arctic wolf, a mountain lion, a fox, a grey wolf, and two grizzly bears on the grounds that they "did not work out." When I write Hyde asking him to elaborate, he declines to comment.

There are bear men and there are money men.

THE EDUCATION OF THE ASTRINGENT CREEK GRIZZLY

■■ A plume of steam sways in the pulsating breeze, which skitters across the snow-covered meadow. It is late April in the remote backcountry of Yellowstone Park. A tiny, warm creek cuts a dark swath through forty inches of lingering snowpack. Three brown bears—two tiny cubs following a three-hundred-pound female grizzly—amble down this narrow passageway, padding along the bank, sometimes splashing in the shallow water.

The grizzly family stops underneath the column of white vapor hissing from a four-foot cone of travertine. A trickle of hot water drains from the thermal vent. The surrounding earth is free of snow, melted by the heat rising from the giant mass of molten rock that underlies the

Yellowstone plateau. Buffalo chips litter the open ground where bison lingered during the frigid days of winter.

A raven croaks overhead and flies south. The meadow joins a defile between low pine-blanketed hills. The bird follows the narrow creek a mile down into a giant meadow complex. More hot springs mark the periphery of Pelican Valley. Across the snowy expanse lies a zone of forest and, beyond, the largest lake on the continent at this elevation. A white skin of ice, now fractured by dark leads, still covers Yellowstone Lake.

For bears, early spring is a tough time of year. Food is hard to come by. The grass and sedge they love to graze have yet to sprout. The winter was too mild to kill many bison or elk, and spring carrion is scarce. For reasons known only to the mother, the grizzly family left the winter den late this year. Perhaps she knew April would be lean.

The grizzly noses the barren ground surrounding the steam vent. Her appetite has returned from the long fast of winter. The receding snowbanks yield a thin fringe of vegetation. The sow nibbles the first green-up poking up through the warm soil. There isn't much of it. The sow remembers this place. The remains of rodent holes snake across the naked earth. During the winter, pocket gophers burrow up into the snow, excavating from nests to seed caches, and leave a dirt tunnel behind. As the snow melts, these casts are left on top of the ground. To the mother bear, this means dinner.

For the next two hours, she digs along networks of burrows, discovering grassy nests and caches of seeds that resemble white chocolate chips. She licks up the onion seeds. The cubs follow close behind, curious, nosing her leavings. One nest is full of young gophers. All three grizzlies scramble after the escaping rodents, pinning them, playing with them. Only mom gobbles them down; the tiny cubs are not yet eating solid food.

Finally the mother grizzly lies down in the sun and presents her paps to the hungry cubs. The faint burble of bears nursing resonates against

PORTRAIT: **THE EDUCATION OF THE ASTRINGENT CREEK GRIZZLY**

the forest. The tiny grizzlies fall asleep next to the sow. Normally the female would make her day bed hidden in heavy timber. But here, in the remote backcountry of Yellowstone, she feels secure. Only a few other grizzlies roam this snow-filled valley and, more important, no people visit this early in the year. The spring sun is warm on their fur.

Gray dawn reveals the grizzly family on the move. They cruise atop the crusted snow, the cubs sometimes running to keep up with their mother. The big bear knows travel will become arduous once the mid-day sun softens the scab of ice; they will break through and flounder. Grizzlies walk on the soles of their feet, and this plantigrade gait bears but a fifth the pressure of an elk hoof, enabling them to travel atop the surface at times when ungulates and other mammals (such as humans) would wallow in the belly-deep drifts.

In an hour they cover the distance that brings them to the immense valley. The family turns west and contours along the tree line, still ambling with ease over the hard snow. A pale disc of morning sun squints through the gray cumulus. The sun pops out for a few minutes, illuminating the hint of a silver collar behind the mother's hump. One of the cubs, a female who keeps close to her mother, is a bit smaller than her brother, who lags behind. The dark male cub has a white spot on his chest that spreads along his neck like a necktie. The little female is uniformly brown. The cubs are tiny, a scant ten pounds.

Another three miles on the snow and the grizzlies come to a sizeable creek on the edge of a big thermal area that has a dozen plumes of steam issuing from vents and hot springs. The mother slows her pace and cautiously approaches the snow-free ground. She carefully scents the air, circling the sparsely timbered area from the leeward. The sow snorts in an encyclopedia of information.

The mother bear has spent almost all her life within twenty miles of this thermal area known as Vermillion Hot Springs. She knows hundreds of hidden niches in which to find something to eat. Bears are omnivores who evolved from meat eaters. Their digestive tracts are longer than those of cats or wolves, and this allows grizzlies to absorb energy from some plant substances, but not cellulose—the inert carbohydrate of the yellowed grasses and dry forbs. These are inedible to bears now.

What this bear wants most is meat. She knows that as the snow melts away, she can quarry out rodent caches with their stores of seeds. She will savor the fresh, green vegetation when it sprouts. The bear can also sniff out edible roots and corms, the underground parts of spring beauty, and biscuit root plants. But now, vegetables are her second choice. The female grizzly scents a dead bison.

The three bears step into the thermal area. The cubs, happy to be off the snow, begin to wrestle. A cuff from mom abruptly ends their play. Danger loiters here. A game trail leads away from the creek across the sinter washed down from the hot springs. Many bison and two moose have passed this way. Imprinted on top of the hoofprints is the rear track of a huge bear. The footmark is nearly twelve inches long. It was made yesterday morning. The sow looks over her shoulder, scouting out the area for further sign. She knows this male, the dominant bear of this complex of meadows. His huge range includes the twenty-some square miles of Astringent Creek, the watershed the bear family just walked out of and in which they do most of their foraging.

This male grizzly is one of the last great predators surviving from the years when Yellowstone's bears fed at government garbage dumps. After the dumps were closed in the late 1960s, most dominant and aggressive grizzlies were shot or otherwise removed from the population. This huge bear survived by his aversion to humans and his skill as a hunter of bison, moose, and elk. Now in his twenties, his spring weight has dropped below seven hundred pounds. For a Yellowstone grizzly, he is very old.

Grizzly predation upon elk is not uncommon. They get them in the winter-weakened spring, as calves in June, and when the bulls rut in fall. But Yellowstone bison and moose rarely fall to predators; these beasts are generally too powerful for grizzlies, who are usually not efficient hunters. The old boar from Astringent Creek is an exception. He ambushes young bison in these thermal basins. He sometimes catches yearling moose at the edge of deep snowdrifts, rising on the crusted snow to break their necks with his jaws. The carcass of a two-year-old bull bison lies in a shallow, warm creek two hundred feet from the mother and cubs. The boar has made a kill.

The bison is now mostly hide and bones. That's why the boar is not bedded close by, defending his food store. There's meat left, but not much. She claws off the sticks covering the remains of the bison and shakes the dirt from the kill. The boar cached the carcass before he moved on, meaning he could come back. Perhaps he made another kill—maybe not. The mother bear considers this information; the need for food outweighs the risk.

The cubs watch their mother tear into what's left of the bison. They are alert to the big grizzly's every move and gesture—the lessons reaching beyond any material reward—as if arming themselves with tools for yet unimagined challenges.

For the next thirty-six hours, the sow feeds on the bison. She nurses the cubs during breaks and while bedded nearby at the foot of a large pine tree. Mother bear maintains her vigilance. When she has stripped the carcass clean of meat, the three bears move on.

The grizzly family wanders widely during this season. They find a moose carcass up Astringent Creek and another bear-killed bison yearling near the head of the Raven drainage. Mother bear grazes on fresh grass and sedge wherever she finds it and nibbles leafy emerging cow parsnip that grows in wet areas. The cubs are dependent on their mother's milk, which is ten times richer than cow's milk, and often suckle for ten or fifteen minutes a half dozen or more times a day. But they also pay close attention to their mother's feeding activity. Much of grizzly behavior is learned, and the little brown female in particular ponders the sow's every move. The two-and-a-half-year tutorial of the young grizzly, augmented by a special mother-daughter relationship, will be the key to her long-term survival—her ability to adapt to the profound changes that will sweep over the vastness of Yellowstone's wild heart.

■■ It is late May in Pelican Valley. Along the crests of benches and terraces, white cornices of snow snake across the great meadow. Deep game trails cut these arcs of remnant snow. Tiny orange bison calves dance around grazing buffalo herds. Elk have returned to the valley, the cows heavy with unborn young. Spring green-up grows along the creeks and below melting snowdrifts. It is the time of birthing. The starving season is over.

The grizzly family ambles out of Astringent Creek and along Pelican Creek. The sow eyes the grazing animals, knowing the fiercely defended orange bison calves lie beyond her predatory reach. The elk are another story: Earlier this month she charged a herd of cow elk and brought one down, only to have the struggling ungulate break loose and bound away. Now the elk are strong again, and the deep snow that slowed them down has melted away. As a big game hunter, mother bear has failed this spring. But her time is coming.

The two little bear cubs climb atop a bank of snow and then leap with abandon off the steep side, sliding and rolling, four legs in the air, head over paws, all the way back down. They begin again. The sow makes a disciplinary lunge toward the cubs, ending their play. Danger lurks: They might have rolled into the creek, its treacherous currents surging with floodwater. But there is a greater peril. Male grizzlies now crisscross the valley.

The mother moves upstream and leads her family across the necks of the creek's meandering bends with the wind at their backs. To their south, a broad meadow opens up. A narrow ravine hugs the western fringe, close to the timber. The mother bear reaches the mouth of the draw, where the tiny drainage dumps into Pelican Creek. She looks back up the gulch. A big dark grizzly emerges from the trees and ambles into the draw. In the stiff westerly wind, neither adult bear can scent the other, though they are but a hundred yards separated. Now the boar raises his head and looks directly at the family group. The larger bear rises onto his rear feet and stands erect. For a second, all movement freezes.

The sow suddenly pivots and drives one cub into the other, herding them down the valley. They race along the creek, the mother looking back over her shoulder to see what the big boar is going to do.

The male blows a loud *whoosh* into the stillness of the valley. He slams his forepaws onto the muddy ground and explodes into a full-blown charge. He hits the creek and turns downstream, flying along the bank in pursuit of the tiny bear cubs. The little female grizzly falls behind her mother and brother. The boar closes the distance; he is but several yards behind.

The young grizzly feels the boar's breath on her backside and in desperation leaps across a deep cut on the bank of Pelican Creek. She falls short and slides into the water. Ahead, her mother breaks to a stop, sliding on the mud. The female cub flails away in a dark eddy trying to stay afloat. The flooded, boiling creek waters carry the cub out into the powerful current. She is swept rapidly downstream.

The sow instantly spins on her heels and charges the boar, whose attention has been distracted by the struggling cub and sees the mother bear coming at him only at the last moment. The sow charges hard into the bigger animal and knocks him off balance, holding on to his scruff with her jaws. The boar roars and throws the sow back with a toss of his neck. They lock jaws and rise on two feet, trading bites and circling each other. The male cub retreats down the creek. Roaring into each other's faces, the two adults back off slightly. At the periphery of her vision, the mother bear sees her tiny cub flounder in the middle of Pelican Creek, disappearing swiftly around a bend and out of sight. The entire scene has unfolded in seconds.

The big bear bellows a diminished roar and turns his huge body to the side. He is done fighting today. The mother grizzly wastes no time; she turns and runs down the bank, gathering up her one cub and then looking for the other in the creek.

The little bear cub no longer thrashes away trying to stay afloat. Strength and stamina have abandoned her tiny body. Only her nose remains above the surface of the water. She drifts into a frothing chute and is engulfed by a standing wave, which pushes her to the bottom of the river. The rapids spit her out and she again gasps for air. Next time, she will go under for good.

The sow and male cub continue for another quarter mile, hurrying down the raging creek as it wanders and meanders out into the valley. No sign of the little female. She has vanished. From their point of view, it seems that the rising, muddy waters of Pelican Creek have swallowed her up.

Instead, the cub is being swept along the left-hand bank. Ahead, the creek takes a hard turn to the right. The creek bank erodes rapidly during flood season. Large chunks of sod have slumped into the water. A few tussocks of grass anchored to muddy columns barely break the surface of the surging water. The flow drives the bear cub directly into a piece of collapsed bank. It slams her hard into the tussock, and the current holds her there. She wraps her weak paws around the earthen pillar and digs her tiny claws into the grass. With the last of her fading might, she inches up on top of the grass, all four legs clutching the platform.

It is impossible to read the frame of mind of the mother bear. The mood of a grizzly can change instantaneously. Could she already be resigned to the death of her cub? Maybe the tragedy has triggered hopelessness, some deep bear sadness. At any rate, the sow now moves sluggishly into the valley, her surviving cub slowly trailing close behind. They follow the run of the creek.

A piteous bawl rises from the din of rushing water. Somehow the faint cry reaches the sow. She halts and lifts her head into the gentle breeze.

She hears it and dashes to the source, at the edge of the raging current. Two feet from the bank, the female cub clings precariously to the tussock of grass. Mother bear drops into the creek and, using her teeth, lifts her cub up by the back of the neck. Holding the little bear in her jaws, the sow claws her way back up on top of the bank. She carries the cub far from the creek and lays her down. The cub is too spent to nurse.

From a timbered terrace just south of the creek, a man watches the little female grizzly with binoculars. The human has been watching the bear family since they emerged from Astringent Creek. He witnessed the entire dramatic escapade, and thinks he has seldom seen anything in nature so heroic. He is drawn to the female cub that almost drowned. He examines her with his field glasses: In the sunlight, the beginning of a blond band wraps around her middle; the brown of her head grades subtly into the lighter shade of her rear. He writes the description in a notebook because he wants to keep track of these bears. Sometimes he gives them names. The male cub is distinctive by the white yoke on his neck. He knows the mother. Below the description of the brave little female he writes "the Astringent Creek Grizzly."

■■ In June, warm weather and the first human visitors of the year come to Pelican Valley. To avoid people and aggressive male grizzlies looking for mates, this mother and her cubs retreat to the recesses of the great valley, exploring widely up Raven then Pelican Creek to a hot springs complex north of Tern Lake. She avoids the large meadows along upper Astringent and White Lakes. Something bad happened there three years ago, when the sow was a young mother traveling with a previous litter of cubs. The place swarmed with armed rangers during early August. A person was killed there. A woman camper was bit on the head and dragged out of a tent by a bear. Another bear—no one knew which or how many bears were involved—climbed twelve feet up a tree and retrieved some human food. Later, a bear fed on the dead body. The big boar from Astringent Creek left his tracks nearby.

The female grizzly reveals no awareness of these events beyond that she has rigorously shunned the area ever since. Adult grizzlies don't climb trees except under extraordinary circumstances, such as chasing an offending human. The mother bear, like most other grizzlies, will not approach a backpacker's camp or tent at night or any other time. The fact that human flesh was eaten is perhaps least surprising; anything, once dead, is food to a bear.

For the sow and her cubs, none of this is extraordinary. The grizzly's world is decorated with the textures of danger: roads, killer bears, armed humans, developments, and people with cameras. The mother bear checks out the area and proceeds accordingly.

The small meadow at the head of Sour Creek yields only a few days of grazing, and the bear family moves back south, again scrupulously avoiding the White Lake area. Snow clogs the high passes, and the bear family spends most of June in the lower valleys, following the snowmelt where the youngest, most tender shoots grow. The young bears take it all in. The exceptions to the vegetarian diet are ants, pocket gophers, and elk calves.

The trail south leads along a narrow defile drained by a roily creek. Elk and bison sign cover the muddy bottomland. Mud pots and sizzling hot springs thump and hiss as the bear family passes by. The sow has slowed her gait. The wind blows into her face, and she can detect no sign of danger—no scent of humans or male grizzlies. Her cubs watch as she noses the droppings and urine of cow elk. Her curiosity seems excessive to them. But the sow is excited; she dances around a trail of elk pellets and thrusts her great snout in the air. Suddenly, she bolts into a nearby timber patch. The abandoned cubs are puzzled and start to follow. Before they reach the lodgepole, the mother bear emerges carrying a spotted elk calf in her mouth. She trots to the creek bank with her prey. The cubs stay close.

A shrill bark shatters the mountain stillness. A cow elk breaks from the timber and prances directly at the big grizzly. The ungulate approaches to fifteen feet, slams her hooves into the mud, and barks another snort at the bear. The elk stamps her feet. This is her newborn calf. The cubs cower before this formidable elk mother. The big grizzly rips into the calf and feeds for a few minutes, then stands and faces the cow elk. The two fierce mothers take stock of one another. At first, neither moves; then the cow slowly circles the carnivore that is disemboweling her off-spring. The bear stays between her kill and the mother elk. Even long after the grizzly has finished off the calf, the elk is still there.

A couple of days later, the sow captures another calf, this time by charging into a small herd of cow elk and calves. She sprints into the meadow, scattering the herd, and quickly singles out one of the tiny ungulates. The grizzly closes, grabs the calf by the neck, and runs back to her cubs with her kill. They retreat to the timber at the edge of the great valley.

In the next week, mom runs down and captures three more elk calves. Others escape. The cubs, fascinated, join the hunt and run along-side her; the chase has stimulated the cubs' instinct for predation.

▬▬ In late June, the family begins to undertake a major journey. The bears cross Pelican Valley at daylight; the mother knows people are unlikely to hike here this early in the day. In late morning, they retreat to the forest where the mother bear finds a big fir and scrapes out a saucerlike basin at the foot of the tree. The cubs imitate their mom and paw out small pits. All three bed. They nurse and sleep out the day.

The next day, the bears pick up a hiking trail and continue their pas-sage south. By midmorning, they reach the edge of a large butte. The sow stops and identifies the scents blowing up the trail. The clamor of human chatter and the jingle of bells have been audible for the last half hour. The mother grizzly leads her cubs up the side of the butte and sits on a ledge a hundred feet from the trail. The cubs, knowing what is expected of them, copy her. They watch silently as the noisy party of three men and a woman pass below them. The people never look up.

The bears wait twenty minutes and return to the trail. They don't go far. Ahead is a heavily traveled road. The sow listens to the traffic and nudges her cubs off the trail with some urgency, driving them down into a creek bottom. She must somehow convey to the cubs that here is a deadly human hazard of a different sort. All day long the sow demands strict obedience from her cubs, as if she wants them to file away in permanent memory the considerable danger of the paved road.

The bears wait and wait. The long day of summer lingers. Traffic doesn't fall off until dark. A couple of hours later, toward midnight, the bear family dashes across the road and into the trees, arriving safely on the far side.

Early July finds the grizzlies near the eastern shore of Yellowstone Lake. Along the several feeder creeks draining into the lake, a number of grizzly bears have gathered to eat spawning cutthroat trout. A subadult female fishes only a couple hundred yards from another female with two yearlings. A young male grizzly is also in the area. The grizzly family with cubs of the year seems comfortable with these five bears; the mother knows them. Larger male grizzlies frequent a different creek, where the fishing is better.

The grizzly bear's capacity for social behavior has been poorly understood and greatly underestimated. Early portrayals of the adult bear as strictly solitary (except when mating or with family) and exclusively territorial are flat wrong. The mutual intolerance seen among adult grizzlies is readily broken down by the promise of food. It happens not only at dumps, salmon streams, and around carcasses but also with abundant berry and even sedge crops. The mother bear from Pelican Creek knows she can coexist with her cubs in this small gathering of grizzlies. The presence of a large boar or humans would be a different story. For now, there is enough bear food for all.

The trout fishing tapers off in midsummer, and the grizzly family moves eastward, toward the high peaks of the Absaroka Range. The protein available to bears from plants is highest in preflowering stages—a brief time span after they first sprout up. Plants ripen progressively later with elevation. So the bears move up and continue grazing. The sow also digs for roots and laps up ants.

The weather heats up, and the plants explode into bright flowers, neutralizing their food value to bears but garnishing the alpine meadows with a brilliant mosaic of yellow, red, and blue. By the time the bears arrive at timberline, the high scree fields of the mountains are covered in flowers.

Mother grizzly stalks up through the fields of lupine, columbine, and fireweed. She reaches the foot of the talus slope and rummages the slabs and wedges of angular andesite. She paws over a big flat rock. Insects scurry about. She noses them like an entomologist, then licks up the bugs. The sow moves upslope, turning over rocks and lapping up the ladybugs and moths; this year they are mostly army cutworm moths, especially on the higher rubble slopes. The bugs are good to eat. The cubs follow, flipping smaller slabs. By evening, the moths are crawling all over the place. These aestivating insects arrive here from places like Alberta and Kansas, where they are considered agricultural pests and are sprayed heavily with pesticides.

Again, other grizzlies are attracted to the abundant food source—especially female grizzlies, several with litters of young. Two other bears have cubs of the year. By the end of the week, two of the families have intermingled, the mothers feeding but twenty feet apart, their respective cubs sniffing at one another. Rough play is reserved for siblings, although the brown female cub from Astringent Creek chases the cub from the other family. They race through the flowering meadow at the foot of the scree field, running in circles, exploring each other's wildness.

The Astringent Creek Bear is learning a sociability that pushes the limits of ursine tolerance, and, concurrently, she is developing an agility of adaptive behavior that will allow her to coexist with other grizzlies, human beings, and strange new mammals from the outside.

■■ In September, the grizzly family begins a journey. They leave the high scree fields and start back north. At the head of the cutthroat trout stream, a long lake lies alongside the paved road. Tables and garbage cans occupy a picnic area just upstream. The bears will cross the road there.

The bears come to the head of the lake in the late morning. They hear traffic on the road. The mother grizzly can see the picnic tables; a couple of vehicles are parked in the area. The sow decides to bed. They can cross the road after dark, when the picnic area is deserted.

The bear can smell the rich fetor of human foods emanating from the garbage cans and picnic foods laid out on the tables. She knows garbage is nutritious, and she is aware of her own hyperphagia with the approaching winter. But people are notoriously tied to danger. The picnickers are linked to rangers with traps and guns. The mother grizzly balances the hazard with the puny reward; she sinks into her forest bed.

By midafternoon the cubs are fidgety. They wander a few yards from the day bed and start to wrestle, rolling over and over in the pine duff of the open forest. Mother lifts her drowsy head and sees her cubs in plain sight of the picnic area. Just beyond the cubs, a tall, pale human approaches rapidly. Behind the man ramble two children. The cubs now freeze with fright.

The man carries a video camera but doesn't seem interested in using it. He turns and shouts something at the children. The pale man comes to a stop four feet from the terrified cubs. He reaches out with one arm, as if to pat them on the head.

In an instant the sow grizzly rises, standing on all fours, gnashing her teeth, her ears flat back, her carnivore nervous system overloaded with conflicting instructions. The protective maternal instinct takes command.

Mother bear charges, covering the short distance in seconds. The cubs jump out of the way as she flies by. Somehow, in the space of a few feet, the sow slides to a halt, just inches from the human. The man seems unperturbed, as if he were at the county zoo. The tall human turns and hollers excitedly at the kids. The grizzly approaches a step and sniffs at the human's pant leg. Then she issues a growl and, spinning, races off into the timber with her cubs.

The three bears cross the paved road in the black of night. They move uphill, away from the road. The forest is dripping from the heavy rain of the previous week. The dewy ground cover of kinnikinnick (bearberry) and whortleberry is decorated with colorful fungus. Yellow chanterelles, red russulas, and pale brown boletus poke out of the green moss. Other species of gilled mushrooms and coral fungi abound. Mother bear greedily grazes on a tall cluster of brown slimy fungus. In a half hour she has eaten a bellyful. The cubs investigate and sniff about, curious why their mother prefers this particular mushroom to others, which she avoids—like the abundant *Cantharellus cibarius* and *Boletus* so favored by human beings.

The grizzlies climb up through the lodgepoles into the zone of whitebark pine. The food available to these grizzlies is different from a place like Glacier, where huckleberries abound. In Yellowstone, late summer and fall feeding centers around insects and pine nuts. But crops of whitebark pinecones are fickle. Some years there are only a couple of cones per tree. And there are essential middlemen—the red squirrels. Mother bear looks around. Two years ago, when there was a tremendous harvest of cones, the caches were huge. This year, she finds the stately trees barren of cones.

The family moves north, contouring below the high peaks of the Absaroka Range, prospecting the country for food. They find squirrel caches with a few whitebark pinecones and more insects. It is rugged country with extensive scree fields interspersed with subalpine swales and alpine parks. The andesitic soils of the meadows are especially fertile, producing the plants whose underground parts are packed with edible carbohydrates. The grizzlies are fat; the cubs might now weigh sixty pounds apiece.

On chilly mornings, the yellow grasses glisten with a bright patina of hoarfrost. The elk are bugling and the weather is changing. On the fall equinox, a winter storm blows in. The female grizzly senses the barometric low and, the day before the blizzard hits, leads her cubs west down Sedge Creek, across Pelican Valley, and up Astringent Creek toward the backside of Stonetop Mountain.

By the time they reach 8,500 feet in elevation, it is snowing hard. Mother bear seems to know where she's going. She drops off the north side of a ridge and finds a hummock of stunted trees clinging to the side of the slope. The three bears step into the thicket and begin to claw out day beds. The adult female leaves the cubs snug in their beds, steps out into the snowstorm, and investigates the mountainside. A few big trees cling to the crumbly slope. She tries digging under one of them. The rotten rock collapses. Finally she finds an ancient whitebark pine with big roots splaying out into the decaying bedrock. She excavates for hours between forking roots. Snowflakes bleach her fur coat. Finally, she looks back at her cubs, who have wandered from the thicket. They retreat to the relative shelter of the grove of trees to slumber in their beds, the small white puffs of exhalation drifting off on the wind.

For the next two days, the adult grizzly works on the den. The cubs, playing nearby on the slope, dig little holes of their own. The tunnel now bends almost six feet through the branching root system of the old tree. The entrance is just big enough for the fall-fattened sow to squeeze through. The passageway runs a little uphill.

Mother has denned on this mountain before. She generally prepares these dens weeks before actual hibernation.

The days soon turn fair and, leaving the den, the grizzly family hits the trail again. They cross the big river in the night and continue northeast to Hayden Valley. The warm springs along the southern boundary of the valley nourish horsetail and watercress. Yampa, a nutritious root, grows in the bottoms and biscuit root out in the sagebrush. Elk roam all over the place. The sow checks out the herds. Some bulls are preoccupied with rutting and are vulnerable to predation. The mother watches them and bides her time.

Her moment comes at dusk, in a small clearing where the great valley yields to the thermal complex around Mud Volcanoes. Three bull elk have been bugling back and forth from the timber surrounding a small meadow. Though the season is late for rutting, the biggest bull tends a harem herd of females and yearlings.

The big grizzly stalks along the tree line, shadowing the smallest of the three elk, still quite a formidable animal with a five-point rack. Mother bear steps clear of the pine forest and advances toward the ungulate. The elk ignores the bear until she stands fifty feet away. He makes no attempt to flee. The bull paws the dirt with its front hooves and turns to face the grizzly—the sharp tines of its rack lowered. They stand facing each other for the good part of a minute, the cubs stationary behind their mother.

The sow charges the bull, who stands his ground and even takes a small step forward. At the instant before contact, the grizzly rises on her hind legs and reaches over the head and antlers of the elk. She grabs his neck with her jaws. The grizzly has all her weight on the forequarters of the elk; he shakes his head and circles, churning the ground with his hooves. The bear hangs on with her claws and bites the bull on the face and ears. They go down kicking, and the ungulate almost breaks free. The sow bites again and this time clenches the spinal column with her teeth. The bear picks up the bull by the neck and shakes it. The bull shudders then lies still.

The elk kill caps the nutritional year for the three bears. Its considerable protein will see the grizzlies safely through their hibernation. They treat it like a gift, the big female dragging the carcass of the bull into the trees, where they cache the leftovers with sticks and dirt and bed close by to defend this valuable food source from all interlopers.

They feed on the carcass for most of the week. Coyotes, a red fox, innumerable ravens, a black bear, two subadult grizzlies, and a hiker approach the carcass. The sow runs them all off, including the human, who seems to know that the stench of rotting meat late in the fall means a dangerous grizzly will be bedded nearby. The hiker stops two hundred feet from the carcass and intentionally lets his scent blow into the thicket, where he imagines the bears to be bedded. Mother grizzly acknowledges his presence; she stands and shows herself. The bearded man safely retreats. By the time a large adult male grizzly shows up to check out what's left of the elk carcass, the family is ready to move on.

A major storm begins to push into the Yellowstone ecosystem. This will be the snow that makes winter. The three grizzlies trek back to the high country across the river. They find the den on Stonetop Mountain and paw out little beds on the fine detritus at the mouth of the hole. They are done feeding for the year. The bears can scarcely keep their eyes open; they stare sleepily into the approaching grayness of the northern sky, awaiting the snow that will cover the den and seal them in their winter home until next spring.

A storm of another kind will soon be on its way here, a humanly unimaginable one that will devastate the lives of countless plants and animals, and will take the grizzly family to the absolute limits of physical survival.

■■ The mother grizzly arouses in early April and peers out toward the Mirror Plateau. The rolling timbered high country is covered with snow. Although the fractured landscape looks much like it has for the past dozen springs, the bear sniffs the mountain as if searching for an unexpected clue of what the season might really hold. She is groggy. The sow eases down the slope, checks out the copse of trees, and returns to the den, curling up with her two yearling cubs for another week of sleep.

But the bears are waking: Their metabolisms quicken and their pulse accelerates although their appetites have yet to bounce back from the slow starvation of winter. Finally, they leave their winter home behind and travel west over the deep snow, down a narrow creek choked with downfalls to the big river.

A huge rapid here boils over large boulders. The stranded carcasses of bison are hung up in the rocks. The sow cautiously tests the air; a half dozen drowned buffalo are wedged in the shallows. She smells the recent visitation of other bears. A paved road runs along the far side of the big river.

The grizzly family finds a bison carcass washed up along the near bank. The pine forest here hugs the river and provides cover and protection. They begin to feed, slowly at first. In a week, hunger reasserts itself.

A month later, snow squalls give way to showers. The weather seems almost normal. For a while, the grazing is good. Then the rains stop. By June, the driest summer in recorded human history arrives. Mother bear senses something is up. The usual forbs and grasses are shriveled. She seeks alternative food.

They travel far to the east, up into the high country. They check out the scree slopes of the Absaroka Mountains for moths, finding a few meals. The sow notes only a couple of pinecones growing in each whitebark pine tree. Ants are plentiful. Off to the west, thunder rumbles and lightning crackles; no moisture falls with these early storms. The drought brings on an outbreak of spruce budworm in the Douglas fir areas. The larvae are in turn eaten by wasps that nest under logs or in the duff at the foot of trees. The mother bear has fed on the adult wasps before, but this particular year the insects abound in the denser forests.

The dry lightning storms continue; their pyrotechnics light up the western thunderheads almost daily. Still, no rain falls. By mid-July, the sow can detect the smoke of several separate forest fires. A week later, an ominous pall hangs over the entire plateau, the blistering summer sun filtering through the forest with an eerie amber haze. Ghostly elk and bison herds mill nervously in the smoky meadows.

The mother grizzly draws on all her experience to find food. Buried in her memory, learned from four years of traveling with and then trailing her own mother, are a thousand secret places—tiny springs where forbs grow, thick woods with wasps, or a secret grove of whitebark pine. But there is danger in this timbered terrain. The fires are burning beyond any notion of human control, and the grizzlies must tiptoe around blazing grasses and smoldering downfalls. The sow has to be aware of escape routes at all times. The afternoon winds are the most hazardous. She knows fire and is fearful of getting caught in a forested gulch by a crown-jumper that might cut off her flight.

At the end of the third week in August 1988, Yellowstone's mammals experience the most terrible firestorm anyone has ever witnessed. A ferocious wind stokes the several wildfires into tremendous blazes that hop-skip northeast, burning huge chunks of the forested plateau. In a single day, more than 150,000 acres would be consumed. The inferno catches the grizzly family traversing the high country just north of Mount Chittenden. They are contouring north at the base of a sheer cliff, moving fast, just short of panic speed, when the trees explode in flames. Giant fireballs ignite the country, blowing over the divide east into the national forest. The cubs follow their mother; she drops into a narrow creek bottom and races up the defile toward the scree slopes of Cathedral Peak. Fire breaks out in the timber along the gulch. The bears run through it, dodging flaming branches that drop off the treetops. The smoke itself would be suffocating if not for the tremendous winds mixing the air currents and churning the giant fire plume that rises a thousand feet into the crimson sky.

The creek tops out onto a small flat. This open pass is on fire. The family must run through it. The female yearling gallops tight behind her mother, a patch of burned fur on her rump still smoking. The male cub bellows with pain; he shakes a burning coal from his paw and struggles to keep up with the females. The bears are engulfed in the conflagration. Why the sow keeps running north, directly into the inferno, is a mystery; their survival appears hopeless.

The male falls behind, bawling, his feet badly burned. Suddenly, the sow loops back and scoops him up. He hobbles forward a hundred yards behind his mother. The burning pass drops off into the head of another creek. It is timbered but the trees are not on fire.

The grizzlies reach the unburned creek bottom. Imitating her mother, the Astringent Creek Bear encourages her brother onward, pushing him forward with her nose. They could continue down the drainage, but the yearling with the white patch on his chest can't keep up. He lies down in the trickle of water, the moisture cool on his wounded paws.

The fires rage all around them. The burning ridge just to the east runs four miles, trapping the family against the flank of the mountain. The bears are in a deadly predicament. If they stay where they are, a single blast of erratic wind could incinerate them. But brother bear cannot travel. To abandon him would be a death sentence for the yearling cub.

The mother grizzly must choose the course of action. She notes the tempestuous blaze rising in multiple rose-colored plumes all around. The fires have created their own weather, driving hurricane-force winds over the peaks. Cathedral Peak seems to be deflecting the storm behind them; that fire isn't getting any closer. The fireballs are hurtling east, over the divide.

The grizzly family hunkers down in the creek bottom. For forty-eight hours it is touch and go. They find a pool of water deep enough for brother bear to submerge his hundred-pound body. The bears might survive a crown fire here by lying down in the water, but fortunately the flames never make a run down the creek.

The male grizzly can barely hobble far enough up the creek bank to find a few huckleberries. One rear paw is so badly burned he doesn't put his full weight on it. He moves with excruciating pain; the odds of him surviving the year are remote.

But the sow doesn't abandon her maimed cub; she sticks by him, remaining in the tiny drainage, exposing both herself and her female yearling to the forest fires that burn around them for the next two weeks. Sister bear is increasingly independent, making brief forays on her own to look for forage. On September 11, snow falls on the plateau. Dodging the forest fires has been a nutritional drain; the bears must find food to ready themselves for hibernation, or they all will starve.

The bears smell carrion on the wind and travel south, moving slowly so the male yearling can keep up. At the little divide, the family encounters a solitary boar grizzly. The big male advances, his gait stiff legged and aggressive, across the flat to within a hundred feet of the three smaller bears. The sow knows her burned yearling cannot run and her ears go flat. The boar reads her aggressive body language and abruptly ceases his approach. But she charges him anyway, and, as he spins and tries to race away, she catches him, biting his flank. The male finally throws her off and escapes at a gallop into the smoldering timber.

The little male cub hobbles after his sister and mother down into the ravine, where the fire almost killed them three weeks ago. A herd of fleeing elk was not so fortunate. Six charred carcasses are scattered at the head of a rocky gulch. The grizzlies scent other distant carcasses down the drainage, a bonanza for scavenging animals, beginning with bears.

Brother grizzly has a shot at survival now. With a rich concentrated protein source, he doesn't need to roam. The bear family feeds for two weeks in the little valley, moving from one unfortunate elk to the next scorched victim, giving the yearling cub a chance to mend his paws. Other bears pass through, but not even the boars displace the fierce mother, who now defends her cubs and their food with dangerous determination.

The Astringent Creek Bear is aware of the change in her mother's behavior. The sow has become extremely aggressive toward other bears. She seems to know that it is a matter of her family's life or death to stay anchored to this gulch with its treasure store of elk meat. The female yearling files this insight away; it will be useful in the coming years.

By mid-October, they stand near the divide. Mother bear hears the far-off discharge of a rifle coming from the national forest. She knows the gunshot means a fresh elk gut-pile. Sometimes the hunters take only the head of the elk, leaving behind hundreds of pounds of food. The sow has been down there before. All the humans carry guns and are eager to use them. Many grizzlies have died in that valley. The circumstances constitute a situation too dangerous for the cubs, even if both were healthy.

But they are not. The male's rear right paw suffered third-degree burns. It could have been worse: The quick cooling in the creek no doubt reduced the severity and the depth of the burn on the other paws. His wounds are miraculously free of infection. The little bear now walks with a pronounced limp, putting his weight on the outside of the maimed foot.

Snow now dusts the high country; winter is on the way. Instead of making the long journey east to their previous den west of Astringent Creek, the bears cross the 9,400-foot buttress and travel but a fraction of a mile down the north side of the ridge. The sow finds a huge whitebark pine tree and excavates a hole in its root system. By the time of the first big snow of November, the family is sleeping in the den.

During the year following the great fires, life shifts for the three grizzlies. Food isn't a problem because so many elk and bison died during the winter. The wildfires stressed these grazing animals, and they winter-killed in large numbers.

But their mother is acting differently. She is downright grouchy toward her two-year-olds. By late May, the adult bear is actively running off her young; she snarls, bites, and chases them away. The two subadults sit on a sagebrush-covered knoll, puzzled, and they watch their mother graze from two hundred yards away.

The little bears realize that they are on their own when a threatening big male comes courting their mother. They move off, wary of bigger bears during the breeding season. The two-year-olds feed, play, and bed together for six more weeks. In July, the twins follow their mother's old trail down to Yellowstone Lake. Despite last year's fires, the spawning creeks run clear. Bears have gathered there, but the fishing is poor. The subadults probe the local social hierarchy while they interact with the other grizzlies. They find their status enhanced by working as a unit; together they are able to dominate solitary bears and displace them from the better fishing sites. The Astringent Creek Bear seems precociously aggressive for a female grizzly of scant two hundred pounds.

But the two-and-a-half-year union of the young grizzlies soon uncouples on the shores of the great lake. The Astringent Creek Bear wants to follow her mother's footprints back into the high country. Her brother seems to know the abrasive scree of the Absaroka Range will be too sharp for his scarred paw.

Climbing up into the mountains, the Astringent Creek Bear passes through a square-mile patch of burned trees. The grass is just coming up here. She stops to graze, stepping on mushrooms. There are thousands of morels, false morels, early boletus, and countless other fungi popping up everywhere in the burn. She samples them, wolfing down a few morels, then settling on a coarse gilled mushroom that resembles the kind that her mother preferred. She eats a bellyful.

On the high slopes, the bear finds that the whitebark pine trees—the ones that survived the fire—are loaded with cones. She feeds on the caches of squirrels for the next month. Other grizzlies pass through. One day she spots her mother raking pinecones a quarter mile away, on the north flank of Cathedral Peak.

The young female grizzly, now a luxurious light brown silvertip in the amber sunshine of autumn, begins a unique passage in her life: She will shadow her mother, tagging behind at a respectful distance, but very much within the sphere of influence of the older female. In the wake of the great fire, the whitebark pine trees sag under the weight of a huge cone crop. The rich, concentrated food probably opens the window to the renewed relationship between the mother bear and her subadult daughter. The instruction will continue.

When the sow moves east to den on Stonetop Mountain, the Astringent Creek Grizzly trails behind. The mother has a den already prepared near the old site. The Astringent Creek Bear pokes around and tentatively starts excavating rocks at the foot of a dead tree a quarter mile downhill of her mother's den. By the time the blizzard arrives, the subadult lies snug in her grass bed at the end of a four-foot tunnel.

■■   In mid-April, the three-year-old female spots her mother leaving the den with three tiny new cubs. All five bears head down Astringent Creek, the family roaming three hundred yards in advance of the solitary grizzly. The two bigger bears seem comfortable with this degree of separation. Throughout the spring, the sow with the three little brown cubs is seen feeding or nursing within a quarter mile of the light brown subadult grizzly, who now wears a distinctive blond band around her middle.

The weather warms up. The sow departs the high country for the big valley. The three-year-old bear lingers for a week and loses track of her mother. No matter; she will find the older bear back on this mountain come autumn.

September rolls around. A dusting of fresh snow crowns the higher peaks. Five bears amble over the alpine tundra. The older female bear leads her three new cubs into a mountain pass. The Astringent Creek Bear trails two hundred yards behind. The bears travel east down a long valley into the national forest. During morning and evening, gunshots reverberate up and down the beautiful drainage. It is big game hunting season. The younger grizzly has never been down there before. Her mother taught her that people are dangerous, that the ones with rifles are the most deadly, and that humans in the national forest are not the same as those in the national park. These two-legged predators should be avoided at all cost.

But mother bear and her cubs have nutritional needs far beyond what the younger female can comprehend. The rifle shots mean elk carcasses and gut-piles. They need the food. The older grizzly must risk it.

The grizzlies slink through the gathering shadows. Sticking to the timber, they bypass horse corrals and clusters of wall-tents with loud

Grizzlies are more tolerant of humans and each other where food is abundant, like this salmon stream in northern British Columbia. (Photo courtesy of Round River Conservation Studies/Doug Milek)

Trophy hunters have killed at least 275 grizzlies during the past two decades in the Taku River drainage of northern British Columbia and southern Yukon. With the help of Round River Conservation Studies, the Taku River Tlingit purchased the local guide license in order to end the hunt. (Photo courtesy of Round River Conservation Studies/Doug Milek)

Tank the Bear (of Wasatch Wildlife in Heber City, Utah) helps staff from the Wind River Bear Institute train Karelian bear dogs for field work with wild grizzlies. (Photo courtesy of Wind River Bear Institute/Scott Sine)

Don Thomas, a bow hunter and physician from Lewistown, Montana, considers grizzlies to be the "most impressive single-game species in the world." He killed this bear with a longbow along a beach in the Russian Far East. (Photo by Doug Peacock)

The treatment of captive bears, like this male at a facility in Rexburg, Idaho, is governed by a patchwork of state laws. (Photo by Doug Peacock)

A social "contract" governs grizzly-human relationships at this salmon weir in northern British Columbia. (Photo by Doug Peacock)

Mother grizzly Star and her two cubs are captured in a culvert trap after breaking into homes in the Polebridge, Montana, area in search of food. The grizzly family now lives in captivity. (Photo courtesy of Zooprax/Derek Reich)

The rear track of a bear (here along a sandy beach in Alaska) eerily resembles a human footprint. (Photo by John Burbidge)

An impatient driver in Denali National Park demonstrates why security from humans is the most important component of grizzly bear habitat. (Photo courtesy of Zooprax/Derek Reich)

The relationship between Doug Seus and Bart the Bear pushed the limits of modern possibilities for grizzly-human bonds. (Photo courtesy of Wasatch Wildlife/Doug Seus)

This Glacier National Park grizzly pretends to ignore the photographer in lieu of aggressive action. (Photo by Doug Peacock)

Without the berry crops of more wet climates, bear families like this one in Yellowstone rely heavily on whitebark pine nuts, which have all but disappeared in this ecosystem. (Photo by Doug Peacock)

The original Astringent Creek Grizzly was a formidable male bear and, unlike most grizzlies, a great hunter of big game. (Photo by Doug Peacock)

Grizzlies living in Glacier National Park get most of their important fall nutrition from the region's renowned huckleberry crops. (Photo by Doug Peacock)

people and barking dogs. It is getting dark. The subadult bear seems nervous; she follows her mother reluctantly.

Shots explode in a nearby meadow. The hunters have killed a bull elk. One man pulls out a knife and begins butchering. He pulls out a pile of intestines. The other hunters twist fearfully in their saddles, checking out the gloomy forest for creatures of the night. The three men abandon the elk, making no effort to cut it up or drag it off. It's too dark. They ride off to camp.

The bears go to work. The two bigger grizzlies rip open the carcass and feed for two hours. Mother bear drags the huge elk almost to the tree line. They eat again, and then the sow covers the dead ungulate with sticks and dirt. They bed in the timber two hundred feet away.

The five grizzlies are brutally awakened by gunshots and snarling dogs. The appropriation of the elk has made the hunters angry, and they fire blindly into the trees. Bullets crash through the underbrush. The sow makes no move to defend the carcass; she flees into the forest with her three cubs close behind. The Astringent Creek Bear runs for her life. The men incite the dogs to join the chase, urging them on, shooting over their heads into the timber. The canine pack closes in on the family and snags one cub by the leg. The dogs tear into the little bear. The sow turns to fight them off and takes a .243 slug in the hip. She limps off with her two other offspring. The remaining cub is ripped to pieces by the dogs. The men on horseback circle around and watch them finish off the tiny bear. The three-and-a-half-year-old grizzly covers the entire distance back to the Yellowstone divide in a few hours. The Astringent Creek Bear will not find her mother from this time forward. Her maternal education is complete.

■■ Five years pass. The cycle begins again. The Astringent Creek Bear roams the old family homestead with cubs of her own. The two little bears constitute her second litter. This 350-pound sow is now known by other grizzlies as a force to be reckoned with and, by the humans who know her, as a dangerously protective mother.

A thin, jagged scar runs from her left eye down her snout. One ear wears a deep notch. This combative disfigurement is unusual in a female grizzly. Older boars are normally the ones carrying wounds from challenges by other males during the breeding season. The Astringent Creek Bear is exceptional; all other bears know of her ferociousness in defending her cubs or a hoard of food.

With people, she is more cautious. She is aware that humans in Yellowstone Park are largely benign compared to the gun-toting killers in the national forest. But part of grizzly aggression is innate, a reflexive response to threats to her cubs. Whenever possible she avoids the two-legged mammals, but during the summer they are everywhere. Once, she made physical contact not far from the Pelican Valley trailhead. She was digging roots in a finger meadow separated from the hiking trail by a fringe of trees. As the early summer day warmed, the Astringent Creek Grizzly and her cubs ambled toward the trees to bed, crossing the trail on the way.

As soon as she reached the human pathway, she saw them coming. Two garishly clad people were running down the trail straight for the grizzly family. The two male joggers skidded to a stop thirty feet from the agitated sow. The man in the lead froze at the side of the wide path. The other man behind turned and broke into a run. The bear charged past the man standing in the trail, brushing him aside in pursuit of the fleeing jogger. Just as she closed on the man, he hit the ground and lay still. The Astringent Creek Grizzly stopped on top of him, straddling his leg with her forepaws. The man didn't move. The bear sniffed the man but didn't touch him. She spun as the other jogger took advantage of the five-second pause to sprint down the trail in the opposite direction, directly past her cubs. In a heartbeat, the bear was upon him; she knocked him to the ground and stood directly over him, ready to deliver a killing bite to his head. At the last microsecond, she hesitated; her jaws closed a quarter of an inch from the man's skull.

The sow rested one paw on the jogger's shoulder and turned back to check on her cubs; they cowered beside the trail. Neither human stirred.

The big grizzly bolted back and gathered her cubs, all three running off into the timber. The man was unhurt. Later that day, armed rangers came looking for her. But by then, the grizzly family was long gone.

■■ The Astringent Creek Bear uses her vast store of knowledge and hard-learned lessons to find adequate food for her cubs and still avoid humans. Because of her dominance in the bear community, she can occupy quality habitats remote from two-legged visitors; other, more subordinate mothers and subadults are forced to feed near roads and major hiking trails.

She also knows she has choices; aggression is a tool she can use to explore fresh situations, pioneer relationships—with humans, other bears, and strange new predators. Eight years into her life, an ancient carnivore has reappeared on the scene.

She first sees them drifting through the trees like shadows, black and gray ghosts fluidly rolling over downed timber, effortlessly flowing through the forest. The beasts seem poorly stitched together with spare parts: huge paws attached to long spindly legs, ungainly even, except she has never seen a four-footed creature move so gracefully.

The Astringent Creek Grizzly smells them. She knows the type—the family of coyote and fox. But these animals are different. They kill many elk. She watched as they brought down a bison. They are masterful hunters whom the grizzly now trails much as her mother trailed the treacherous human elk hunters in the national forest, hoping for a carcass or a gut-pile. But the female bear does not fear the four-legged predators as she does the dangerous humans. The canines inspire something different; the caution she exercises around these creatures of the forest seems to stem from the most ancient variety of respect. Wolves and grizzlies—they are kindred.

The bear meets the wolf pack on an elk kill. The wolves have fed on the animal throughout the late summer day. Now they sleep under the pine trees at the edge of the meadow fifty yards from the elk carcass, which lies out in the sagebrush. The canines flick mosquitoes off their ears and watch the mother grizzly and her two cubs approach the kill from the open.

Three wolves stand, as if to greet the bears, and fan out on the edge of the meadow. The cubs ball up behind their mother; the larger wolves weigh more than a hundred pounds each. The three adult wolves stalk into the sage and stop forty feet from the grizzlies. Wolf and bear stare at one another; there is no visible sign of hostility.

The sow eases up to the carcass, almost in slow motion, her cubs close behind. Two wolves sit, the other lies down. They watch the bear family feed on the elk carcass. After a half hour, one wolf steps forward for a closer look. The female grizzly moves out to meet him. They are ten feet apart. The wolf slowly turns and joins his pack at the edge of the timber.

Some of these wild dogs have been brought down from Canada, where wolves and grizzlies vie over kills. In their canine memory, they know that as a pack, they could back a grizzly off a dead moose or elk, but only at some price. The new wolves of Yellowstone are still finding their place. The elk are plentiful and food is no problem. The Astringent Creek Grizzly finds she can easily displace the wolves and appropriate their kills. She holds her aggression in check. It isn't necessary.

■■ The situation changes the following spring. The pack has learned to prey upon bison, attacking them while the buffalo are in deep snow. Yellowstone bison have had no real predators since they were brought back from the brink of extinction. In 1800, some sixty million buffalo ranged throughout North America. By 1902, only twenty-three wild bison were known to exist: They lived here, in Yellowstone, in Pelican Valley.

Spring food is scarce, and the wolves stiffen their resistance; they are more reluctant to relinquish the kill to the grizzly. They growl and snarl at the bear, which lunges in return. By now her young are yearlings and better able to defend themselves from the wolf pack. She trails the wolves for a month, waits for them to make kills, and then appropriates the carcasses. The sow must make the most out of her ferociousness.

One day, the Astringent Creek Bear is on hand while the pack brings down a yearling bison. She sees and scents the man with the beard—the same man (also the one who saw her almost drown) she first saw when she was a cub in Hayden Valley—in the distant tree line watching with binoculars. The mother grizzly moves in on the wolf pack. She glances over her shoulder at the human intruder. The man smiles back. He thinks this might be the first time in a century that a human has witnessed a wild wolf preying on a wild American bison. With the Astringent Creek Grizzly watching it all, he thinks life has come full-circle; that a great historical wrong may be mending.

THE POLITICS OF
BEAR BIOLOGY

■■ On December 17, 2004, Louisa Willcox of the Natural Resources Defense Council convened a collection of U.S. grizzly bear advocates in Bozeman, Montana, with a call to arms. Under threat of lawsuit from the governor of Wyoming, the U.S. Fish and Wildlife Service planned a fast-track removal of Yellowstone's grizzly bears from the protection of the Endangered Species Act. Convinced that such a move—under the sorts of conditions proposed by the agency—could send the park's grizzlies on a downward spiral toward extinction, Willcox figured the activists and lawyers gathered had about a year to either derail the process or get ready to sue.

Those responding to her call were the heavy hitters of northern Rocky Mountain nonprofits: conservation lawyers who had successfully defended Yellowstone's wolf reintroduction program and had built a tenuous consensus around the idea of reintroducing grizzlies to the remote Selway-Bitterroot Wilderness of central Idaho and western Montana; and attorneys from the firm that won the case (if only temporarily) for Bill Clinton's roadless initiative, that stopped Crown Butte from digging its New World Mine cyanide heap-leach gold mine at the northeastern corner of Yellowstone, and that won its case to phase snowmobiles out of that park.

It was not, however, an amiable gathering. Within minutes, old alliances and grudges reared their ugly heads. One former protégé of Willcox's proceeded to sabotage the agenda, which Louisa had meticulously pieced together during the preceding weeks, while another announced he'd be opposing his former mentor on the issue. The temperature in the meeting room of the public library seemed to rise with everyone's tempers; by early afternoon, the group was reduced to thinly veiled personal insults.

For Willcox and her allies, the idea of taking Yellowstone's grizzlies off the endangered species list is a bad gamble in the face of declining food sources, genetic isolation, and habitat gobbled up by trophy homes, logging, and oil and gas development. Proponents of Fish and Wildlife's plan point to the grizzly's numeric and geographic rebound and the political needs of the Endangered Species Act. All have put in time on the ground, humping through grizzly country with a pack on their backs and with a love for the land in their hearts. But in the heat of the debate here and across the region, a fire nurtured through three decades of disagreements and mistrust, the bears themselves are reduced to abstract mathematical equations and pawns in an elaborate game of science, power, and prejudices taking place far from any wild country a bear would recognize as home.

▪▪ The modern grizzly debate finds its roots in the summer of 1967. On one August night, two women camping in two different parts of Glacier National Park were killed by two different garbage-fed grizzly bears. Though these were the first such human mortalities in the park's history, the Night of the Grizzlies (as it came to be called in a book by the same name) sent the National Park Service into a panic. Against the advice of pioneering grizzly biologists, brothers Frank and John Craighead, Yellowstone decided in 1968 to close its garbage dumps abruptly, forcing grizzlies who had learned to depend on human refuse to go cold turkey. The park service feared legal liability and didn't want any more generations of bear cubs picking up the bad habit of associating people with food. The Craigheads argued against the rapid closure scenario, advocating a more gradual phaseout to give the bears time to adjust. As it turned out, the Craigheads had a good point: The Yellowstone grizzly population crashed. Exact counts vary, but at least 229 grizzlies were killed in the five years following the dump closures as hungry bears ranged into towns and campgrounds in search of food. (That figure could be low; the Craigheads counted 270 dead grizzlies.)

Regardless, by the mid-1970s there were only about two hundred grizzlies left in Yellowstone, and the dump closures marked the beginning of a decade-long decline, according to government biologists. If nothing was done, the Yellowstone grizzly would likely go extinct. In 1975, the federal government intervened and classified the great bear as a "threatened" animal, placing it under the protection of the fledgling 1972 Endangered Species Act. Though the full power of the law has rarely (if ever) been brought to bear on violators, killing a grizzly, except in cases of self-defense, carries a theoretical penalty of up to $25,000 and six months in jail.

The economic and social repercussions were nonetheless significant. Hunting ended, and ranchers lost the option of shooting predator grizzlies on sight. Sheep were phased out of many nearby national forest grazing allotments. Timber companies and oil and gas developers working on public land had to clear the hurdle of showing that their projects would not degrade any landscapes with even the potential to support grizzlies. As a protected species, grizzlies proved a powerful tool for conservationists hoping to slow down the expansion of civilization's trappings in Western wildernesses. A host of federal and state agencies teamed up under the auspices of the Interagency Grizzly Bear

Committee and Study Team to embark upon a monitoring program of epic proportions in an effort to find out everything they could about how grizzly bears live and die in the Northern Rockies.

Under these conditions, Yellowstone's grizzlies spent the next thirty years regaining their numbers and recolonizing the park and some of the national forestland surrounding it. By the best educated guesses of government biologists, somewhere between four hundred and six hundred or more bears are now living in and around Yellowstone.

Though the population has been genetically isolated for the last hundred years, a 2003 study of Yellowstone grizzly DNA suggests any damage resulting from the population crash of the 1970s has yet to reveal itself. Two decades ago it was rare to see a grizzly. Now anyone willing to work at it has a decent shot of at least finding sign: a muddy footprint on a boardwalk, a day bed nestled in tree roots next to a meadow, overturned rocks or digs for biscuit root and yampa in a high alpine basin, or fresh-smelling grass scat left in a pile in the middle of a trail.

In 1993, the U.S. Fish and Wildlife Service set itself a list of targets designed to meet the requirements of the Endangered Species Act for a "recovered" species: an average of at least fifteen females with cubs of the year over a six-year period; sixteen out of eighteen so-called "bear management units" occupied by females with young; and a human-caused mortality limit not to exceed 4 percent of the total population on a running six-year average, with no more than a third of those deaths to be females. (Grizzlies have one of the slowest reproductive rates of any mammal on earth, so females are considered—to borrow a phrase from prominent grizzly biologist Dave Mattson—"especially special.")

While these targets were deemed to be "arbitrary and capricious" by a federal judge in 1995, the agency nonetheless has continued to use them as a goalpost (a fact that is likely to be an issue in any future delisting litigation).

Saying those goals had been met as of 2001, the Interagency Grizzly Bear Committee developed a blueprint for taking grizzlies off the endangered species list, a 160-page draft Conservation Strategy that forms the backbone of the post-ESA management plan for grizzly bears.

Basically, the nearly six-million-acre "recovery zone" has been renamed the "primary conservation area" (PCA) within which grizzlies will be afforded the most protection. Outside that zone, the fish and game agencies of Montana, Idaho, and Wyoming will make the rules (within certain mutually agreed upon guidelines), theoretically geared toward maintaining a population of about five hundred bears. The plan was formally and finally approved on April 30, 2007, and immediately challenged by Earthjustice attorneys. Resolution of the case was still pending as of late summer 2008.

"The PCA will be a secure area for grizzly bears, with population and habitat conditions maintained to ensure a recovered population is maintained for the foreseeable future and to allow bears to continue to expand outside the PCA," reads the executive summary of the plan. "Outside of the PCA, grizzly bears will be allowed to expand into biologically suitable and *socially acceptable* areas." [Emphasis added.]

Those two words are probably the most important in the entire document. In grizzly country, there are plenty of opportunities for trouble. Bears and people tangle over livestock (especially sheep); hunters leaving a carcass at sunset will often return the next morning to find it has been appropriated by a bear; those who move to grizzly country and plant orchards or feed the birds will likely find a bear on their back porch eating the dog food; and the proliferation of recreational off-road vehicles, as well as oil, gas, and logging, all bring people and grizzlies together, often to the detriment of the bear. The 2005 *Wildlife Monograph* published by the Interagency Grizzly Bear Study Team finds that humans were responsible for more than 85 percent of Yellowstone-area grizzly bear deaths between 1983 and 2001 (the causes ranging from grizzlies shot in self-defense or mistaken for black bears, to those hit by cars or killed purposefully by wildlife managers and illegally by poachers).

That monograph further found that grizzlies die at a much faster rate outside the recovery zone for the simple reason that people cannot carry guns inside the park. But these areas where bears die, called "population sinks," are precisely where managers propose to give the greatest discretion, saying that people must feel safe in order for the plan to work.

"Successful management of nuisance grizzly bears is paramount to the success of overall grizzly bear conservation," reads Idaho's management plan. "Outside of the PCA, significant consideration will be given to humans when grizzly bears come into contact with people or private property including livestock."

Montana's guidelines are the most bear-friendly, allowing grizzlies to occupy more or less whatever landscapes the bears find appropriate. Wyoming, on the other hand, takes the "socially acceptable" phrase to its extreme and has drawn a line on the map: Grizzlies crossing it will be killed. Idaho lies in between, but all three states plan for a hunting season on grizzlies.

There is only one other remotely healthy population of grizzly bears in the lower forty-eight states, finding its core refuge in the public lands of Glacier National Park and the Bob Marshall Wilderness area, lands that form what biologists call the Northern Continental Divide Ecosystem. While Glacier-area grizzlies are still considered threatened and will remain under federal protection for the time being, conservationists see the fate of Yellowstone's bears as predictive for the species as a whole.

▓▓ To the ranger who approached us, we must have looked like any other tourists having a midday snack at the picnic area. "You all should know there's been a grizzly around," he said. We smiled at him. The ranger shifted from foot to foot. "A *bear*," he emphasized.

"Oh? Where is he?" one of the women responded.

The ranger looked puzzled; we clearly were not reacting the way he anticipated. He mumbled something about being careful with our food, and left us to confront the beast on our own.

The ranger seemed to sense he was not talking to a group of casual visitors. This was a gathering of a branch of the Craighead clan and assorted friends. With us was a man who'd been chasing bears likely before the ranger had been born. In the spring of 2000, it was one of Frank Craighead's final trips to Yellowstone, where he and his brother essentially invented the science of grizzly bear research forty years earlier.

These days there are far more grizzly advocates than grizzly bears, but when John and Frank Craighead first took to the rolling hills of Yellowstone in 1959, they were the vanguard. "At that time nobody knew much about grizzly bears," says Lance Craighead, Frank's son and a respected biologist in his own right. "There was a whole Western mythology around bears, but there were basically no scientific studies of what bears do and what they need."

Perhaps even more important, few people cared. Missoula biologist Charles Jonkel also got his start in the grizzly business that year (a profession made practical with the invention of the tranquilizer dart gun), hired by the state of Montana to oversee all things bear.

"People then, they shot bears all the time just to see if their rifle was on," Jonkel says. "They weren't valued whatsoever. Nobody cared about bears." Between 1850 and 1920, grizzlies were killed back to less than 5 percent of their range in the United States (a figure that has since dwindled to less than 1 percent) and were treated by settlers as predators and competitors. By the time Jonkel and the Craigheads got into the bear business, there was only a handful of healthy grizzly bear populations left south of Canada.

As biologists, Jonkel and John Craighead gave birth to contemporary grizzly politics in another way. The two mentored a young man named Chris Servheen. It's been Servheen's job to shepherd grizzlies in the lower forty-eight states from near extinction to recovery. As head of the U.S. Fish and Wildlife Service's grizzly bear recovery program for the past twenty-five years, Servheen's entire career, nearly all of his adult life, has been tied to the fate of the great bear.

Both Jonkel and Craighead were Servheen's professors at the University of Montana in Missoula in the 1970s. Servheen moved out west to go to grad school at UM after seeing the National Geographic Society feature on the Craigheads' work in Yellowstone, so the chance to study under John was a dream come true for the young man. Jonkel was instrumental in furthering Servheen's career, recommending him for the job he holds today.

A quarter of a century later, both men are critical of their former protégé. Craighead, ninety years old in the summer of 2005, is more politic in his assessment, saying he has respect for Servheen; in fact, he likes the man. "His biggest problem is he wants to be the top . . . He doesn't take other people and groups into consideration very much. He tends to make the decisions on his own."

Jonkel, however, makes no secret of his bitterness. After Servheen was put in charge of grizzly recovery, Jonkel lost both his job with the state of Montana and his funding. Rightly or not, he laid blame at Servheen's feet.

"He got real into power and control and became very detrimental to bears," Jonkel says. "I think a lot of good people walked away because they didn't want to put up with it, [his] talking down to people, and such. I remember one time early on, he was doing a talk up in Hamilton, and somebody asked a fair question. He said, 'I don't need to explain that to you. You wouldn't understand it anyhow.' Well, there are probably a hundred people who are still—fifteen years later—madder than hell about that. Rural people don't forget.

"I knew he had those characteristics when he was a graduate student. But he also would help me when I had reports due, and I needed to get this done and needed to get that done. Everybody else wanted to go run the trapline and run the ridges and let the wind blow through their hair. Chris would help me. I appreciated that."

Many others echo Craighead and Jonkel's criticism of Servheen. Years ago, someone nicknamed him "Self" as in "Self Servheen." Like any nickname with the ring of truth, this one stuck, and even field biologists could be heard saying things like, "I wonder what Self would think of this?" But Servheen's greatest critic by far is not a rancher or anti-grizzly politician, but the diminutive, wiry woman named Louisa Willcox, a resident of Livingston, Montana, who has made grizzly conservation her life's work.

I was writing for the weekly *Missoula Independent* in 1997 when I first met Willcox socially. She phoned me one day to say she'd heard a rumor that Servheen was holding a meeting of some importance in Missoula. After calling his office all day without getting a response, I got up early the next morning and sat by his door on the University of Montana campus until he came in.

"Who told you about this meeting?" he demanded. Willcox hadn't requested anonymity, but I didn't think her identity mattered and told him so. We went round and round, getting nowhere. "Was it Louisa Willcox?" he finally asked. I had to admit Willcox was my source. "It's not a public meeting," he snapped, and our conversation clearly was over.

Seven years after my first awkward meeting with Servheen, he agreed to talk with me. People say he's mellowed over the years, and if this second encounter was any evidence, he has. The conversation was cordial, enlightening even. We talked for nearly an hour about grizzly politics before I broached what I knew was a sensitive subject: I asked him how his relationship with Willcox became so damaged. "Louisa Willcox has gone out of her way. She's tried to get me fired; that kind of goes beyond the issues of grizzly bears," he says. "I'm not sure why she's got that burr under her saddle. I mean, I don't think any other environmental group has tried to get me fired. She's got that unique approach to things."

Willcox, however, says she never tried to get Servheen fired, and that Chris has told other people the same thing. But when I ask her about the bad blood between them, she has no answer. "I've tried repeatedly to reach out," she says. "I have a whole correspondence file where I've tried to ask questions.

"At one point I drove over there and just showed up in his office and said, let's talk. I feel like I've tried to break down his barrier. But if there's any comfort, it's not just me. Look at the number of scientists who are in the same boat."

A few scientists have had very public spats with Servheen: Dave Mattson and Janet Roybal both had their stories publicized in Todd Wilkinson's book on the subject of censored government biologists, *Science Under Siege*. Others acknowledge their schisms off the record, not eager to open old wounds or damage a fragile working relationship.

Willcox moved to the region at about the same time as Servheen. She had worked in Lander, Wyoming, for the National Outdoor Leadership School in the mid-1970s. After a stint in Yale's graduate forestry program, she returned to sign on with the Greater Yellowstone

Coalition. "I did my major paper—it must have been 1983—on grizzly bears in Yellowstone. That was the year that there was a leaked memo from the Department of the Interior that indicated that there may be as few as forty-seven reproducing females left," she says. "That got me pretty interested, the whole sense that maybe these bears wouldn't be around."

Willcox worked her way through the ranks of conservation groups and now heads up the grizzly office of the Natural Resources Defense Council in the small town of Livingston, Montana, about fifty miles north of Yellowstone. Servheen, on the other hand, stuck with government work and was hired to run the U.S. Fish and Wildlife Service's Grizzly Bear Recovery Office out of Missoula.

"If I was going to scale or rank two people who I felt had worked around this issue for a long time, who had extraordinary interest in the welfare of the bear, Chris and Louisa would be at the top of the list," says biologist Tim Kaminski. "If you ask the next question, which is, gee, why don't they work together? I would say it's because they don't agree on anything."

Which is not exactly true. One of Servheen and Willcox's shared strengths is their vision. Louisa has been a driving force behind the development of grand-scale grizzly conservation. Bear advocates envision the day when grizzlies inhabit all the wildlands between Yellowstone and the north country of Canada—skirting cattle ranches and dashing across highway under- and overpasses (built just for that purpose) to the relative safety of the vast central Idaho wilderness, where they could establish another stronghold. The adventurous among them could keep going, grazing their way through the developed narrow river-valley bottoms of western Montana, crossing more two- and four-lane highways to hit Glacier and beyond. With two thousand grizzlies living in the lower forty-eight states and connected to stable populations in Canada and Alaska, advocates theorize that the bears would have a decent chance of surviving just about anything thrown at them: global warming, disease, changing political climates. "The conservation initiative is a broad vision that embraces this concept not just for grizzlies but for all wildlife species," says biologist Lance Craighead. Getting there is not rocket science but a matter of social and political will. Conservationists have a name for this plan: They call it Yellowstone to Yukon. It is, like communism, a beautiful idea with serious logistical problems.

In reality, grizzlies haven't been allowed much beyond the bounds of Yellowstone's recovery zone and its immediate surroundings. Those making a move—subadult males, mostly (the grizzly equivalent of a teenager)—have been shot or trapped, tranquilized, and helicoptered back home. In effect, the recovery zone has been a protective prison.

A proposal to reintroduce grizzlies to the Selway-Bitterroot Wilderness of central Idaho, a logical corridor for genetic interchange between the Yellowstone and Glacier populations, stalled politically with George W. Bush's election to the White House in 2000. Even if regional politicians had been willing (and they certainly were not: Former Idaho governor and Bush Interior Secretary Dirk Kempthorne characterized the plan as the federal government foisting "antisocial, flesh-eating" monsters upon the citizens of his state), the climate in Idaho was, and is, openly hostile.

On the north end of the Rockies, biologists say that Alberta, Canada's, grizzly bears are in such bad shape—stressed by hunger and by dodging humans in a landscape dominated by oil, gas, and tourist-related development—that their body chemistry appears to be changing. "These are not fat and happy bears. These are skinny, food-stressed bears all the time," says Canadian biologist Mike Gibeau.

But Servheen has foresight similar to Willcox's and wants to see grizzlies in these wildlands as well. His agency was the lead architect of the plan to move grizzlies back into the Bitterroots, and he believes that day is going to come. "The habitat is there. The need is there. We know we can do it," he says. "It's just a question of political will. Things will change. We go from one administration to another, swaying back and forth, and I think eventually we'll get to it."

If they don't get to it, the Conservation Strategy goes a step further, mandating that the feds fly grizzlies into Yellowstone from other ecosystems (two bears per generation, probably subadult females from Glacier or British Columbia) to augment the population's isolated gene pool. That is, if there's no evidence that bears are making the trip on their own in the next twenty years.

Putting aside the questionable wisdom of moving grizzlies around like livestock, Willcox says the premise of the Conservation Strategy itself is flawed: Yellowstone is not likely to remain ideal habitat for grizzlies over the long-term, especially with changes wrought by global warming. She suggests allowing grizzlies to colonize new ground, essentially letting the four-legged experts determine what areas are "biologically suitable," with humans granting some quarter in the "socially acceptable" realm.

"The Wyoming Range comes into play," Willcox says of the mountains south of Jackson Hole, on the western edge of Sublette County, Wyoming. "They've got some of the most healthy, big chunks of whitebark pine that's in unoccupied habitat. Promoting grizzly bear use of some of these outlying areas where whitebark pine is still healthy would be a smart idea, instead of drawing a line in the sand and saying you're going to shoot every bear that tries to get down there."

Political reality intervenes here. Sublette County commissioners passed in 2002 a resolution declaring grizzly bears and gray wolves to be "economically and socially unacceptable," following on the heels of similar resolutions in nearby Fremont and Lincoln Counties, which prohibited the presence of these animals outright. While these resolutions have no legal standing, they are nonetheless a clear statement of local sentiment.

But politics is Servheen's game, and he plays it well. He's woven a complex web of alliances, including Wyoming's Game and Fish Department, and attempts to bring in conservationists by appealing to their loyalty to the Endangered Species Act. "We've had very few successes under the act," he tells me (and every other reporter who's come calling of late). "There are a lot of people who say it's just a failure, and it needs to be revised or changed or even eliminated. Unless we start showing success, those people will gain more credibility and more of a following."

His office has developed reams of paperwork outlining detailed monitoring programs in which he appears to have complete faith. The tough questions about food, habitat, and mortality are all answered with a nod to the piles of reports lying on and around his desk.

"We have a pretty good handle on where bears are now. One estimate right now [is that] there are 588 bears as of last year in the system, and about 10 percent of those occur outside of the recovery zone. We've got, like I say, 10 percent of the bears with radios on. But if we start to see changes in the distribution of home ranges, in association with changes in the foods, we can adjust the boundaries to places where bears need to go and protections in those areas in order to minimize mortalities.

"I feel comfortable that we've got a good idea, we've got a good system to monitor all the important things, and we've got a responsive, dynamic system that will change in response to needs."

I suggest to Servheen that conservationists' concerns about delisting are rooted in mistrust: We all hear the bar talk about killing wolves and grizzlies. "Maybe they'll all get parvo [a canine virus] and we won't have to shoot them ourselves," was the hopeful conclusion at one dinner party, where the conversation turned to wolves. And the fact is, our grandparents and our neighbors' grandparents did drive these animals to the brink of extinction. Servheen dismisses these worries as paranoia. "This idea that somehow nefarious people could start to do bad things and nobody would know about it is not the case," he says. "Mortality limits still exist after recovery and delisting. And there's still a management program to manage that. It's a public process with public meetings and public exposure. So it's not like people can start shooting grizzly bears or the states can decide, okay, we're going to forget what we agreed to.

"It's almost like having a teenager and he or she wants to drive," says Servheen. "They get their license and you say, okay, here are the keys. Keep the car out of the ditch or you won't be able to drive again. So the incentive is really on the teenager now to do the right thing. If he drives into the ditch and wrecks the car, the problem for him is he's not going to be able to drive again. The states are essentially the teenager in this approach. They want control of the bear. They know the things they need to do to manage the bear properly. And if they drive the car into the ditch, it's going to be a very public wreck."

But it's not just their neighbors that conservationists worry about. The government's Conservation Strategy provides very little in the way of a safety net in case of trouble in the grizzly world. The feds are setting up a committee of federal, state, local, and tribal representatives to keep watch over the entire program. But changes on the ground could happen very fast (researchers believe the difference between an increasing and declining population could hinge on a mere handful of deaths a year), while the regulatory mechanisms take a long time to kick in.

If the mortality standards are exceeded, for instance, it will take at least three years to trigger a breach in policy (as managers plan to work off a three-year running tally of deaths). In such a case, any member may request that the committee consider a "biology and monitoring review." If the committee votes to conduct such a review, it has to be completed within six months. The end result is not action of some sort—say, a hiatus in the hunting season—but a report. "If the situation, after completion of the biology and monitoring review, is such that all or some of the desired population and habitat standards specified in this Conservation Strategy are not being met, and cannot be met in the opinion of the [committee], then the [committee] will petition the Fish and Wildlife Service for relisting."

Now, the Fish and Wildlife Service has a backlog of proposals for listing under the Endangered Species Act that stretches across 279 species, which, according to one analysis, have been waiting nineteen years on average for a decision. (At least forty-two of these species went extinct waiting for protection: eleven species of terrestrial snails, ten birds, nine flowering plants, six freshwater mussels, two amphibians, and one each—stonefly, freshwater snail, and a mammal—the Little Marianna Fruit Bat). Given those conditions, it's easy to see why conservationists fear a grizzly population in trouble could go extinct waiting for help.

"It's sort of a matter of arranging deck chairs on a boat instead of developing backup systems in the engine room, which is what they should be doing," Willcox says. "They're setting up a whole monitoring system that doesn't have any trigger mechanisms . . . Litigation, even if we're successful, it may be too little too late because when you've already eliminated 99 percent of bears from their former habitat, you're playing with fire with the last 1 percent. You'd think we should have learned something about how easy it is to kill bears and how hard it is to grow them, and I think there's an enormous amount of hubris in this whole endeavor."

Furthermore, the entire process requires that people trust authorities to act not according to political expediencies, but with the best interests of the grizzly at heart. Servheen, for instance, has a long, acrimonious history with the main opponents of delisting. They don't trust him. A change in the acceptable mortality limits in June 2005 illustrates how these feelings were perpetuated.

Mortality and population (births and deaths) are the underpinnings to the success of grizzly recovery. They're dependent on things like food, habitat—especially habitat—and security from humans, but whether or not grizzlies will survive depends in the most basic sense on how many bears there are and how fast they die.

Dozens of biologists have spent thousands of hours devising ways to pin these numbers down. When the Fish and Wildlife's Conservation Strategy was released in 2003, officials decided to shoot for a population of five hundred grizzlies. Biologists calculated that such a group of bears could sustain a human-caused mortality rate not to exceed an annual average of 4 percent over a six-year period. This was presented as a conservative figure, based on a benchmark study by Richard Harris in 1986, concluding that a population like Yellowstone could probably sustain a loss of grizzlies at 6.5 percent annually. "The current ratio of known and probable-to-unknown mortalities is 2:1; therefore an upper limit of 4 percent documented mortality allows for an actual mortality limit of 6 percent," the Conservation Strategy explains. While .5 percent may have been a slim comfort margin, it was a margin nonetheless. On June 18, 2005, the Associated Press reported that Servheen was recommending the annual mortality limit be raised to 9 percent for females, 15 percent for males:

[A] federal wildlife official said Friday he doesn't expect deaths to rise much as a result. Rather, Chris Servheen said the planned change is intended to allow wildlife officials to better track how—and how many—bears are dying. "The goal is to do a better job of accounting for mortalities," said Servheen. Servheen said the proposed method, backed by the Interagency Grizzly Bear Committee, would also track all bear deaths, not just those caused by humans.

When I ask Chuck Schwartz, who heads up the Interagency Grizzly Bear Study Team (the research arm of the government's grizzly bear management agencies) about the change, he points me to his group's 2005 *Wildlife Monograph*. In one chapter, Harris—who set the original 6.5 percent mortality limit—compares the two methods. "The current approach to grizzly bear management in the GYE [Greater Yellowstone Ecosystem] is for management agencies to consider all forms of mortality, but to establish an annual limit only for human-caused mortality," he writes. "We proposed that rather than counting human-caused mortalities, management agencies should focus on survival rates irrespective of the cause of death."

Harris lays out a series of mathematical formulas and computer models that he says comes up with comparable survival rates for both the 6.5 percent method of counting only human-killed grizzlies and the higher limits for counting all dead grizzlies.

Previously, the idea of counting every dead bear couldn't pass the straight-face test. A 1991 study by biologists Dave Mattson and Richard Knight estimated that natural deaths account for 69 percent of backcountry mortality; two other studies, by John Craighead in 1974 and Richard Knight in 1984, calculated that the government records only 40 to 60 percent of actual grizzly deaths. But in the 2005 monograph, the biologists conclude that natural mortality is unusual these days because they documented only five such cases out of sixty-four deaths.

Accepting these changes, it seems, is not about trust: It's about ego. What makes us think we can know every bear that lives and dies merely by calculating its existence?

Willcox suggests that the raising of acceptable mortality rates is motivated by politics, not biology. Yellowstone comes so close to that 4 percent figure on a regular basis that once you add in dead grizzlies from legal hunting and the state's management activities, there's little hope of maintaining it; she thinks the feds are raising the limits to head off that issue. "This is my sense of the real purpose," she says. "Also pushing hard on upping the limits is Wyoming Game and Fish."

According to Jonathan Langer, who worked for Willcox at the Natural Resources Defense Council, Wyoming wildlife director John Emmerich attended the June 2005 Interagency Grizzly Bear Committee meeting and pushed the committee to allow the state to have its own mortality limits, saying that low mortality in one area (like the park) could compensate for higher mortality in other areas (like his state). Several months after the fact, Emmerich declined to confirm this version of events for me, saying instead that Wyoming would accept the government's mortality rates with an eye toward keeping his state's grizzly population from getting any larger. "Some shifts in population distribution will occur, but overall management direction would be designed to hold grizzly numbers at current levels in Wyoming outside of [the park]," he says.

Further driving a wedge of distrust between the government and some grizzly advocates is the impression that the government's Interagency Grizzly Bear Study Team has diddled with the numbers for years. Probable deaths (deaths that were likely due to a shooting, car accident, or the like, but in which a corpse was not recovered, as opposed to "known" mortalities where a body is found) were not counted until 2000, nor were orphaned cubs of the year (who are almost certain to die once their mother has been killed) included in the body count until that year. Grizzlies killed more than ten miles outside the recovery zone still are not counted toward the total.

Finally, the calculations themselves are somewhat convoluted.

For example, people killed 19 grizzlies in the Greater Yellowstone Ecosystem in 2004. With a population estimated at a minimum of 431 grizzlies, a death toll of 17.2 grizzlies would exceed 4 percent of the population. But two of those grizzlies were killed more than ten miles outside of the recovery zone. "Both of these instances involved male grizzly bears that were misidentified and mistakenly killed by black bear hunters over bait," according to the study team's annual report. So the official total was only 17 grizzlies, under the 17.2 limit. However, 17 dead bears is not the number used. The number used is 13.3: That's because biologists don't count the annual total alone in determining whether the limits have been breached for any given year, but simply add it to the six-year running average of human-killed grizzlies, and then use that number. And since the 13.3 figure (the six-year running average as of 2004) is under 17.2, the limit for dead grizzlies in 2004 officially was not exceeded.

"It's not very clear," biologist and team member Mark Haroldson agrees when I admit to confusion. "I get lots of questions on this."

If all known and probable human-caused grizzly deaths were counted—and counted annually instead of on a running six-year average—the mortality limit would have been exceeded in seven of the last twelve years, including four of the last five (when probable deaths and cubs became statistics). But by the study team's calculations, only 1995 proved to be an overly lethal year.

The fact remains that for all the science, no one really knows how many bears live and how many die. Dozens of papers have been written, plugging factors of food, mortality, road densities, and the like into computer models that all spit out formulas that invariably conclude grizzly bears don't fit into computer models.

■■ It's a three-day hike to reach the Two Ocean Plateau from Jackson Hole, south of Yellowstone Lake in one of the wildest parts of the park. In the fall, there are hunter camps in the Thoroughfare to the south, just outside the park; tent cities reportedly equipped with whores and whiskey bars are catered to wealthy elk hunters and guarded like fiefdoms by politically well-connected outfitters. But here, 10,000 feet above sea level, few humans travel, and no one lingers. You can plan a trip, and if you arrive too early, the high country may still be enveloped in snow midway through the summer. Doug and I hope to see bears, grizzlies who come here to graze on green grass sprouting just at the edge of the melting snow. Doug has been here nearly a dozen times. "There will be a bear bedded in every patch of trees," he predicts, based on his previous experiences. He thinks they, too, come here for the solitude.

But by mid-July 2003, we are too late. Temperatures soar into the eighties, and the grass is brown even at the edges of the few lingering snowbanks. With the exception of a mother with two cubs, and maybe another subadult hanging around, the predominant animal life is mosquito and blackfly. We explore stands of stunted, windblown trees (whitebark pine, subalpine fir, and Engelmann spruce), examine old day beds, bathe in a tepid, buggy pool, and get used to the idea that we're alone. Doug thinks the extraordinary heat is a sign of Yellowstone's changing climate and that there was no chance for the bears to feed here this season.

Most years, grass isn't the most important food for grizzlies, though they routinely eat it. Researchers have identified four sorts of food that are vital to the Yellowstone grizzly population as a whole: cutthroat trout, whitebark pine nuts, army cutworm moths, and ungulates like bison, elk, and moose. Unlike many other places where grizzlies live, there are few berries here. While grizzlies are master pioneers, there's not much opportunity to develop new things to eat. And their larder is growing thinner by the year.

Dave Mattson is easily the current preeminent biologist of grizzly bears in Yellowstone, among the several dozen who have made the study of the park's bears their focus. The results of his fourteen years of grizzly-related fieldwork stand out as the premier independent body of work defining much of what we know about the life of the region's bears in the post-Craighead era. And he says that while the grizzlies seem to be doing all right now, trouble looms.

In the spring of 2004, Mattson is speaking to a group of journalists gathered at a ranch nestled in a high basin at the south end of Montana's Paradise Valley at the invitation of Louisa Willcox. She's been fighting for grizzlies for decades under the various auspices of the Sierra Club,

Greater Yellowstone Coalition, Earth First, and, briefly, her own non-profit Wild Forever. She wages one side of that battle every year by inviting reporters from across the country to a weekend retreat on the north end of Yellowstone National Park. Participants in 2004 range from the likes of the *Boise Weekly* and *Salt Lake Tribune*, to the *Washington Post* and scouts from *60 Minutes*. Everyone drags him- or herself out of bed each morning to hit the Lamar Valley (about a two-hour drive from the ranch) at daylight—around 7:00 a.m. this time of year, late April—in the hope of catching grizzlies and wolves on the move. The afternoons are filled with lectures, the evenings with stories.

Mattson has published more than seventy papers on the lives and doings of grizzly bears during the last two and a half decades. But from his talk tonight, I gather that his real love is food. Now, bears will eat nearly anything with nutritional value: mushrooms, dandelions, roots, and tubers. "At this time of year," Mattson says, "they're grubbing for biscuit root up on these high ridges. You can see paw-size excavations.

"They also dig a lot of yampa [a white-flowered perennial with nutritious tuberous roots] later in the year. They eat a fair number of carpenter ants that they dig out of logs like this one," he projects a photo onto the screen in front of the fireplace. "These are distinctive because they have a high ascorbic acid content, and I've recommended numerous times to people that they should try eating ants because they're actually really pretty tasty. Honestly.

"I have to confess that I've eaten a lot of what the bears eat, [but] not all. They're fairly reliable guides to what's good cuisine. I draw the line at rotten meat and maggots."

There are those fellow biologists who say Mattson's science, his research, is the best out there (though one colleague, who asked to remain unnamed, cautions that the appearance of partisanship can taint just as badly as true bias, implying that Mattson is unwise to speak at gatherings like this one). But despite innuendos about his loyalties, no one questions the value of Mattson's work; in fact, practically no modern grizzly bear researcher can write a paper about Yellowstone's bears without citing him. So this snowy spring evening in 2004, as his colleagues lay the groundwork to remove the grizzly from the endangered species list, Mattson picks apart their argument piece by piece.

He indicates that there was a spike in the use of the bear's four main food groups through the 1980s (due at least in part to an increase in those foods with management policies like catch-and-release fishing and an end to herd-reduction programs for bison and elk), which Mattson believes has probably helped the grizzly population grow to its current size. The problem with delisting, he says, is that these spikes are very likely temporary, cyclical by nature, and the results, to some degree, influenced by biases in the study methods. "The point, though, is that when you put these all together, [these four foods] are accounting for 80 to 90 percent of the energy the bears are getting out of this ecosystem," Mattson explains to the dozen or so journalists gathered. "What we'll notice, though, here, is the absence of the archetypal bear food: The bears around here eat virtually no berries, which is really, really unusual. This diet is rare in North America.

"If you're going to find bears anywhere in the world that have a diet that really closely resembles the diet of grizzly bears in Yellowstone, you have to go to Siberia, where again you'll find bears that are eating seeds of the stone pine [of which the whitebark pine is one], ungulates, salmon, and, in most places, relatively few berries. The point is that the bears here are unique; they have unique behaviors and a unique diet in a unique ecosystem. So in that respect, they are especially special."

To canoe across Yellowstone Lake, you've got to leave at daylight. At 7,733 feet above sea level, the water is always cold, often still partially covered with ice in early June. If a storm blows up, there's little time to make shore. As my husband is fond of saying, "They call the lake a man-eater, but in fact it's an equal opportunity killer." We get a late start due to a side trip to the Lake Clinic to put fifteen stitches in Doug's head after he trips on his shoelaces and bashes his skull on a rock. "Take it easy for a few days," the doctor cautions, so we hit the water.

As each stroke leads logically and rhythmically to the next, stretched over hours, the surface of the lake comes alive. The sun strikes patterns in the waves, textures that are mesmerizing, changing, dizzying, hinting at the power and force of a living being under the surface. My imagination is not so far off—there are other worlds here. Scientists studying the lake's underwater secrets find a landscape of hot springs, geysers, spires, and canyons. The lake also nurtures Yellowstone's cutthroat trout—fish that dozens of species depend upon, including grizzlies, white pelicans, and river otters.

It's a toss-up, which grizzly food is in more trouble: cutthroat trout or whitebark pine. The cutthroat is a native Western fish sporting a red slash at the base of its throat, which gives it its name. It's not a big fighter and is good (if politically incorrect) to eat. While the U.S. Fish and Wildlife Service has so far declined to list cutthroat as an endangered or threatened species, regional conservation-minded anglers sport bumper stickers that read, I RELEASE CUTTHROATS.

"As an all-around sport fish it has few peers: It grows to a fairly large average size, is highly vulnerable to sportfishing, even by novice anglers, and it has a high susceptibility to repeated catches when released," former park historian Paul Schullery and retired chief scientist John Varley wrote in a 1995 report to the superintendent of Yellowstone. "Cutthroat trout, more than any other trout species, is the archetype of western trout fishing."

While they've been in decline in much of their range, cutthroat maintained a stronghold in Yellowstone Lake. Then, in 1994, the park service discovered that someone had surreptitiously slipped some lake trout into Yellowstone Lake (Mattson and biologist Dan Reinhart hypothesize the lake trout came from Lewis Lake, seven miles away. Historically empty of fish, Lewis was stocked with lake trout in 1896). The problem is, lake trout eat cutthroat and have a history of displacing these natives in other Western lakes. They are credited with the decline or extinction of cutthroat, for instance, in Lake Tahoe, Jackson Lake, and Heart Lake in Yellowstone. In the West Thumb area of Yellowstone Lake, where the most lake trout have been found, spawning cutthroat have fallen off to near zero.

Unlike cutthroat, which are caught by bears as they spawn in the shallow cobblestone creeks and streams, lake trout are deepwater fish and don't swim where bears can catch them. The loss of cutthroat doesn't just affect the animals who eat them, but the entire ecosystem. After catching a fish, a grizzly (or osprey or otter) will usually haul it up away from the water to eat, unwittingly participating in a process that biologists call "energy flow to consumers at higher trophic levels." In other words, grizzly scat and what's left of the rotting carcasses provide nitrogen-rich compost for plants and other animals beyond the banks of the river.

Furthermore, the loss of Yellowstone Lake's cutthroat fishery would have significant financial implications: The Schullery and Varley report entitled *The Yellowstone Lake Crisis* put the potential loss at $640 million over the course of thirty years if lake trout were not controlled.

So the park service declared war on lake trout in 1995. Anglers catching lake trout are obligated to kill them. The park has launched an aggressive deepwater gillnetting campaign in the hope of preventing as many lake trout as possible from reaching reproductive maturity. Cutthroat will decline no matter how hard the park works to kill lake trout, but biologists predict measures to control lake trout could reduce that loss by up to 50 percent. The problem is, these programs are expensive (the park service spends at least $300,000 annually on lake trout eradication), and to be successful to any degree, they will have to go on forever.

Fish and Wildlife grizzly bear recovery coordinator Chris Servheen is less concerned about the loss of cutthroat in terms of their value as grizzly food. He says that relatively few bears eat cutthroat trout at any point in their lives. "It seems that about 12 percent of the bears in the entire ecosystem eat fish at one time or another," he says. "And almost all of those are males. We know that bears eat fish at certain times, but a small percent of the population eats fish."

I e-mail Mattson to ask about Servheen's interpretation of the research, and he writes back saying such an exact number is not appropriate. Numbers of bears and numbers of bears eating fish are both estimates, he says, which when combined don't lend themselves to a clear answer. "The current range of uncertainty in that estimate is huge, so

I find '12 percent' quite strange coming from a credentialed scientist," he says.

Furthermore, Mattson says, what we're seeing is not representative of historic conditions: With cutthroat already in decline, fewer bears are eating them. "Haroldson et al. (2005) think it most likely that the changes in use of trout by bears is due to an overall decline in numbers of spawning trout, resulting in fewer stream reaches offering high-quality fishing opportunities for bears, with male grizzlies better able to dominate these opportunities under current conditions of scarcity," he writes. "Females would have the added incentive to avoid a limited number of profitable stream reaches if they were likely to lose their off-spring to predatory males . . . leading to an overall decline in consumption of trout, with a shift from females to males." This is, in fact, the trend biologists have documented.

Which brings up an important point. Grizzlies eat certain foods for different reasons. Males grizzlies in particular like to bulk up on meat, Mattson says, because it gives them an advantage come mating season. Females, however, are clearly dependent on whitebark pine nut crops to put on fat. Researchers have found a strong correlation between the quality of a given year's nut crop and the females' reproductive success, with nearly twice as many cubs being born after a good whitebark pine year. Conversely in poor crop years, grizzlies range closer to civilization looking for food and are, therefore, more vulnerable. In those years, humans kill more grizzlies—about two to three times as many, according to the 2005 *Wildlife Monograph*.

"That translates into pretty dramatic differences in overall population growth rate," Mattson tells his audience of journalists. "During a year when we have a good seed crop, the population increases on average by about 7 percent. When we have a poor seed crop, it declines by about 5 percent.

"The bears are not living or dying because they're starving. The primary effect of whitebark pine seeds on bear death rates is in the extent to which it governs where bears are on the landscape relative to people. Whitebark pine occurs only at very high elevations in this ecosystem, up above about 8,200 feet. When bears are up high using whitebark pine seeds, they are safe from people for the most part. In contrast, when you have poor seed crop years, bears tend to spend more time at lower elevations, nearer people. And what we've found is that when grizzly bears are near people, near roads, they die at nearly twice the rate that they do when they're in the backcountry."

Kate Kendall was the first biologist to take a close look at grizzlies' use of whitebark pine nuts. A Glacier-area biologist now compiling a portrait of that park's bear population using DNA analysis of hair samples, Kendall got her start in Yellowstone after being inspired by the Craigheads' work.

What Kendall discovered was a web of cooperation: Whitebark pinecones don't open on their own, and they need two years to germinate. They are harvested by red squirrels, who stash their pinecones in great mounds called middens at the base of trees. Grizzlies raid these middens—squirrels protesting (and occasionally getting eaten along with their stash) all the while—crunch open the cones, and delicately pluck out each nut with their tongues. Whitebark pine is a slow-growing tree, taking fifty to seventy-five years or more to produce cones. But it grows in the most desolate, windy, dry, mountainous places imaginable. As such, it's what biologists call a "keystone" species, a tree that by its very existence nurtures a whole host of other plants and animals. Diana Tomback, a biologist with the University of Colorado in Denver, has made the whitebark pine her life's study.

"In other words, whitebark pine in the greater Yellowstone is relatively low in abundance, but its impact is much greater than its abundance," she says. "It provides wildlife habitat. Elk go up there; deer go up there. It's at the uppermost limits of tree growth. It will grow where other conifers can't. Because of that tolerance, it actually plays an important hydrological role."

Whitebark pine slows snowmelt and thus controls erosion; it feeds nuthatches, grosbeaks, crossbills, several woodpeckers, and others; it acts as a nurse tree for spruce and fir, providing shelter for the fledgling starts. It's one of the first species of trees to begin growing back after a wildfire. And it's under assault from three fronts: mountain pine beetle, climate change, and blister rust.

Mountain pine beetles are native pests, a "true predator in that they must kill their host to successfully reproduce, and they often do so in truly spectacular numbers," write Jesse Logan and James Powell, of the U.S. Forest Service's Rocky Mountain Research Station based in Logan, Utah. They can kill whitebark stands at rates approaching 40 percent. Pine beetle epidemics fluctuate; though no one is sure why, Logan and Powell speculate that global warming is playing a role. While the beetles used to primarily attack lodgepole pine, they appear to be moving up in elevation and hitting whitebark as well. The only responses researchers have come up with are "all expensive and labor intensive," Logan says. The best, according to Tomback, involves sending hikers out with pheromone packets, costing about $20 each, which when nailed to a tree twice a summer will protect it for the season. (Since our initial conversation, Logan says more recent data on whitebark pine's vulnerability to pine beetle has revealed much higher rates of infection, with upwards of 90 percent mortality among cone-bearing trees in places where infestations have run their course. A number of factors appear to be driving the beetle's success: climate change, the close proximity of an alternative host (lodgepole pine), and the fact that blister rust makes whitebark trees more vulnerable to pine beetle attack. In addition, while whitebark pine is primarily dependent upon Clark's nutcracker to harvest and distribute its seeds, the nutcracker can make a fine living on other conifers and could abandon whitebark without trouble. "It is conceivable that the combination of these factors could drive whitebark pine to extinction in the Greater Yellowstone Ecosystem," Logan writes. "Functional loss in the short term is, in fact, *almost a certainty.*")

The climatic changes that may be encouraging pine beetle infestations are also likely to squeeze whitebark pine out of the zones in which it can grow in Yellowstone: above 8,500 feet, where it is free from competition with other conifers, and below 9,500 feet, where temperatures get too cold. William Romme and Marcia Turner, in one of three papers published on the subject, examined three climate change scenarios in a

1991 article for *Conservation Biology* magazine: warm and dry, warm and wet, and an intermediate set of circumstances in which temperatures increase but precipitation is stable. In all three, they concluded, whitebark pine habitat is likely to decrease, possibly by as much as 90 percent. The other two papers predict similar scenarios.

Then there's blister rust. It's a fascinating organism all on its own, but it's a scourge to the biologists who normally might have an intellectual fondness for the Asian fungus. Blister rust first hit the western coast of North America in Vancouver in 1910, traveling on the back of some eastern white-pine seedlings ordered from France. Although European five-needle pines are resistant, North America's pines are not, and the disease has been spreading—slowly in dry areas, more quickly in humid climates—ever since.

"The spores land on pine needles of five-needle white pines, and they actually grow down into the stomates [minute pores] of the needle into the twig, and then it takes, oh, about two to three years to start forming this canker," Diana Tomback explains. "The canker grows year after year until finally it girdles the branch. It kills the branch.

"In the meantime the living part of the branch is down below the canker. The canker grows down the branch toward the trunk of the tree. It follows the reverse flow of sap, basically. When the canker gets into the trunk of the tree and develops and grows and encircles the trunk, it will kill the tree. The problem with five-needle white pines, and particularly whitebark pine, is that the cones are formed high in the canopy in the branches. So you can effectively kill all of the cones, or most of the cone-producing branches, five years, ten years, before the tree itself is dead."

Blister rust spores travel on the wind; biologists have documented an outbreak three hundred miles away from its source. They can go dormant for years, which in a dry climate like Yellowstone means the odd humid summer is enough to revive the spores and escalate infection rates. Scientists have plotted out forty-five randomly placed samples in the greater Yellowstone in recent years and found 71 percent of those had some evidence of blister rust infection. Furthermore, biologist Mark

Haroldson says, nearly a quarter of the trees surveyed died between 2002 and 2004, mostly from mountain pine beetle, though the data appear to indicate that the rate of loss has slowed. Whitebark pines have about a 5 percent resistance rate to blister rust, though researchers have not yet been able to identify the gene that confers this protection. The plan for now, Tomback says, is to cultivate seedlings from these resistant trees, expose them to a heavy dose of spores, and see how they respond, then plant the healthy ones back out on the landscape. Tomback and her colleagues have formed the Whitebark Pine Ecosystem Foundation to try to save these trees. They promote a local approach, with regional foresters, biologists, and botanists collaborating to save their own forests.

"Blister rust will spread geographically. There's no stopping it. Not even aridity, not even drought apparently. All it takes are these wave years climatically," she says. "We are very concerned that blister rust will in fact spread throughout all of the five-needle white-pine range, and also Great Basin bristlecone pine, the limber pine, and get down into Mexico.

"And we'll end up with ghost forests, ghost forests of five-needle white pines."

■■ The chronology of the relationship between grizzlies and their third vital food, army cutworm moths, is something of a mystery. Bleached mule and horse bones at moth sites on the high talus slopes of the Absaroka Mountains southeast of Yellowstone indicate outfitters once slaughtered old livestock and hunted grizzlies over their carcasses. While bears eating moths is a well-known and documented phenomenon in the Mission Mountains of western Montana and on Rainbow Peak in Glacier National Park, researchers only rediscovered Yellowstone's moth sites in 1986. (They labeled it a *rediscovery* by the bears as well, though no one knows if grizzlies were eating moths all along.) But does that mean bears weren't eating moths prior to that? Some observers speculate that the moth population was hit by pesticides (moths are considered pests in the agricultural farmland of America) that made them unavailable as a food source to bears during the 1970s. Others wonder if the moths were there but laden with DDT, suspecting that grizzlies knew better than to eat the poisoned bugs.

Regardless, biologists believe moths may play the same role as whitebark pine in terms of keeping grizzlies in remote areas, away from people, and, therefore, indirectly helping to keep those bears from being killed. And, like whitebark, moths may also be vulnerable to changes in global weather.

Moths spend their summer days slurping the nectar of tundra flowers in the alpine meadows; at night they lie under rocks. From mid-July to mid-September, grizzlies frequent these slopes, flipping over rocks and licking off the moths.

"They're relatively chilled because at this elevation these rock slopes are just like refrigerators. So it's really no problem at all for the bears then to get their noses down in there and use their tongue to just lap up moths," Mattson says. "And moths, in the words of another researcher, are little fat bombs. They're 75 percent fat. An individual bear can consume up to forty thousand moths in a day."

The biologists' discovery of these moth sites is important because official estimates of the grizzly bear population in the ecosystem are based to a large degree on the sighting of mothers with young cubs at these locations; those estimates rose dramatically following that discovery.

But does that mean there are more bears? That the bears are simply more visible and therefore easier to count? Or that biologists are now looking for bears in places where they previously hadn't?

Numbers are embedded in our psyche: They are concrete, and they can be cited in papers and lawsuits and fed into computers. The numbers game, Mattson believes, is a red herring. "[Grizzly conservation] really is about habitat, not numbers," he says, explaining that the amount of wild land with good food drives the trajectory of a population. "But we're playing the numbers game. So these are the kinds of trends that you're going to be shown."

Biologists don't count all the bears but use two main indicators to make an educated guess at the size of Yellowstone's grizzly population: sightings of females with cubs of the year and dead bears. Mattson runs through a series of graphs, crunching numbers from 1977 through 1993. The gist is that government biologists counted increases in the number of mothers with cubs and increases in the number of dead bears and concluded that this means there are more grizzlies. But Mattson has developed alternate explanations, and he thinks all these may be playing a part in shaping how we perceive the grizzlies' demographic trends.

"We could be seeing more females, we could be finding more dead bears because we're biased in our methods. It's just as simple as that. It also could be because simply there are more humans in and around grizzly bear habitat, so what grizzly bears that are out there, we're seeing more of . . .

"We could have increased agency efforts to observe bears. If the agencies are spending more effort and time to find more bears, they will. We could also have a redistribution of bears into areas nearer people. Same population of bears, same numbers, we're just simply having a redistribution.

"Also, we could indeed have an increasing and expanding population."

Mattson proceeds to demonstrate with bars and graphs that agencies are spending more time and effort looking for bears and that more tourists are visiting grizzly country. As far as redistribution, he points to the fact that the 1988 fires destroyed substantial numbers of whitebark pine stands, equivalent to a loss of 25 percent carrying capacity for grizzlies in the center of the ecosystem. At the same time, grizzlies were allegedly rediscovering moths at the south end of their range. "So with that in mind, has there been a redistribution of bears toward the periphery of their range, without any population increase?" he poses the question for his audience of journalists. "Probably yes," he answers himself.

Then comes the more complicated question: Do the ways in which we look for bears affect the number of grizzlies we find?

Mattson puts another chart on the screen, this one gauging the likelihood that a bear will be seen, depending upon what it's doing: sleeping, feeding on pine seeds, digging roots, walking the open talus slopes of the Absaroka Mountains looking for moths. "That's really important because the probability of seeing a bear when it's on a moth site consuming moths is almost 100 percent. We're going to see virtually any bear that's on moth sites eating moths.

"By contrast, if it's in the forest eating ants, chances of seeing it while it's doing that are down around 5 percent. Huge difference in the probability of sighting bears, depending on what they're doing.

"So let's go back to this business of numbers of females with cubs of the year we've sighted going from 1977 to 1993, seeing these jumps. What you see in red," he said, indicating the screen, "are the numbers of moth sites on which we observed bears excavating moths. A really dramatic increase during this period of time, a drop, and then another very dramatic increase corresponding to this period of time," he says, pointing to leaps of red on his bar graph. Coinciding with these are green bars, showing the percentage of females with cubs of the year on moth sites in a given year. "Another spike here, another spike here," he points out the correlating years. The jumps in green and red are mirror images of each other. "So are there systematic biases that affect our ability to see bears? Count bears? Absolutely yes."

Mattson allows that the scenario that Yellowstone's grizzlies are increasing in number and expanding their range is possible, though he doesn't find any certainty in the data. What he does conclude is that even if the population is up, the future for Yellowstone's bears looks increasingly difficult as their high-quality food sources diminish.

"So the bottom line: What's the prognosis for Yellowstone's grizzly bear foods? Almost certain decline for pine seeds and cutthroat trout, potentially catastrophic decline in whitebark pine seeds, probably substantial for cutthroat trout. Very likely we're going to see a decline in moths for another reason that is a result of climate change."

Everyone in the business of grizzly conservation agrees that if Yellowstone—the core of grizzly habitat—cannot support the number of bears it has in the past, those bears will start moving out into the national forests and private lands in search of food. (The 2005 *Wildlife Monograph* shows a migration already happening, though those authors speculate it is not due to a decline in habitat but to an increase in population.)

Regardless of the underlying factors pushing bears out of the park, one thing is certain: Life outside of the former recovery zone carries a much greater risk of early death for grizzly bears.

■■ Even so, Chris Servheen tries to reassure the critics of delisting by saying it would be a mistake to think the government is approaching problems in the grizzly world in a cavalier manner. While his "dynamic management" plan doesn't go into specifics as to what kinds of problems will trigger what sorts of solutions, he maintains that he hasn't worked all these years just to see the bears die out.

"Fundamentally, [grizzlies] are symbolic of the pieces of nature that still remain in the wild country of America. We have broken that piece really badly in the past," he says. "We've got grizzly bears down to a fraction of their range. We had no concern for them whatsoever . . . We now have the power to fix that, and I think we now have the recognition that, boy, we came really close to losing them.

"I want my kids to be able to go out and see grizzly bears on the mountains and to look up in the mountains in western Montana and know that grizzly bears live up there."

Regardless of the backroom and courtroom political wrangling, Servheen has a salient point (a quote that comes off as practiced despite its truth): "The most important habitat for grizzly bears is the human heart." It's neither the scientists nor the bureaucrats who have ultimate power over the grizzly's fate; it's the people who live in grizzly country who will either push the great bear to extinction or find the courage and generosity to share the remnants of a wild landscape we all call home.

HUNTING GRIZZLY

The bear is the first thing you notice in Keith Atcheson's office. He's standing off to the side, in a corner really, but he draws your attention from everything else in this modest-size room at Jack Atcheson & Sons hunting guides headquarters in Butte, Montana.

The grizzly stands about ten feet tall; he might have weighed a thousand pounds or more the spring he was shot, in the foul-weathered volcanic mountains of southern Alaska. More than a decade after his hunting trip to Aniakchak Bay on the Alaska Peninsula, Keith Atcheson recalls details with clarity. "The wind always blows on the peninsula, very strong. It's not a question of whether it's going to be blowing. And you have to land there in this particular spot, in a low-wing aircraft, when the tides are out. The wind was probably blowing thirty or forty miles an hour. We came in real hot and landed. That was pretty exciting in itself."

Atcheson has killed other grizzlies. He may kill more. But this one was the climax of one of the best hunts of his life. Nearly every day of that hunt, he says, something extraordinary happened. As he tells the story of this bear, it's clear that Atcheson savors not just the kill, but also the events of each day leading up to it as an integral part of the experience.

The first afternoon of the hunt, as Atcheson watched with a scope from camp, two hunters started up a steep ridge; he figured they were in pursuit of something. He continued glassing the mountainside, spied on some caribou for a while, and then heard shots. "I could see a big brown bear above these guys running down the hill at them in full charge, and they were kind of on a knife-backed ridge. Just as the bear got to them, they split. One went left, one went right. The bear went between them down into the brush. The hunters came back together and sat down. I always surmised how they were feeling at the moment, and what the adrenaline must have been flowing like at that point."

Although Atcheson is an experienced hunting guide himself, in Alaska, nonresidents are required by law to hire a guide. So on day two, he and his guide set up on an open ridge near camp; they watched another set of hunters pursue and shoot a grizzly from a distance. He saw a bear wander into a high mountain valley behind the camp and speculated that it might be a good place to go hunting. But the head outfitter had warned Atcheson and his guide against it, saying the terrain was too rough. "Don't ever go in there, you guys, because that's a real hellhole."

By day three, Atcheson and his guide were still on their ridge, just watching. Waiting, he says, is 90 percent of bear hunting. The other 10 percent, he adds, is "pure excitement and terror." As they sat waiting that morning, they saw a bear walk over the top of a mountain a couple of miles off. "All of a sudden, it kicked loose an avalanche, and the bear was in the avalanche coming down the mountain. It was a slow-moving avalanche, and it was just kind of swimming down through the snow. You could see it disappear; then it would reappear and disappear. Come down about a thousand feet and stopped at the bottom. The bear just kind of stood up and looked back at the mountain, shook itself off, and kept going on its merry way."

The wind kicked up the next day as Atcheson and his guide returned to their ridgeline to watch some more. A cow moose with two young calves wandered across their viewpoint, downwind about eight hundred yards away. Atcheson recalls joking to his guide that the moose family would make good bear bait. A little later, they noticed a brown bear on the same ridge, about halfway between the hunters and the moose. "As soon as the bear got downwind from the moose, he smelled them, just turned into the wind, and started galloping up through the alders right up toward the moose." When the bear got within a hundred yards, it began a catlike stalk, Atcheson says. At twenty-five yards, the mama moose figured out something was going on. "She must have given out some sort of signal to the calves: One went left, one went right." They ran off about twenty-five yards and stood absolutely still. "About that time, the bear just charges in and grabs a hold of the mama. They start this huge fight. It was a heck of a fight. Alders were swinging left and right. Pretty soon the moose finally stood up and broke loose; the bear was attached to this moose's brisket. She's trying to get away, running down through the alders, and the bear's flailing away at her side."

Eventually the skin broke loose, and the long-legged moose easily outran the bear. The grizzly walked back up to where the fight had begun, and the mother moose circled around past the hunters, a big piece of skin and hair ripped out of her chest, claw marks on her side. Atcheson says that moose calves have almost no scent, so if they remained still, the bear might not have seen them.

"One of the calves couldn't stand it any longer and it bolted," he says. "The bear ran over in three or four bounds and he was right on top of it. I could hear the bear killing the calf. You could hear it bleating over there. We thought about firing some shots over there to try to save its life, but there was really no sense of it. It's just Mother Nature; the bear's doing what he does.

"So he ate that moose for about two hours; there was blood all over the place. He just went up on this big snowy knob, laid down, put his head over his arms, and went to sleep."

By the next day, Atcheson was ready to cover some ground. He eyed the canyon that led to the high mountain valley behind the camp—the one he'd been told to avoid—and decided to take a chance. He and his guide followed a bear for a while—climbing up one side of the canyon, dropping down another—before getting close enough to see that the bear was too small. Rather than climb back up the way they'd come in, they tried dropping further into the canyon until the drainage turned to steep, smooth, slick rock that made for dangerous walking. They turned back.

"I shaved, changed my T-shirt. Not that I'm superstitious, but I thought maybe a little change of pace would bring some good luck," Atcheson says. He left behind his twelve-pound .375 rifle that last day of the hunt and took a lighter .300 Magnum, a seven-pound sheep rifle, instead. Atcheson and his guide headed out to their usual ridgetop viewing area, and right away they saw the bear. It was a big one, and as they watched, it headed into the thick drainage behind the camp.

The drainage, he says, was only a couple of miles long. He could hear a pack of wolves howling at the upper end. He couldn't see the bear anymore, but neither could he see how the bear could get away from them. So he decided to make a stalk.

Atcheson and his guide climbed down into the canyon, wet with snow, where Atcheson left his backpack and his extra coat. They eased up a ridge where he expected to find the bear and—nothing. Only three or four feet of snow and lots of alder. "We're right where we're supposed to be, but there's no bear. We can't figure it out. He must have winded us or something."

Then, as he peered into the alder, Atcheson spotted the tips of two bear ears at about seventeen paces. He motioned to his guide, whispering, "He's right there." Then the wind shifted, swirled, and the bear got a whiff of the hunters. "He exploded out of his hole. It was a full-on charge coming straight at us."

The bear woofed at the hunters, clacking his jaws in agitation as he charged. Atcheson says the snow impeded the bear's progress, which gave him time to shoot. "I hit him in the left front shoulder, and he really didn't react to that other than turning 90 degrees, trying to run away from us. I remember shooting and reloading and shooting."

When Atcheson was down to his last shot, he hesitated, thinking he might need to save the bullet in case the bear turned and charged again. As it was, the grizzly ran about ten more yards, then dropped over dead.

"I felt this incredible, out-of-body experience start to come over me. I turned and looked at [the guide] and was like, did that really happen? We started hootin' and hollerin'. We were very pumped up, adrenaline-wise."

The bear had fallen in a creek covered with snow, which collapsed under the grizzly's weight. They worked skinning him for hours, struggling in the icy water with the wet hide. It was late, and the two men were exhausted, so they packed the skull and buried the hide in the snow, planning to retrieve it the next day.

The next morning, the guide couldn't handle the weight of the pack and suggested cutting the hide in two. Atcheson refused. "I don't like carrying real heavy loads, but I was in good shape then and I was younger. I put the thing on, and I probably only weighed 155 pounds at the time, and it weighed easily 130 pounds," he says. "But I didn't want my bear hide chopped up." So he shouldered the pack and made the hike back to camp a few steps at a time.

It was May 15, 1994. "Now," he tells me, "you know why I remember that bear."

■■ Grizzly hunting is big business in the places where it is legal: British Columbia and coastal Alaska in particular. Successful hunts can cost upwards of $17,000. Most often, only the head and hide are taken by the hunter (the guide might cut off the paws and carve out the gallbladder to sell for medicinal purposes), and the rest of the bear is left on the ground. In Alaska, hunters kill an average of sixteen hundred grizzlies annually (out of a population official estimates place at between thirty-five thousand and forty-five thousand); upwards of three hundred are killed annually during trophy hunts in British Columbia. Such expeditions run the gamut from fair-chase hunts like Atcheson's to guides who set their clients up in tree stands to shoot at grizzlies on salmon streams or at bears who have been trained to come to bags of doughnuts set out by the outfitter.

The phrase "fair chase" has a very specific meaning in the hunting world. The Boone and Crockett Club defines it as "the ethical, sportsmanlike, and lawful pursuit and taking of any free-ranging wild, native North American big-game animal in a manner that does not give the hunter an improper advantage over such animals." This means fair-chase hunters pursue their quarry on foot; hone their skills so they make quick, clean kills; and obey not just the law, but local customs as well. It also means not participating in "canned hunts," where animals are kept in captivity for the purpose of hunting them, or hunts of animals baited with food. In essence, fair chase implies the need for hunters to learn about the land and the animals they pursue, to spend time developing not just their shooting technique, but also their wilderness skills so that their trophies are not measured in points but as landmarks in a lifetime of learning.

My husband, Doug, also prefers strict standards for hunting dangerous big game: The animal should have an equal chance to kill you. So ideally, one ought to hunt buffalo with a spear. On foot. Doug put his principle to the test fifteen years ago when he was asked to "walk point" on an expedition into polar bear country. He was accompanied by two of America's most famous adventurers, Rick Ridgeway and Doug Tompkins, so he knew he had to be on solid ground, both ethically and practically speaking. After a little research, he designed a pike. Attached to one end of the eight-foot-long wooden shaft was a nine-inch iron point. In case of attack, he'd wedge one end of the spear in the ground, and the polar bear theoretically would impale itself on the other. It was a risky proposition, and everyone on the expedition was probably relieved that there was no opportunity to try it out in the field. Doug, nonetheless, felt pretty good about the whole scenario. "I think you'd lose ninety-nine times out of a hundred," he says, adding, "But we didn't live there and the white bear did. The spear made me feel like an ethical invader."

Of course, in Doug's case, the group wasn't hunting polar bears but merely wanted some protection in case a polar bear came hunting them. Therein lies the irony, and probably the attraction, of predator hunting. The animal in question, given the chance, could decide to become the hunter. Certainly, there are all kinds of ways to hurt yourself while hunting (with falling out of a tree stand being at the top of the list). But mule deer and antelope and elk generally don't fight back. It's that possibility of becoming prey that makes the hunt interesting. When it happened to Jebb Lackey, it changed his life.

Lackey has hunted black bear with a bow and arrow for at least a decade; he's never shot one, is not sure he's ever intended to, but liked the idea of an encounter.

"The thought of sneaking up on a bear did intrigue me," he says, "just to see how close I could get, see what would turn out.

"I've had several opportunities, and in my soul they didn't feel right. So I passed up those opportunities. Deep down inside I wonder about these opportunities that I chose to not take, whether there's some sort of metaphysical connection there."

Lackey wonders about a connection because in the spring of 2005 a mother grizzly spared his life. Lackey was hunting alone on the east side of the Hungry Horse Reservoir in Montana's Flathead Valley. His usual hunting companions had other things to do that day, but Lackey didn't mind; he likes being alone in the woods.

"I walked up the trail about, I'd say, a mile to a mile and a half. Knew that I was really getting into bear country and figured I'd go to the bathroom before I got up into where I really thought they were thick," he says. "So I put my bow down and was really relaxed. It was a great morning, a beautiful sunny morning, and I was just so happy to be in the woods again. I was on the side of the trail, and I was just zipping up my pants. I had just buttoned my top button when I heard these crashes."

He spun around and in the split seconds available to him, saw two grizzly cubs running up the trail away from him and their mother in full charge at him. "I had a pistol, a .44 Magnum, and as I reached for my pistol and gave it a tug, I realized that I never had the opportunity to buckle my belt. The holster, my belt, and everything kind of ripped off, and I was never able to draw my pistol. It all came loose. I put my hand in front of my face and tried to guard my vitals because I knew, I basically assumed, that I was not going to live too many more minutes.

"Then she slammed into my ribs with a force that [was] like a Volkswagen hitting you at twenty miles an hour." Lackey fell face down, the wind knocked out of him, dazed by the impact. Although as a former Forest Service employee he'd been trained on how to behave during a bear attack, none of those lessons came to mind. He just did what felt right, which was nothing. He could feel branches moving as she circled him.

"Right when I thought I might get out of this, she put both of her paws directly on my shoulder blades, pressed me down into the brush. Then next thing I knew she put her nose on the back of my neck and down my spine. She was sniffing me really hard and making this kind of a gurgling sound—not a growl—but she was really trying to get a smell or something. In that instant, when she touched her nose to my neck, I was preparing myself. Talking to God a little bit; I assumed that was my last moment on earth. That she would crush my skull and that would be the end of it."

Instead, she left him alone. He felt the release of pressure, heard her gallop down the trail, and lay there for about five minutes gathering his wits. He hiked back to his truck, certain he was badly injured and in shock. Once Lackey figured out he was only bruised and scratched from the fall, he realized he'd left his bow behind. "In hindsight, a $300 bow doesn't matter. But obviously I wasn't thinking very clearly." He hiked back in to get the bow and made it back without incident.

In retrospect, he's been able to dissect the anatomy of the attack. He was walking next to a creek, and the noise of the running water likely camouflaged his presence until he urinated. "That was a big part, I think, of why it was such a close encounter. We couldn't hear each other. The wind was in my face. I was making sure that the bears I was after couldn't smell me," he says. "It was thick brush where she was, but it wasn't quite as thick where I was. So I couldn't see down in there whatsoever.

"I truly believe that the smell of my urine just gently drifted over in her direction. We were in such close quarters, and neither one of us knew it. I think she just got that nose full and was like, this is not right. I think that's why she was in full charge right off the bat. Of course, she could have been down there clicking her jaws and grunting, but I wouldn't have heard it anyway."

The Flathead Valley where Lackey lives and works as a carpenter is a community in flux. Multimillionaires build their dream homes here; locals both benefit from the construction jobs and suffer from inflated property values. A radio talk-show host has inflamed collective anger at what many people see as an intrusion on a formerly quiet lifestyle and directed it—with violent rhetoric—at conservationists (scapegoats for everything from the declines in the Forest Service's logging program to changes in the global economic landscape). So when Lackey says he feels kindly toward the mother grizzly, he does so in a highly charged environment. "I was an intruder in her domain. As far as I'm concerned, she had every right to kick my ass," he says. "Like I tell people a lot recently, if there was an intruder in my living room, I wouldn't stand for it. If there was a bear in my living room, I couldn't have that either. That's how I think of it. It's respect for nature, and respect for the fact that I don't own the woods; I don't have dominion over any of it. I'm blessed to be able to go out among them.

"I have these smudged, weird grizzly prints on the back of my shirt as a reminder. I don't know why she never bit me, she never slashed at me at all, which is really rare from what I understand. There were no puncture wounds of any sort, which is amazing to me. I was very, very lucky."

Lackey says he is done hunting bears. "That bear spared my life. I could never take a bear's life at this point. It just wouldn't feel right deep down inside."

■■ Humans have probably never pursued grizzlies merely for food. There are, as one hunting guide told me, simply too many easier ways to catch dinner. From the scattered surviving stories on every continent where bears and people shared a home, it appears most likely that indigenous people hunted bears only occasionally, often in the bears' dens, and with spiritual and ritualistic intent. Despite the shrinking wilderness and the invention of rifles and scopes that can make bear hunting a relatively safe endeavor, the reasons men pursue bears remain largely the same: Killing such an animal can confer its power upon the hunter. To stalk and kill a grizzly in a fair-chase hunt is the ultimate test of a hunter's skills in North America. Especially if, like E. Donnall Thomas Jr., you're doing so armed only with "a stick and a string."

Don Thomas is a traditional bow hunter. He uses a longbow—no scopes, no fancy compound bow—and his hunts may come awfully close to Doug's idea of fair chase. After growing up in the Pacific Northwest, Thomas attended medical school during the late 1960s in Berkeley, California, and felt he owed someone two years of his life in exchange for the deferment that kept him out of Vietnam. He volunteered for the Indian Health Service and wound up in Fort Peck, Montana. He'd grown up rifle hunting with his dad, the Nobel Prize–winning doctor for whom he is named. Once he moved to Montana, he made the switch from gun to bow.

"I realized that, for me, one of the essential aspects of being an outdoorsman was voluntarily limiting my means of take in the field," he says. "Because that made it harder, it made it fairer; it allowed me to spend more time in the woods. And it gave me an excuse to learn a whole lot more about animals. You don't learn much about an animal when you're looking through a telescopic sight at three hundred yards. But to do this with a stick and a string, you essentially have to learn to operate within natural predator distance. I operate at the distance that wolves and mountain lions operate at."

Thomas's house is homage to a lifetime in the field: Mounted birds decorate the walls; a mountain lion prowls the living room, forever frozen mid-stalk. There are skulls and spear points and disembodied wings. A brown bear stands on all fours at the top of the stairs.

The bear is why Doug and I have driven to Lewistown to talk to Thomas. He shot this one with his longbow in the Russian Far East; we want to know why.

First, he tells us, hunting a bear of any species is different from hunting ungulates. And the grizzly, he adds, "is probably the most impressive single-game species in the world." This comes from a man who's hunted all over the world. He's been up close to elephants and cape buffalo in Africa. He's hunted in Australia and killed an Asiatic buffalo. The grizzly's attraction, he says, is in its intelligence, its complicated social life, and the difficulties it presents as prey. "A very experienced Alaskan guide I knew said he could guarantee a sheep to basically any hunter who's in shape. But even with a good hunter, who's a good shot, who's in good shape, there's no way he could guarantee that person a big bear.

"Killing a bear with a traditional bow, a longbow, or a recurve, on the ground, stalking, no bait, no dog, no tricks, is a very, very difficult thing to do." Thomas has hunted bears in Alaska (where he lived for eight years) and killed a number of black bear, but he is careful to point out that bow hunting is often about not coming home with a kill.

"Hunting bears with bows has made me a better naturalist, it has made me a better woodsman, it has made me a better tracker. I feel like I'm a more complete outdoorsman for having done it," he says. "Why do I do it? I like being close to bears. I describe the hunter as the alert man, and you're never more alert than when you're in a bear's space and he doesn't know you're there. You've got a stick and string; there's no firearm involved. You see the world very differently under those circumstances."

The ideal and the reality, however, don't always meet. Such was the case with Thomas's brown bear. His first trip to Russia with a fellow bow-hunter friend was in August 1990, just as the former Soviet Union was opening to the West. In fact, their trip coincided with a counter-coup in Moscow and a U.S. State Department warning for Americans to stay away.

The hunters had made their plans and decided to go anyway. They flew into Khabarovsk, landing in an airport full of military tanks. They hitched a ride up the coast and talked their way into a helicopter ride. "They dropped us off with some Russian sable trappers. We didn't know whether this helicopter was coming back or not," he says. "I mean, this was on the edge, man. This was over the top."

Thomas's friend knew a little Russian and so explained to the sable trappers that they were interested in hunting brown bears. The trappers took them to a stream churning with spawning dog salmon. "We were walking along, and all of a sudden the Russians got agitated. The next thing I know, they're pantomiming. I looked up, and here goes this grizzly cub right up this tree in front of us." While Thomas looked around for the mother bear, who was sure to be close behind her cub, the Russians urged the Americans to take their shot.

"We backed out, the cub came down the tree. She [the mother] woofed the cub off," he says. "We said, 'We gotta go back to camp and have a talk. We're not shooting cubs, we're not shooting sows, we're not shooting bears in trees. You guys gotta be quiet.'

"And the Russians got all mad; they took all their stuff and went to the other side of the sandbar and sat down, drinking vodka with their backs to us. I mean, this was going to be an international incident, you know?"

Eventually, the bow hunters made their purpose clear and spent another three weeks with the trappers, following rivers and streams in search of a good salmon run and the bears that were sure to be feeding. The Russians assured the hunters there would be a run of pink salmon in a river somewhere before they hit the ocean. "So we asked, 'How far is the ocean?' Well, it's 120 miles. We said, 'All right, let's start walking.'"

They followed the Ul'ya River (which coincidentally, Thomas tells us, was the drainage used by Russian explorers to reach the Pacific at the same time Lewis and Clark were hitting the Pacific via the Columbia River on the other side of the ocean). They found salmon, they found bears, but the situation was never quite right. No bear "asked for my arrow," as Thomas described the situation he was waiting for. No one took a shot. They did, however, earn the respect of their guides, who invited them back for a hunt the next spring.

The next time, they flew into the lower Ul'ya and right into a blizzard, which left behind eight feet of snow that melted and turned the river into a dangerous torrent. They decided to hike about six miles to the beach and see whether there were any bears hanging around there. Here, Thomas cuts the story short: "I made a long stalk and killed the bear. You can read all the details; there's a chapter in my book *Longbows in the Far North*." When I do read the account, I understand why Thomas preferred to let the story rest.

Thomas writes that the stalk begins with a bear, a black spot about a mile away. He works with the wind and with a six-foot trench created by a small freshwater stream cutting across the beach, and guesses at distances and the bear's intentions as he prepares to set an ambush.

"The bear remains a relatively abstract presence at first, as he closes leisurely to a range of one hundred yards. Then the mood changes. This is a real grizzly now, all fang and claw and shoulder hump as he hones in relentlessly on my position," he writes. "For an archer, a frontal shot on an advancing bear is pointless, so my tactical goal is to be twenty yards downwind when he crosses the creek and gives me a broadside. The problem is that the bear is tacking back and forth across the tide line. Every time I move laterally and peek over the top of the ditch, he is bearing straight down upon me. My stalk is starting to seem less a matter of getting within bow range than of surviving the process.

"Forty yards and closing. It is time to start shutting systems down. Our brains come equipped with warning devices that tell us to retreat before we get within what I call pouncing range, the inner circle in which a bear is likely to swat first and ask questions later. If you are going to bow hunt bears, you have to learn to pull that fuse."

Thirty yards, twenty yards, and Thomas readies an arrow. He takes another look above the bank and sees what he needs: The bear has stopped broadside to Thomas, rooting around at the tide line, asking for his arrow. The shot is perfect, the arrow hits right behind the shoulder blade. Thomas says he knew at once he'd killed the bear.

The grizzly roared and Thomas hit the sand. The bear might charge, he might run away. He would, however, fall. But as Thomas waited for that moment, a shot rang out. And although his Russian guide claimed to have shot into the ground to frighten the bear, the postmortem report proved otherwise: While the grizzly was mortally wounded by Thomas's arrow, he also took a bullet to the gut.

Thomas agrees with naturalist Aldo Leopold's notion that the value of the trophy is a direct reflection of the effort expended in obtaining it—not its size. "You know, if you go back to Leopold's dictum of earning the trophy, we had six weeks in the Russian bush. This was not a canned hunt. This was over the top. I just made myself a promise that I would think about that bear every day of my life." Fifteen years later, Thomas says, it's a promise he's kept.

While Thomas talks about the reasons people hunt—for food, as an excuse to get out in the mountains, for the trophy on the wall (and finds a little of each in himself)—he returns several times to the notion of bow hunting as a connection to precivilized humanity, and I wonder if this isn't at the heart of his bear hunting.

Thomas tells us another story. He was hunting black bear in Alaska several weeks before our interview. He'd been stalking a bear along a tidal flat and lost track of it. So he sat under a bank to decide what to do next, when he saw two ears poking above the top of his hiding place.

"There's no way an ungulate is going to reproduce the emotional response to finding yourself in that situation," he says. "All of a sudden, it's three hundred thousand years ago, you're in a cave, there's a little fire going, there's a saber-tooth tiger out there. It just cuts through all the layers of modern technology, communication, and garbage."

Thomas has been a gracious host, offering us dinner and even to put us up for the night. But he knows who Doug is. He's read *Grizzly Years*, and he's been prepared all along for a contentious discussion. He suspects we may be there to argue with him about bear hunting. (Atcheson, incidentally, also was wary and defensive.) But Doug, who "wouldn't shoot a grizzly for a cool million," is uncharacteristically quiet; he is impressed by Thomas's promise to not let a day pass without honoring the spirit of the bear he killed.

In the rural West, hunters are often environmentalists—or maybe the other way around. Most people eat off the land at least some of the time. That, says Thomas, is where the potential lies for modern big-game conservation. "The more people who have a vested interest in this part of North America hanging on to a sustainable, self-sufficient population of grizzly bears, the more likely it's going to happen," he explains. "It's just politics 101. A hundred thousand hunting licenses get sold in Montana every year, and there are eight hundred thousand people in the state. That's a very potent block of people.

"If those people have a vested interest in the presence of grizzly bears or wolves or mountain lions, it's going to be more likely that the right decisions are going to be made when it comes time to talk about roadless areas or drilling on the Rocky Mountain Front." Wolves are a great example, he adds. The reintroduction of wolves to Yellowstone National Park has proved tremendously polarizing, pitting ranchers against conservationists in ways that don't often make sense. If the state were to sell a few wolf hunting licenses, Thomas speculates, a lot of that anger would dissipate. "The fact of the matter is, there are plenty of hunters who will gladly see fewer elk next year in order to hear some wolves howl. That's where you gotta go with this, if the big top-end predators are going to survive."

Doug posits to Thomas that human evolution was sculpted by hunting. "We evolved as hunting animals," he says. "One of our first notions of awareness was of being meat."

Thomas readily agrees. "I think hunting was intimately involved in the development of human language, cultural organization, cooperation," he says. "So many people say let's get back to our natural roots. Those are our natural roots." He tells us of a tribe he hunted with in Africa called the San. As they walked through the brush, he realized their language had evolved to sound like grass and leaves in the wind; they talked and he heard no human voice.

Doug often compares the fear and adrenaline rush of combat to that produced by a grizzly's charge and says the former lacks the "gift of life" inherent in the latter. Estranged from death, we fear everything that might bring it. Yet we might learn from the caribou who does not fear the wolf, he thinks, as humans so obsessively fear the shadows on the edge of their former world. Caribou evolution did not lead to escaping their fate as wolf meat but to an appropriate offering at a suitable time.

Yet the question remains whether it's proper under any circumstances to hunt grizzlies, when they are a species increasingly isolated and under assault from humanity. Doug finds his power in the beauty of the living bear and spirituality in the grace conferred when a grizzly chooses to walk away rather than attack. And when modern weaponry—including guns capable of bringing down B-52s—is added to the equation, the purpose of the hunt seems lost entirely. Yet he is reluctant to eliminate the possibility of a good hunt from our lives. Finding our place in the natural world—and participating in its elegant struggle with humility— may be key to our continued life on this planet. Doug, Thomas, and hunters of all species know this: When death comes in the form of a wild beast, at that moment there is no more intimate relationship than between predator and prey.

LIVING WITH
GRIZZLIES

■■ The wind howls through East Glacier, Montana. It whips off the mountains of Two Medicine Valley in Glacier National Park, and in a race for the high plains it stunts trees, blows cars off the road, and tears apart abandoned buildings. It's a land of coulees, intermittent creeks, dinosaur bones; a place where prehistory lives: Blackfeet, buffalo, and grizzly bears. Those who would protect the Rocky Mountain Front from oil and gas developers point out that nearly every species of animal—from lynx and cougar, to bighorn sheep, mountain goat, and wolverine—that lived here when Lewis and Clark arrived still persists.

East Glacier is a reservation town, sustained by summer tourists and populated by a healthy mix of Anglos and Indians. Violent bar fights belie the National Park Service's veneer of civilization. There are

Blackfeet who, resenting the park's existence, regularly and illegally let their cattle graze over the edge of the boundary, so the animal foraging on the side of Spot Mountain could as easily be a cow as a grizzly bear. In a reverse drama of cowboys and Indians, there are local white men who talk of shooting the cows. A few dead cattle would encourage ranchers to keep their livestock off this sacred ground, they theorize.

Doug and I arrive by accident, late in the fall of 1998, all hotels on the west side of the park closed or the few rooms kept open for the winter taken. I knock on the door of the Whistling Swan motel just after dark, our last chance of avoiding a long ride back to Helena at night. A friendly man in his early thirties answers. Yes, he has a room. Are we here for business or pleasure?

Both, I respond. Doug is on assignment for a men's magazine, writing about grizzly bears. "Well," the man says, "I'm a ranger, and I know a little bit about grizzlies. Let me know if you have any questions."

I hesitate. My companion, I tell him, is Doug Peacock. He blanches, speechless. As we settle into our room, the proprietor, Pat Hagan, comes knocking at the door with a copy of Doug's *Grizzly Years* in hand. I don't remember what he said, only that it marked the beginning of a series of deep friendships. When we meet for breakfast the next morning, Hagan tells us about a local man who had been eaten by grizzlies earlier in the season; while the man was a relative newcomer to a town populated by immigrants, he had nonetheless made a number of close friends whose loyalties were tried by the idea that a beloved bear had killed a beloved friend. Hagan was then testing the theory that the man died from other causes, maybe hypothermia; another suggested he'd taken a fall. Though all mourned him, at the edge of their grief was the suggestion of rightness: that a person who'd found his true home was lucky to die in it, no matter the cause.

The grizzlies who fed on the man were dead, killed by rangers. This struck the dead man's friends as wrong: The mountains are dangerous; people are drawn to them and die in them. Why fault the bears?

There is perhaps no more complicated landscape shared by humans and grizzlies than Glacier. Known alternately as the Northern Continental

Divide Ecosystem, the Crown of the Continent, and the Backbone of the World, it's breathtaking country that draws nearly two million tourists every year.

After a season of wildfires, the national forests on the park's west side teem with gun-toting mushroom pickers. On the south, the park abuts a great stretch of wildland in the 1.5 million acres of the Bob Marshall and Great Bear Wilderness complex; someone down there in the land of tiny lakes and log cabins otherwise known as the Swan Valley appears to be poisoning grizzlies. At least three, maybe five, have died. The Flathead Valley to the southwest is gone, gobbled up by the vacation homes of multimillionaires. There is no room for bears there.

To the east, ranchers run cattle and sheep at the edge of the wilderness. There also live the Blackfeet, formerly among the fiercest and most feared of the northern plains tribes, some of whom revere grizzlies, others who shoot them. North of the park, in Alberta, Canada, grizzlies are struggling to survive amidst tremendous human development: Mortalities, say biologists, far exceed births. "We have the lowest reproductive rate of any population of grizzly bears yet studied," says biologist Mike Gibeau. "A bear barely replaces herself in her lifetime."

There is nothing about Glacier's landscape or its inhabitants that lends itself to control and management, which makes the jobs of those who try rather tricky. On the east side of the park, where the rolling plains of the Blackfeet reservation hit the mountains with violent contrast, biologist Dan Carney wrangles grizzlies for the tribe. Officially, he's Director of Threatened and Endangered Species, which means he's the guy you call in the middle of the night when a grizzly is breaking into your chicken house.

"I left my cell phone in the truck, but it could be ringing right now. It's that sort of a deal. I get called at two o'clock and four o'clock in the morning," he says. "Sometimes it's a bear, sometimes it's a dead cow, sometimes it's a dead pig. Who knows? I go and see what we need to do and help them out."

While Carney has trapped, moved, and killed his share of grizzlies during his years with the Blackfeet, like many wildlife biologists he says his real job is managing people, not animals. His colleagues speak of him with a degree of awe: It takes a special person to balance all the demands of this job.

"I call it sittin' and whittlin'," says Missoula biologist Chuck Jonkel. "It has to be just the right kind of guy, one who loves talking to ranchers and understands how to view their version of their plight. Listening. Dan Carney's that kind of guy. How many people could work for sixteen years for the Blackfeet? In a controversial position? Dan's done it. He has the right personality for it."

There's no bravado to Dan Carney, no posturing. He answers questions like a man more used to gauging others. Aside from the reservation's unique cultural landscape, Carney says the conflicts he deals with are universal to grizzly country: garbage, birdseed, and livestock.

The previous season had been a terrible huckleberry year, a vital food for grizzlies in Glacier. Normally a relatively moist region compared to most of Montana, Glacier was seeing the effects of the same drought affecting much of the western United States; a meager 2004 berry crop did little more than dry on the bush. Furthermore, firefighters in 2003 had destroyed some of the park's best berry habitat with a massive backburn intended to save the claptrap buildings at West Glacier from what had been a modest wildfire. Experts suggested that the charred huckleberry rhizomes might take a century or more to regenerate.

When Doug and I arrived in East Glacier that fall, our friends were full of stories of grizzlies in town feeding at restaurant garbage cans.

While the solution would seem an easy one—bear-proof dumpsters—Carney tells me it's not so simple. Replacing every dumpster and garbage can on the reservation with bear-proof containers takes money, and given the battering they take by frustrated bears, they need to be replaced regularly. In addition, these special dumpsters require special trucks to empty them.

"What I'm hoping to do," Carney says, "rather than just keep throwing bear-proof dumpsters into a bottomless pit, is have some areas set aside where we can put up a fence—a chain-link fence or electric fence around that—and just have all the dumpsters in town moved to there."

This doesn't much help restaurant owners like our friend Mark Howser, in whose diner Carney and I sit. He and others stay open late in the summer, making up for nine months of snow, wind, and no customers. "We're still going to need something else," Carney says, "because a restaurant like this, you know, if they close at ten o'clock or eleven o'clock at night and they've got a truckload of garbage, what are they going to do between now and eight o'clock tomorrow morning, when the garbage dump opens up?"

Oddly enough, convincing people to properly store their birdseed and pet food is even more complicated than the garbage problem. These foods act as springboards: One day the bear's eating sunflower seeds with the magpies, the next he's breaking through your kitchen window and reaching for a pot of soup. Carney says he's done everything from writing articles for the local newspapers to shooting grizzlies in the backyards of horrified homeowners to get their attention. None of it seems to help. There are those who get the message, he says. But too many others refuse to change, acting as though the wilderness out their window is no more than a big TV screen.

"People move to places like this because they want to see the wildlife, and bird feeders are a great way to see wildlife," he says. "Some of the people are the biggest conservation-minded folks around, but it doesn't matter if I tell them, 'You know what? You're killing grizzlies.' They've still got to have their damn bird feeder."

Livestock is a much more complicated issue. It's not like the arid West is great cattle country: There's just so much land, we can't seem to resist setting domestic animals to graze. Cowboys and cattle drives are deeply embedded in our self-image, defining to a large degree that which makes Americans feel unique—the Wild West. So when grizzly bears, themselves symbols of wilderness, kill cattle and sheep, such predation takes on meaning all out of proportion to a simple meal.

On the face of it, grizzlies who eat livestock are cast as an economic issue, ready-made for manipulative bureaucrats, says grizzly recovery coordinator Chris Servheen.

"They compete with humans for space. They kill livestock occasionally, occasionally they kill elk calves, you know, something that people want. So people look at them as somewhat of a competitor," he says. "Politicians tend to use things that are competitors with people to their own ends. Some governor can raise the issue about meat-eating carnivores and another that, you know, *it's a states' rights issue. It's our decision versus the federal decision on grizzly bears.* All those things are out there, but a lot of this stuff isn't about grizzly bears at all. It's about control or loss of control."

Further beneath the talk of economics, buried within our desire to control, swirls a whole mix of emotions drawing upon thousands of years of coevolution. "It's an animal that's always pushed our buttons," the Natural Resources Defense Council's Louisa Willcox believes. "We've always been afraid of them. It's an animal that can eat us, it's an animal that invades our dream-life.

"So I think this animal works on many levels. Everything from the teacher image and the guide, to the predator, to an animal that we probably followed around and learned a great deal from . . . It's weighed down now with different kinds of symbolic trappings, particularly with the Endangered Species Act. Not only do you have an animal that requires lots of space and tends to eat domestic sheep if given a chance. It's got a double whammy of wearing around its neck the weight of communities' views of the federal government and its role in their lives."

Within that context, ranchers Sam and Roseanne Anderson say, it's damn near impossible to have an open discussion about wolves or grizzly bears. "The belief system about what's important almost takes on more significance in a lot of conversations than the facts," Sam says. "You've probably heard it. Somebody will say, 'Yeah, there's a grizzly up there on that cow,' and then the next line might be, 'You know, there's far too many bears here.'"

The Andersons' ranch consists of fifteen hundred acres in Tom Miner Basin, just north of Yellowstone National Park. It's high, cold country; spring in the valley takes a long time to reach up here. Roseanne guesses there were twenty or thirty families running livestock in the basin at one time, but the Depression and two world wars took their toll; now there are five working ranches and innumerable trophy homes, a fact that led the Andersons to put a conservation easement on their land. "This will never look differently; there will be no more buildings," she says. "I mean everything around us may change, so maybe that was not economically smart for other people to benefit from looking down on us, but it felt like the right thing to do."

The Andersons are sophisticated people. Roseanne is a college professor, and Sam worked for years in the financial world. But Sam's roots grow from the soil on which we sit and talk. His parents moved here in the 1950s, immigrants from Wisconsin who bought the land from a family who had ranched it through the Depression. He says it was a great way for him and his two brothers to grow up, and while his own kids were raised in Connecticut, Los Angeles, and Chicago, he and Roseanne brought them here as much as they could. Grizzlies, he says, have always been part of the equation.

"I remember a big neighborhood event when I was about five years old. A grizzly bear had been caught. My father and the neighbor with the government trapper had shot the bear, brought it down, and leaned it up against a tree. We were all around it, and I remember having my picture taken. The bear was in the middle, I was on the right-hand side, one of our neighbors was on the other side. We were each holding a paw. And he moved the paw on his side, and for some reason my paw moved. And it was pretty scary.

"But the reason I point that out is that I think it's an example of a ritual of yesteryear. Long ago. You know, a cattle-killing bear was shot, the neighbors gathered round and sort of admired what had happened. I honestly cannot remember in the last forty years a grizzly bear that was killing cattle in this area being dealt with in that way."

Sam and Roseanne moved back here full-time in 1989. They renovated the bunkhouse, where Sam's parents chose to move. He and Roseanne, who teaches religion and philosophy at Montana State University in Bozeman, remodeled the homestead for themselves. The result is an elegant homage to ranch life: stone floors and a huge kitchen and dining room made for parties, all ringed with windows that bring the outside in.

The Andersons do not strike me as typical ranchers, but then my idea of typical is informed by a combination of myth, media, and bar talk. Urbane and articulate, they profess tolerance for the occasional predator and say most ranchers are like them: not so close to financial ruin that one or two dead cows make a difference.

Grizzly encounters, grizzly sightings, even occasional grizzly predations are still within the bounds of normal. Most ranchers, they say, enjoy having the big bears around.

"Realistically, there are almost no ranchers left here who are truthfully scraping by to the point that every animal might make the difference between making it or not," Sam says. "So that old, somewhat stereotyped attitude of, 'they're a predator, what the hell kind of use are they anyway? And by the way, nothing's going to kill my cattle'—I just think there are fewer of those people around.

"Most of these ranches around here now are owned by people who don't make a living off the ranch and actually cherish the bears. And I don't mean to say that the former owners didn't cherish the wildlife either, but there's no economic impact, there's no real concern for their livelihood."

That's not to say the ranchers don't care one way or the other. Roseanne says she has great ambivalence: She's thrilled whenever she sees a grizzly, but cried when one broke into her chicken house, killing the hens and her favorite rooster.

Another time, a grizzly got into their calving yard. It was mid-April and Sam was walking around the pasture, just checking things out. It was a dark, snowy night, he says, and he couldn't see anything beyond the beam of his flashlight. "I saw a cow that I thought might calve. Went back out an hour later, and I hear this tremendous ruckus down in the pasture. So I go running down there, didn't go two, three hundred yards from the corral, through the hollows and bogs and willows, and there in my beam is a grizzly bear chasing about a week-old calf." The Andersons were able to run the bear off, but the cries of the calf tore at Roseanne as much as the sight of the bear buoyed her.

Sam's father found a couple of big grizzlies eating an old horse one year; his mother lost a set of rams to another bear. The point is, Sam emphasizes, these are the exceptions, not the rule. The grizzly that killed the rams turned out to be an old bear. "It was in the fall, he's just not making it in terms of fattening up. He's an old bear and he gets desperate. So it's a sad kind of a story because that bear was destroyed. But it's not normal behavior; it's an extreme situation. An old bear, a sick bear, and it seems to me that that's the kind of thing that you generally hear of related to interaction."

The Andersons say things are a little different on the south end of the park, where a friend of theirs ranches. "Of all things, I was watching *60 Minutes* or something one night, and there was a deal on about all the interaction around Cody [Wyoming]," he says. "And I found myself just a little bit dismayed at the superficiality of that report. Basically, in a simple way, yuppies in their trophy homes out along the river were objecting to the fact that their kids might encounter a grizzly on the bird feeder."

Sam points out that there's not much decent grizzly habitat around Cody to start with; the mountains are so steep that people and bears share the valleys. And with city people moving there at a record pace, grizzlies find themselves face to face with humans more than they might choose. It was under these circumstances that Sam's friend had some trouble with a cattle-eating bear on his ranch.

"Grizzlies are really a daily part of their lives at certain times of the year. They don't lose many cattle to them, but they're in the hay fields; they're really around all the time," he says. "There was a problem bear, I think it was last summer, that killed five or six of their calves, a dozen of the neighbor's calves. It was a real problem. And they had real trouble finding it. But when they finally killed that bear, nobody lost any more cattle. It was one bear that was zeroing in on calves."

That, says Blackfeet tribal biologist Dan Carney, is typical. "There's probably 5 percent of grizzlies out there that are eating beef or killing cows to get beef, and we've just got to manage those bears," he says. "But there are always going to be 5 percent or 10 percent of them out there who just like to kill livestock. I don't see any way around that."

Cattle-killing grizzlies challenge our sense of place and test our generosity. Americans have so convinced themselves of the sameness of every community, we become irritable when confronted with evidence of differences, cultural or otherwise. The *60 Minutes* suburbanites who so offended Sam Anderson were California immigrants who built their dream home along a river, the lifeblood of the wildlife that has been here for eons. They didn't bother to learn the difference between a grizzly and black bear and so sent the TV program a photo of a black bear chewing on their hot tub as evidence of their grizzly troubles.

"This region's getting more affluent; you'd think there would be a sense that we can afford to share the space, but it seems like in some ways the climate has gone the other way," Louisa Willcox observes. "This country is becoming in some ways increasingly conservative and more concerned about private property rights and less concerned about sharing."

Changing that, she says, means taking responsibility for our impact on others and cultivating a sense of altruism. "Responsibility in that this is an animal that has nowhere else to go. It's down to the last 1 percent of its range in the United States. If it requires us to take some steps, make some sacrifices, we should be willing to make them because there aren't many choices for the grizzly bear in the lower forty-eight states."

▨▪ The fact remains that grizzlies are troublesome. We can kill them, we can make them afraid of us, but our power ends there. Within those bounds, a few biologists and self-styled naturalists struggle to redefine what it means to live with grizzlies, what that relationship should—or could— look like.

Canadian naturalist Charlie Russell grew up on a cattle ranch around grizzly bears. The wisdom of the Alberta communities of his youth was that grizzlies are dangerously unpredictable and should be made to fear humans. Russell did not grow up in a typical ranching family, however. His father was an author, naturalist, filmmaker, and hunter. Russell says childhood expeditions to Alaska and Yellowstone set his imagination to work: Wasn't it possible to have a different kind of relationship with grizzly bears?

"I had a lot of chances to watch them, and I saw them as peaceful animals," he says. "It's not too hard to see that man is the perturber in that situation; man is the one stirring up trouble . . . I always wondered, what if you could create a situation where the bears lived and only have good experiences with humans?

"If they didn't have bad experiences, they didn't have the violence of hunting and the biologists snooping around and whatever they do with them, and if these animals just have a pleasant time around people, how dangerous would they be in that situation?"

Russell decided to undertake an unconventional experiment: He would find himself a population of brown bears with little or no knowledge of humans and see what sort of relationship could be forged absent a history of antagonism. The task of finding such a group of bears proved harder than he expected, but he finally settled on a remote region on the Russian peninsula of Kamchatka. He and his partner, artist Maureen Enns, built a cabin in 1996 near Kambalnoye Lake, where they spent the next seven summers.

Russell posits that we prefer grizzlies to be fearful of us because we are so afraid of them. And as for their predictability, he likens them to humans: "They get angry, and it might take them twenty years of bad treatment by humans 'til they blow their top. *I've had enough of this— whack!* So I wanted to explore those questions."

Russell's experiment took an interesting turn the second summer; he and Enns were offered the chance to raise three orphaned brown bear cubs. He downplays the importance of this development, saying that his real "work" was still about living around wild bears who, as it turns out, weren't interested in having much to do with him or Enns (though one grizzly mother did use them as "babysitters," leaving her cubs with the couple while she foraged more than a mile away). But their experience with the cubs turned out to be fascinating. Russell and Enns taught them to fish, played with them, took long walks together, even fed them when necessary. They were, in fact, the cubs' foster parents, trying to prepare them for life on their own as wild bears.

Like Doug Seus with his captive bears, Russell discovered the cubs to be surprisingly social, loving physical contact. I ask him about touching. There seems something forbidden in this contact, as evidenced by the little video footage that exists of such experiences: Timothy Treadwell reaching out to a subadult who whines and growls at him; Russell touching the head of an anxious coastal British Columbian grizzly sow he named the Mouse Creek Bear.

"With me, I want to explore the limits of trust. I push and I push it," he says. "Sure it's controversial, but by golly, we're in a situation exploring these things, and there's not going to be that many opportunities to live with these animals. I wanted to really look at this question before there wasn't any more opportunity to do it."

What he found is what bear experts will tell you the world over: The limits vary with the bear. A good bear on a bad day, given the chance, will take your hand off. "I think there are days with male bears that are dangerous without any real good excuse to be dangerous," he says. "I always say that you create dangerous bears, and we do a lot. We create dangerous bears by how we manage them.

"But I think there are even cases in males where they become so opportunistic that they can become dangerous. Look, they're huge. They're twice as big as females. Especially if there's a food barrier or anything, and they've got this huge frame to fill up. They've got to be inventive about what they eat." And the truth of the matter is, he says, to a hungry grizzly bear "humans look edible."

Russell and Enns's close contact with the cubs ended after two summers with them, though the cubs returned as subadults to visit with their human friends. By all accounts, their experimental halfway home had been a success. The cubs adjusted to life as wild bears with only one setback: One had disappeared by the time the Canadian couple arrived in the early summer of 1999. Enns found her skeleton and suspected she'd been killed and eaten by a predatory male who had shown great interest with obvious intent in the cubs the previous season. They grieved the loss and were navigating the Russian bureaucracy in the hope of raising more orphans when a greater tragedy struck.

In the spring of 2003, Russell and Enns arrived to an eerily quiet cabin. They called for the two remaining cubs (now adults, who nonetheless remained friendly with their adopted parents); they searched for the other bears they had come to know. There was no response. Nailed to the cabin door was a clue: the gallbladder of a brown bear cub. Nearby they found evidence of a helicopter landing. They suspect that the Russian mafia, in retribution for one slight or another, flew in and killed approximately twenty of the bears they'd been working around. The slaughter put too much strain on their relationship. They split up. Russell has continued to return each summer; Enns has not.

In retrospect, it seems obvious that humans are the ones who are unpredictable and dangerous and that Russell may have put those bears' lives in jeopardy by teaching them otherwise. I ask him if he feels any responsibility for having created the situation. He responds almost angrily, saying others—usually biologists whose jobs are subsidized by the hunting industry—have tried to "get him" with the same question. "Hunters don't want bears being friendly. They want bears to be snarly and mean, so that like I said before, they can be like heroes when they kill them."

But I'm neither a hunter nor a biologist, and my question is an honest one. I push a bit, and Russell responds. "Of course they were killed more easily because they were trusting. But really what it comes down to is poachers and people can kill at great distances with guns. It's a minor point. There's no protection for bears. They're just not safe.

"You know, it was in the middle of a big preserve. It was in an area that wasn't considered a tourist area; tourists were discouraged from going in there. So if everything worked the way it was supposed to work, it was not a problem. And it wasn't a problem for seven years. I guess it was a grand sacrifice."

■■ Gunshots ring out in the night, accompanied by barking dogs and the rhythmic pounding of a galloping horse. At least that's what I hear through the fog of sleep. Doug understands the running animal to be a bear and throws his arm over me in a protective gesture that would have done little good had we been sleeping outside rather than in a cabin. The next morning, the tracks tell the tale: Pushed by cracker shells and dogs, Star, the mother grizzly, ran from the commotion, leaving her cubs in a flight that took her between our cabin and the outhouse, about five feet from our groggy heads.

Polebridge, Montana, is a quiet community on the northwest corner of Glacier National Park. Surrounded by a ghost forest left by the 1988 wildfires and reachable only by a long drive down one of two potholed gravel roads, Polebridge sports a saloon, bakery, youth hostel, and a sprinkling of summer cabins. A few miles farther up the road sits an abandoned border crossing; one can hop back and forth to Canada with uneasy glee at defying the Department of Homeland Security. Polebridge itself is the least-visited entrance to Glacier, populated with the sorts of people who for years have fought efforts to pave the road in the hope of maintaining their solitude.

Here, the state of Montana was taking a chance on a different kind of bear management program, using the Karelian bear dogs of the Wind Rivers Bear Institute. The dogs, Finnish in origin and bred for hunting, are independent and tough, well suited for working with bears. State wildlife officer Tim Manley spent his summer with Carrie Hunt, founder of the institute, to see if they could save the lives of problem grizzlies by teaching them to avoid all things human.

Star (named for the man whose property she first ransacked) was a matriarch of the region and a night bear. She had acquired a taste for human food and was teaching her cubs this bad habit. "That bear was the worst bear we've ever worked with," Hunt says. "She was ripping into cabins. No aggression, but a very serious bear. We worked her through the dead of night for weeks and weeks, but we got her turned around."

Hunt was trained as a traditional wildlife biologist but found the job to be ultimately ineffective. In essence, she says, wildlife agencies solve the problem of habituated bears by moving them around. In fact, she says, these relocations merely prolong a process that inevitably ends with killing the animal.

"It's really easy for an agency to just move a bear. It looks good, like you did the right thing, but it's cruel to the bear. The bear comes back several times, hungrier than ever by the last time it comes back. And then it's a dead bear," she says. "I founded the institute because I got sick of moving bears. I got sick of destroying them. I knew there was a better way, and I knew they weren't being given a chance. As intelligent as they are, they weren't being given a chance to learn what the rules are."

Instead, Hunt employs a combination of punishments and rewards. When a bear does the right thing—stays out of view of the road, away from orchards, and avoids livestock—Hunt and her team reward it with peace and quiet. When a bear does the wrong thing, they harass it endlessly with noisy cracker shells, beanbag guns, and with dogs specially bred and trained for the task. "They work them like cow dogs. They get in there, they bite their butts, they hold them for the hunter. They know how to dance with the bear and not get hurt," she says. "What a lot of people think is that the dogs chasing the bears are the whole thing. And they're not. The dogs are tools that allow us to push the bears so they don't call our bluff. We make the right thing easy for the bear, which is to leave, and the wrong thing difficult, which is to come back at us."

Given the sheer number of people living in grizzly country in the United States and southern Canada, Hunt says hers is the best policy to teach grizzlies to stay away from people, period. Her methods, to a large extent, are intuitive. She's spent a lot of time thinking about the ways bears learn and how they treat each other. Distance is a good example. People always ask her, how far away is far enough? The answer is relative—based on geography and circumstances—but she acknowledges my husband Doug's theory that three hundred yards has a certain significance to the bears.

"A bear looks at distance in a very different way than we do. They look at it in terms of, *if you are a bear, can you catch me?* So what is okay changes depending on terrain, big gullies," Hunt says. "At three hundred yards, most bears know they can outrun whoever's coming at them. I believe they really look at it as, *can that bear catch me? Can that person catch me? Can that animal catch me?* Because they don't know that humans can't run fast."

Unlike Russell's utopian vision, Hunt believes fear is essential; not because grizzlies are so dangerous, but because they are so vulnerable. Because people and bears are forced to live in close proximity, as is the case in the lower forty-eight states, Hunt feels that humanity must be off-limits. "I can't tell you how many times I've had a homeowner say, 'Why don't you leave the bear alone? It wasn't doing anything. It was just eating grass on my front lawn.'

"I'm thinking to myself, you bet, but as soon as that bear moves twenty yards over and is on your deck one morning when you try to get out your door, you won't like it. You like it when you're watching him, but you don't like it when he's confused and thinks it's okay to be close to you.

"I believe when a bear first stops moving away from the roadside or moving away from the trail, he's making a decision as to his status relative to you. He's making a decision as to how he is to operate when you are in each other's personal space. That personal space extends to where the bear can catch you, or where you could catch him. So at what point does he decide that it's okay to be in your personal space because he's dominant? I think when he comes on your front lawn and starts eating your grass, he's taking your food and he knows it."

In Hunt's nine years with the institute, no one has ever been hurt by a bear, and she claims many bears have been saved. The ones who have been killed or trapped afterwards, she says, were victims of her limited funding. Star, the North Fork grizzly mother, was good for a year and a half, Hunt points out. When she got back into trouble, there was no money to send Hunt back out to work with her again. She and her cubs were captured and now live in captivity. Hunt points out that we're standing talking in her yard at the beginning of August, which is prime bear season. She should have all her dogs out working; instead, she's writing grants to buy dog food.

■■ There are places in Canada worlds away from the crowding civilization of Glacier, Banff, and Yellowstone parks; places unlike the volcanic peninsula of Kamchatka, with its brown bears innocent of contact; places where people and grizzlies live more or less peaceably, intimately, and have done so for thousands of years.

Phil Timpany grew up in southern British Columbia but knew with his first trip to the north country, on a family vacation at age thirteen, that this was where he belonged. "I got my parents to stay an extra two weeks. They had to get me back to school the first week of September. I said, no way I'm leaving here. I don't have to go to school. They said, okay, if it means a lot to you, we'll stay. So we did."

He returned as a young man, making a living any way he could. He started out logging and eventually hired on as a hunting guide, setting his clients in tree stands over salmon streams to get their trophy brown bear. When his bosses insisted on increasing the annual kill from thirteen to twenty grizzlies, Timpany balked, and they sold the license out from under him. His biggest regret, he says, was not having the money to buy it himself. Then, in the mid-1970s, he was hired to man a salmon weir on the Taku River, to weigh the kings and count the pinks spawning there.

Timpany at once found himself confronted with a dilemma. He was surrounded by grizzlies all the time, and conventional wisdom said the bears needed to be afraid of him. So he and his crew decided to do a little adverse conditioning.

"Basically, if they tried to get on the weir, we'd put a shell cracker near them and make a lot of racket. If they continued to come, we'd use rocks. If they continued to come after that, we'd just get the rubber bullets out," he says. "Rubber bullets in those days were so useless; you had to be like ten feet away. We did all that. And we left some scars on some bears, but what we discovered that year was they didn't leave the valley, they didn't leave the area.

"They just came at night. They just beat the living heck out of the weir, left holes in it, and it was mostly from their interactions with each other. I'd sneak out there sometimes and watch them. There were so many bears on the weir; they'd be fighting, and they'd be trying to displace each other from the weir, making holes. They'd tear the weir open trying to find a fish."

Furthermore, he says, the grizzlies became more dangerous during daylight encounters because they acted as if humans were the cause of their suffering. "They realized we were the enemy and were trying to hurt them and create discomfort. They were very defensive," he says.

In response, Timpany decided to try to get along with the bears instead. He set ground rules based on the way the grizzlies acted with each other. There would be no bears touching people, no people touching bears. Bears were not to damage the weir, and all human property was off-limits. "We maintained a dominance. We let the bears do whatever they wanted, unless they broke something or got into our gear or threatened us in some way, then we'd come down on them real hard." Then, he says, the cracker shells and rubber bullets would come back out. Timpany describes the result as a "contract." He says the bears quickly grasped the new rules; they all learned the word "no" and basically left the humans to their unfathomable work of catching fish and throwing them back.

My husband, Doug, visited the weir in the summer of 2005. Timpany's experience is almost unique in this world, Doug says. "I was somehow reminded of Timothy Treadwell, except Timpany carries a rifle and knows how to use it if necessary; in the old days, he had to finish off many a wounded bear. When I ask him about this, he nods but won't give me a number or even an example. He remains distant, a bit of a mystery, yet at the same time you realize this man probably knows more about British Columbia's grizzlies than anyone alive.

"Phil knows the family trees of his grizzlies, their personalities, thorny or peaceful. When he hears a subadult bawl in the middle of the night, he knows who it is and why the bear is complaining. He knows how fast they grow and in which years they experience a growth spurt. And when Phil goes into the brush to check on a sleeping female grizzly, you watch a fearless man utterly confident in his knowledge."

For three decades, Timpany has been immersed in the world of bears in which the weir was always central. Along the way he acquired the sort of practical wisdom that is almost unknown today. As such, he discards the notion that grizzlies and humans can't live intimately and has little patience for the sorts of complaints he hears from people living in grizzly habitat in the United States.

"The perceptions of bears now with the media and the sensationalism around them just perpetuates fear. But here we get rid of that. We just coexist," he says. "It's just a comparison between somebody living in a cul-de-sac on the edge of bear habitat: What do they really have to do, compared to what we have to do? What do they really have to do to coexist with the animal? Not very bloody much."

Doug reminds me that Timpany stands on the brink of a great opportunity on the Taku. Timpany has ventured into grizzly bear viewing as a business, bringing paying customers to the weir to watch the bears. At the same time, the First Nations people who live here, the Taku River Tlingit, may regain their claim on traditional tribal territory through the purchase of the local guide license. This is a big guide area, more than two million acres, and the owner controls all commercial hunting within the 4.5–million-acre watershed. An international conservation group, Round River Conservation Studies, has worked in the area with native groups for years and will help with this purchase. In addition, license holders become "stakeholders" in the eyes of the British Columbian government and have leverage in decisions made about resource development on the land.

So the Taku River drainage has a decent shot at remaining unroaded and largely unlogged. Here is one place grizzlies will roam unfettered by humans in naturally regulated populations. Phil Timpany is the perfect educator for those who choose to come here and see the bears. For many, just knowing the grizzly bear lives here apart from the agendas of men will suffice.

Others will recall a line from naturalist Aldo Leopold's *Sand County Almanac:* "Relegating grizzlies to Alaska (or British Columbia) is like relegating happiness to heaven: one may never get there." Elsewhere, the natural world is slipping away in fact and in metaphor. As modern humans search for something to hold on to, the great bear endures as a firm anchor to earth, in flesh and archetype, feeding our legends and prowling our dreams. We also need the grizzly in our immediate lives, throughout more historic range than politicians have yet imagined. The fates of men and bears have always been mingled. We need them on that far mountain across the valley, as well as forever roaming the backyards of our minds.

THE BEAR WHO CROSSED THE FREEWAY

■■ A pale illumination creeps across the long mountain meadow, toward a wedge of moon just rising over the high peaks of the Gallatin Range. It is early morning, a couple of hours before sunrise, still cool in these first days of summer. A small stand of large lodgepole pine grows on a bench above the valley. At the base of one tree, a grizzly bear looks out to the west. He lifts his head at the sound of a distant vehicle shattering the silence of the night. Traffic is nearly nonexistent in the predawn hours here on the northwest corner of Yellowstone Park. It is almost time for him to make his move. He is poised for a long journey.

The bear is a young male, having slept through five winters. He knows where he is going: fifty miles southwest down to the Montana-Idaho border, back to the land where he was raised as a cub, a hazardous trip across two highways, the open Madison valley, and around human settlement. Still, he is restless, anxious to travel. To remain where he is would be precarious. It is the mating season for grizzlies. Three days ago, a larger boar attacked him, biting him viciously on the flank. The glaring red wound is plainly visible through the missing fur. He knows the male grizzly who tore the chunk of flesh off his rear; last September, he followed the trail of the older male up from the Centennial Range. This is not the first time the bigger bear has given him trouble. The young bear doesn't know many other grizzlies because he grew up apart from the core areas of Yellowstone's bear populations. Very few grizzlies roam as far as the Centennials. This particular older boar has been the bane of his short bear life.

The stillness of night returns to the valley. The bear rises from his bed and stretches. Now he moves, down off the bench, across the sagebrush studded flat, toward the willow bottom and the highway that runs along the river. He breaks into a lope and dashes across the asphalt, down the road grade into the willows. He pushes through to the Gallatin River, wades across the shallows, and continues loping all the way to the forest beyond.

Plenty of food is available to grizzlies this time of year—grass, forbs, and elk calves—but for hours the young male doesn't even pause to feed. He seems on a mission; he needs to avoid bigger boars, to be sure, but something else is propelling him into the wilderness, up into the high country of the southern Madison Range.

By midmorning, he ambles into a subalpine basin. Below a snowdrift, a fringe of green vegetation tumbles into a blanket of spring beauty flowers. The bear grazes on the grass and lilies. In less than an hour he resumes travel. The cloudless day warms up. Near timberline, the bear finds a thicket of fir. He crawls in and scrapes out a bed next to one of the larger trees. By late afternoon, he is on the move again.

The days are long in the season just after the solstice. Soon he is negotiating snowbanks in the rolling uplands of the Madison Range. The high country is dotted with lakes, some of which are still shedding their skin of winter ice. The meadows are melting out. The young bear stops to feed on sedges emerging from the raw earth. He grazes and then claws roots out of the snow-free ridges. Stands of whitebark pine decorate the high country. The 325-pound grizzly sniffs the snow at the base of the trees. Last fall, the trees here produced an abundant crop of cones; this year, it doesn't look as promising. The grizzly looks around. He has a long way to go.

A string of lakes leads to a creek that tumbles west off the alpine shoulder of the Madison Range. A hiking trail follows the run of the creek. Snow covers the upper stretches of trail; there isn't much sign of recent travel. The young male bear is accustomed to using these trails and avoiding the people who walk them. He has discovered that humans don't hike much at night.

The grizzly descends in darkness through the forest toward the open valley bottom. Elk and deer have left their hoofprints in the mud. He is aware of a fresh set of large cat tracks. The mountain lion sign is barely an hour old. The bear veers off the trail and finds a thicket, where he sleeps out the middle of the night.

In the dim light of morning, the bear sniffs at the cat track and follows the prints down the creek. The day is clear. Near the edge of the timber, the lion tracks turn and lead north along the edge of the open country. Below lies a sagebrush valley, a paved highway, and a river. The sun is almost up. Humans float down this river in open boats. The bear hesitates, sensing he must wait again for darkness to continue his journey. Crossing the highway and river is always dangerous; a daylight crossing could be deadly. He now leaves the creek and follows the big cat's tracks leading along a game trail at the fringe of the forest.

He doesn't have to go far. Before he has traveled a mile, the bear begins to pick up a scent riding on the morning air. The pungency grows stronger; the grizzly recognizes it. The mountain lion has made a kill. The bear smells fresh blood.

The grizzly slows his pace and stalks along the deer trail with his nose to the ground. The cougar is close. He hears the sound of the cat stripping flesh off the carcass at the edge of the sagebrush. Suddenly, it is quiet; the lion knows the bear is near.

They see each other at the same instant. The lion lies with the white-tail's haunch between his paws; the deer's neck is broken. The cat's mustache and the white of his jowls are red with blood. The male cougar weighs about 120 pounds. His face curls into a snarl; he hisses, cater-wauling at the bear. The grizzly creeps forward, only twenty feet from the cat, his head lowered and ears flat back against his head. The bear inches toward the lion, who steps clear of his kill. The cougar crouches and then leaps at the bear, stopping a few feet short. The grizzly flinches but pushes forward until they stand face to face, snarling and growling. Suddenly, the bear lunges. The cat is quicker and retreats a few yards. The two carnivores stand motionless and stare at each other. After a few minutes, the lion turns and steps back into the trees. The mountain lion cannot risk serious injury. He relinquishes the deer carcass to the bear. The big cat will make another kill.

Throughout the morning, the young grizzly feeds upon the deer. He beds nearby under a pine tree, where he can look out on the valley. Vehicles race by on Highway 287; a few boats drift down the Madison River. He senses he must wait for all traffic to subside, until the dark, quiet hours after midnight. He gets up and finishes off most of the carcass. The bear moves south and passes the time bedding on the border of the sagebrush hills. Before the sliver of moon rises, he starts off toward the highway and river beyond.

The void of night sky casts no shadows. The bear wiggles under a fence leaving behind brown strands of hair on the barbed wire. He dashes across the road and pauses at the riverbank. The water level is still high from melting snow, although two upstream dams mitigate flooding here. The five-year-old boar steps into the river and wades shoulder-deep around big boulders. A deep run sweeps against the west bank. The current carries him downstream as he swims the channel and scrambles up the riprap on the far side of the Madison River.

His journey now leads him south another thirty miles. He wastes no time leaving the open valley. The grizzly crosses another fence line and enters the sheltering forest. He prowls past sleeping cabins. The river branches; the grizzly follows the fork leading south-southwest. Soon he is back in unsettled country. He pushes on southward through the morning, passing over a divide. The land is more open on the south-facing side of the mountains. The bear descends toward a huge valley filled with lakes and wetlands. He is uneasy in this naked landscape during broad daylight. The boar picks up a willow-lined creek and follows it down into the flats. Other kinds of willow grow in tall thickets in the swamps. The young bear finds a hidden dry spot and claws out a day bed. Before he crawls into the brush, he looks south across the great wetland. Brilliant sunlight reflects off patches of snow cornices snaking along the summit of the Centennial Range—his old homestead.

In midafternoon, the young bear wakes and picks his way south through the swampy flats. He stops at the edge of a shallow pond to graze on horsetail and cow parsnip. A pair of trumpeter swans ease away from a hummocky nest. The sun sets. A meandering creek drains a section of swamp, making the walking easy. The grizzly follows the drainage across the flat, bypassing a cluster of buildings, and up into the mountains.

Under the cover of night, the young bear bounds up the cobbled streambed deep into the Centennial Mountains. The creek forks and he takes the one less traveled by humans. The creek pinches out against a rocky slope. The grizzly climbs up and lopes along the ridge on to the summit. In three days he has traveled more than sixty miles. He stands relaxed, his jaws agape, peering out across the forests and darkened landscapes. His expression is much like that of a huge, happy puppy.

He is back on familiar ground, but just as important, he is nearly free of competition with other grizzlies, alone with endless new territory to explore. He is restless, ready for adventure and discovery. Perhaps he was born a roamer.

For the next month, the young male grizzly wanders his old range from the Continental Divide to the Red Rock Lakes wetlands, picking up seasonal food on alpine ridges or the bottoms. A few people live there. The bear does not fear them as he does the ones who herd sheep; his mother taught him that. The bear is spotted several times crossing the dirt road. The humans notice he has a bare spot on his butt. Mosquitoes must play hell on that thing, they joke. The locals name him the Bald-Assed Bear or, sometimes, just Baldy. These people are used to living side by side with wildlife, and it is a rare pleasure to have a resident grizzly in these mountains.

■■ The country in which the young boar was raised—his home range, where he spent his first two and a half years—is centered in a small east-west range known as the Centennial Mountains. The single-chain range rises only about fifteen miles west of Yellowstone Park and runs west forty-five miles to a slight pass through which the freeway I-15 runs. Beyond the freeway, the mountains lead west through remote country for another thirty miles and then hook north into the vast Bitterroot Range.

This huge wilderness region of central Idaho, collectively known as the Bitterroot ecosystem, represents the best unoccupied grizzly country left south of Canada. Longtime survival of the grizzly bear in the lower forty-eight states is largely dependent upon getting the great bear back into the Bitterroots. For many years government biologists, conservation groups, and citizens have worked to reintroduce the grizzly into the Bitterroot: To date, all efforts have failed. The Yellowstone grizzly bear ecosystem is an island that will not endure without connectivity—genetic and geographical—to populations along the Canadian border.

The most direct and practical way to complete this linkage is through the Centennials, across I-15, and into the Bitterroots.

The Centennials, like the Bitterroots, have long been a deadly place for grizzly bears. For most of the twentieth century, herders drove tens of thousands of domestic sheep into every corner of the public lands that constitute these mountains. Bears are inordinately drawn to sheep, which are guarded closely by herders. For the past hundred years, virtually all bears were shot on sight. By the early 1970s, grizzlies were unknown in the Centennials. They had been wiped out. Only in recent years have grizzlies begun to filter back in from Yellowstone.

The young boar's mother was one of these bears. A long maternal lineage of grizzlies—her family—had been gravitating toward the Centennials for many years. That is, the way in which a population of bears extends its range into unoccupied grizzly habitat is through the interlinking home ranges of successive generations of mother bears. As a daughter sets up her own home range on the fringe of her mother's, the collective territory is extended, westerly in this instance, perhaps another twenty miles. This theoretical pattern of recolonization works best where there's good, empty habitat and no obstacles to movement. Unfortunately, those several generations of sows with cubs moving toward the Centennials encountered plenty of problems.

To begin with, other bears occupied the best places in Yellowstone. Also, the most direct route, due west across the Targhee National Forest, was impeded by massive clear-cutting, an industrial outrage visible from space. Some people who lived in the big valley east of the Centennials were inclined to shoot bears. And then there were the sheep and herders who guarded them; these men could be expected to kill bears. In the end, the safest route into the Centennials hooked north into the corridor used by the big cantankerous male grizzly—the same one who bit the young boar's flank and left a bald patch on his ass, legalities notwithstanding.

▪▪ Of course, the bear known as Baldy has a notion of why this big, rich country is devoid of other grizzlies: Sheepherders shot them out. The most important lesson of his life, instilled by experience and his mother over a period of three years, was to avoid these men and their woolly creatures. Four years ago, almost eight miles due south of where he crossed the road, the young bear traveled with his mother and yearling sister along the crest of the Continental Divide. The sow stopped on a broad pass on the Idaho border. A stench leaked up from far below: the reek of sheep that had been dead for several days. The mother bear cautiously searched the breeze for the smell of the sheepherders but detected none.

The sow found the dead sheep—four of them—in a small ravine below a fifty-foot cliff. The three bears fed briefly but voraciously. A rare midsummer carcass couldn't be passed up. The coyotes and ravens hadn't left much, and the grizzlies had been conditioned with a near reflexive aversion to sheep odor. After ten minutes of nervous feeding, the mother and her two yearling cubs climbed the slope and picked up a hiking trail leading back over the pass.

The bears were traversing steep scree when the mother caught the sheepherder's scent. The sow broke into a run. The male yearling raced just behind her with his sister at his heels. A shot rang out. The small female grizzly skidded off the trail down the scree slope. Her mother spun on her rear paws and raced back. Another shot ricocheted off the rocks. The sow lifted up her cub's lifeless head with her snout. The male yearling rocked nervously on the trail above. Mother bear bolted, leaving the dead cub sprawled out on the talus, and herded the little male on up the trail. Both ran at top speed for their lives. At the pass, a last rifle shot cracked in the tree braches just above them. They disappeared into the safety of the forest.

The next year the male grizzly, then a two-and-a-half-year-old cub, again traveled the Centennials with his mother. It was already July, late in the mating season, and the adult female bear was irritable, as she was coming into estrus again. Nonetheless, her big cub trailed along, not far behind. Finally, they spotted another grizzly, a sizeable boar, on a high ridgeline. The male cub had seen this big bear before; the huge bruin had tried to attack him and his sister two years ago. At that time, their mother had fought the boar.

But this time the boar ignored the sow and suddenly charged the young male. The two-and-a-half-year-old raced off the ridge and dropped down a steep slope into a grove of alder and mountain ash. The big male grizzly chased him down the hill but stopped at the thicket.

The young grizzly was now on his own, although he followed his mother, at a respectable four hundred yards or more, for the rest of the year. She copulated with the big boar and denned early. Years later, he would recognize the bigger grizzly that mated with his mother as the same animal who had torn the hide off his rear. There was also a good chance the adult bear was his own father.

The young male bear denned alone his third winter. Not long after spring emergence, he picked up his mother's tracks and followed them. She had two tiny cubs with her. Baldy trailed along, mostly several hundred yards distant, for three months. He noticed once again how carefully the sow avoided the sheepherders. In late summer, his mother and her new litter moved east toward Yellowstone. The four-year-old male grizzly turned back. He never saw his mother again. Later that fall, there was a report that poachers had shot a female grizzly and her cub on Sawtell Peak at the eastern end of the Centennial Range.

■■ Now it is August. The five-and-a-half-year-old bear remembers all the old places, the ones that were good—and the spot where his sibling was killed. He turns west, away from a sheep-grazing allotment, and lumbers up a long ridgeline, feeding as he goes. Yampa grows on the broad, moister sections of the lower ridge. He claws out the tuberous roots, pawing out half a softball-size nodule of Yellowstone obsidian along the way. Long flakes had been struck from this core by prehistoric people. The Centennials have probably always been rich hunting grounds—for humans as well as bears. Baldy digs away at the stonecrop-decorated rocky hillside. Biscuit root abounds here. The bear pulls the tuberlike roots from the chunky soil.

The grizzly looks up the ridge. He ambles up toward a bald summit miles to the west. The crest is half open, half timbered. Carpets of yellow balsam root and purple lupine cover the meadows. Way up high he can see the pallid stands of whitebark pine, the steeper slopes of fir and spruce and the gleaming talus tumbling off a tablelike summit. Majestic mountains roll west along the Continental Divide, the summits more mesas than peaks. Rivulets of timber pour down the north-facing drainages. He is on the move now. The bear wants to pioneer the habitats of the western Centennials, see what's out there, and maybe keep on going. The bear knows the country opens up considerably before the Centennials dip down to where the twin roads run.

Other bears, especially bigger male grizzlies, present potential danger. But there aren't many; in nearly six years, he'd only seen four other grizzlies besides his mother and sister. Only one was a big boar, the one who attacked him. Little competition prowls the ridges: He could be the lone grizzly in this part of the mountains.

Given this road map, the bald-assed bear navigates the difficulties, contouring below the divide, mostly on the north side of the range, using the timbered gullies for cover during the day, and scrupulously avoiding the flocks.

The country is still familiar, but he is nearing the western edge of his mother's former home range. On the other side of the Table Mountains lies terra incognita. Meanwhile, he needs to eat. There's plenty of bear food: A few berries are ripening in the ravines; last year's whitebark cone crop was enormous, and a few groves of pine now carry decent numbers of cones, which red squirrels will be stashing any time now. The male grizzly should be able to put on a lot of weight this fall.

By September the huckleberries, having suffered a hard frost, begin to soften and fall from the bushes. The bald-butt bear travels up to the higher country where the five-needle pines grow. He tops out the divide and walks westward on the summit. He rolls over the undulating landscape and climbs up a huge ridge that runs gently north off the divide. A forest of mature whitebark pine clings to the moderate slopes and reaches upward toward the timberline. The number of cones on individual trees in the Centennials greatly exceeds the crop the bear saw farther north at the beginning of his journey. Arboreal rodents chatter and complain from the trees. He will do all right here.

One crystalline day, the bear looks out across the huge valley toward the snowcapped peaks of the Bitterroot Range fifty miles west. There must be plenty of pine nuts in those distant mountains, berries in summer, and lots of grass and roots the rest of the year. Maybe there are other grizzlies over there. The bald-butt bear looks around. Despite their reputations for solitary existence, grizzlies living within very low densities of other bears seem to have a propensity to seek out one another. These social relationships are naturally unstudied because these bears are seldom observed. This is probably what happened to the last grizzlies in southwestern Colorado, where a tiny population of brown bears survived for decades without humans being aware of their existence.

The second day on the ridgeline, the bear completes his mile-long circle around the pine grove and, alarmingly, crosses bear tracks. But they are merely his own. Still, he is uneasy. More vigilant, the young male keeps on feeding. The wind changes direction; something is wrong. He might not be alone.

Suddenly, he sees it. The suspicion swells into reality: Imprinted on top of his own paw marks is the track of a huge grizzly. The tracks lead in the same direction. The giant bear is stalking him.

A familiar scent lingers in the track. Baldy does not panic, nor does he try to flee. He knows this bear. For nearly six years, the big boar—his adversary—has plagued his days.

It is late in the year, a critical time for grizzlies. The younger boar's fat cells are not yet sending the biological signal that it's time to den.

Though he weighs over four hundred pounds, his metabolism says he needs to keep eating. His instinct tells him that he can't afford to be run out of the whitebark country; it could mean the difference between survival and starvation during the long winter sleep. Baldy is already a big grizzly. Like most bears—and despite the paucity of contact with other grizzlies—he knows his status within the hierarchy of grizzly society. Baldy is on the cusp of his dominant years.

The younger boar now follows the bigger bear's trail through the snow. It leads under the great pine trees toward a minor summit on the ridge. The summit is open. Finally, the big bear's tracks lead off on their own, away from Baldy's day-old trail. He follows the spore of the older grizzly.

The huge paw prints lead over the summit and into the forest beyond. Baldy prowls behind, cautiously scenting the air and watching the trail. Ahead the tracks disappear. A gust of wind carries in a familiar scent; the big boar has circled back and awaits him at the edge of the timber. It looks like an ambush.

Suddenly, there is a roar. The five-hundred-pound boar bounds out of the tree line, swinging his enormous body across the meadow and aiming directly for the younger bear. Baldy rears for a second and then drops to all fours. He charges the bigger boar. When he is four feet away, Baldy slams his paws down and skids to a stop. Then he steps forward, ears flat back, jaws open, and the hair on the back of his neck straight up. The bigger grizzly joins the challenge and comes at him. They stand nose to nose.

The mountains reverberate with bellows that can be heard from miles away. They roar into each other's faces. The bigger bear grabs hold of the fur of Baldy's neck with his teeth. They rise on their hind legs as the younger boar tries to break free. He throws the big boar back, and they stand again, circling like Japanese sumo wrestlers. Both male grizzlies appear poised to deliver a death bite to the other's neck. They parry and rock and roar with open jaws inches apart.

The violent sounds of brawling subside. The two boars still have their paws on each other's shoulders. It looks like a standoff. Abruptly, the bigger grizzly pushes away, drops to four feet, and turns his back.

The fight is over. There are no visible injuries. Baldy also turns his body to the side and steps away. Both bears now stand fifty feet apart in the same small meadow. Neither looks directly at the other. Both pretend to feed, digging clots of soil and roots from the earth.

Some authorities think that male kinship means nothing among grizzlies. Others point out that serious battles between male grizzlies generally take place during the mating season or perhaps in defense of a valuable food source. At any rate, the die is cast: Baldy will complete his journey. His Oedipal wanderings will continue.

Two weeks later, the four-hundred-pound grizzly stands on a peak south of Mud Lake. A blanket of snow covers the higher summits. Winter is on the way. Baldy must think about denning. The country to the west is open. It is elk-hunting season, and the bear has avoided the human camps by traveling at night or down the timbered gullies. Twice he snuck in under the cover of darkness to retrieve gut-piles the hunters left behind.

In this treeless landscape, and with so many armed people about, the grizzly is vulnerable. Far to the west, he can see a refuge, the timbered foothills of the Bitterroot Mountains running north. But in the valley between, five miles away, run the iron rails and the twin highways.

The bear is fat. He wants to find a den beyond the range of the big male grizzly. The bald-ass bear also has a strange urge, a curiosity to explore new land—a restlessness he perhaps inherited from the big boar. The western Centennial Range is all new country, miles beyond his previous range. He will keep going. He will find a den on the other side of the valley.

The bald-butt bear charts a route down timbered ravines and willow-bottomed creeks to the flats below. A light snow begins to fall. He starts out at dusk. The nights are longer now. The grizzly walks west on the open divide for an hour, then drops into the breaks and swings through the sagebrush along a tiny creek that hooks back southward. The snowflakes thicken. He can hear a few trucks traveling I-15. Hidden by the blizzard, the bear moves steadily down the draw.

By midnight the country levels out. The grizzly reaches the iron rails. The freeway lies on the other side. Only a vehicle or two pass by every five minutes, but linked fences make darting across the pavement impractical. Instead, the bear follows the iron rails south into a basalt-walled gorge where no fences run. Juniper trees sag under heavy blankets of snow. The railroad continues south, but the small canyon turns west and runs below a freeway bridge to the country on the far side. Fresh deer tracks lead into the ravine. He follows the hoofprints.

The bear crosses under the freeway. He plows into the enveloping whiteness, the gathering drifts tugging at his hips, on toward the hills beyond. He pushes between the strands of a barbwire fence and begins to climb westward. Behind him he can hear the distant rumble of a truck. Before long, the grizzly has entered a spruce forest. The drifting snow quickly covers his tracks.

■■ The next May, two men from the Red Rock Valley are cross-country skiing the crusted snow lingering on the lower flanks of the Continental Divide southwest of Island Butte. They side-hill up a ridge and stop at the crest to admire the immaculate peaks of the Bitterroot Range sweeping north toward the vast emptiness of the Frank Church and Selway-Bitterroot wilderness areas.

The men are startled to discover a fresh set of humanlike tracks leading down the open ridgetop into the timber below. They study the tracks and determine them to be those of a large bear. The two experienced woodsmen follow the paw prints down. They stop at a particularly clear set of tracks: The front toes are close together and in a straight line, unlike the curved signature of a black bear, and four-inch-long claw marks extend from these front paws. This is the trail of a grizzly. The bear is nearby. They cautiously ski down the line of tracks toward the trees. Neither man has ever seen the sign of a grizzly in the Bitterroots before.

At the edge of a grove of Engelmann spruce, the men stop and scent the air: A fetor rises from the creek bed. Probably a dead elk. Now the men are visibly nervous. Surprising a grizzly on a spring carcass is a perilous situation. They try to back off the far side of the ridge. Below they hear a branch break. The two humans freeze. They hear the conifers rustle, then the brief murmur of brush. A bear bounds across the open creek bottom and disappears into the timber beyond. It is a grizzly bear. The animal has a bald spot on his rear flank.

The danger is over. The two skiers think they have heard of this bear. The grizzly is vulnerable, so they will keep their discovery a secret. The men smile and pat each other on the back. They have just seen something magical.

EPILOGUE: PRACTICAL CONSIDERATIONS IN GRIZZLY COUNTRY

■■ There's abundant literature on reasons for visiting bear country and how to act if you encounter a grizzly. Much of it is at least mildly perplexing and even occasionally contradictory. Part of this conflicting advice comes from responsible officials who assume their clientele knows nothing of bears and who are worried about legally covering their backsides. But some of the confusion is the honest product of the individuality of all bears and the uniqueness of every situation. Though outside the general scope of this book, I thought it might be useful to some readers to discuss the conventional tips given to those who visit the grizzly.

I say "visit" because most of us do not live or work in bear country. Our trips into the wilderness that still contain the great bear are accordingly voluntary and optional. Some advocates argue that the best thing for grizzlies is to leave them undisturbed. Though I agree, this consideration has only recently curtailed my incursions in grizzly habitat. But it's something to think about. I have, especially during the decade I filmed grizzlies, treaded too heavily, taming wilderness and animals with my presence. My advertising their plight with movies was a trade-off, and I quit altogether after 1982.

Of course, an encounter with a bear can be of great value in your personal life. The contention to leave them alone remains counterbalanced with the need for sufficient human contact to collectively grasp the absolute importance of preserving this animal in our modern culture. I never get to the bottom of this paradox.

On a more practical level, the most important ingredient to carry into grizzly country is your state of mind. Depending on how you apply it, your attitude can be a great asset or a considerable liability. A sense of personal responsibility is not a bad way to think about our presence in the wilderness. The grizzly roams the wild because he has been shot out of everywhere else. The bear has nowhere to go outside these areas. Crowding a creature who represents wilderness is a contradictory undertaking and carries a special onus because we humans can go anywhere. The practice of restraint is appropriate, and the reasonable obligation upon us is to learn something about bears before we go into grizzly country.

The main thing to take into grizzly country is an attitude of humility, which constitutes the correct approach for dealing with an animal who can chew off your hindquarters any time he chooses. The "upright ape" is not the top dog in grizzly country. This second-rate wilderness citizenship is a thing to be savored; it takes the heat off people to always be in charge. Accordingly, watch your mind-set as well as how you smell; don't travel into grizzly country reeking of bad karma or old tuna fish. Once out there, be alert. Forget about scenery and try to see from the viewpoint of an animal. Sneak around. Keep your senses searching the tree line and pay attention to detail; see how things interact. Listen to what other animals are saying to one another, especially birds and bears. Note that the most intense communication takes place between predator and prey. The only species of animal that tries to get by in the wilderness without interspecies tact or communication is the human critter. All other animals take stock of what each other is doing and make adjustments in their lives for the presence and behavior of the rest of the animal kingdom.

My advice is to read as much "grizzly literature" as you can stomach, or take your early trips into grizzly country with an experienced bear-person who can point out grizzly sign, food, beds, and travel patterns. (This method is more engaging than sitting in a library.) The knowledge you need is easy to acquire, and it's fun to learn. "Bear advice" books and handouts may be full of contradictions and ambiguities. Read these with healthy skepticism. The idea is to get as much experience as fast as you can so that you are comfortable around grizzlies. Then you can decide for yourself how to act appropriately.

Check out the official reports of bear incidents for guidelines. Sources of information (regarding all kinds of encounters with grizzlies) include reports of the National Park Service, state game departments, and law enforcement agencies as well as statements and interviews of eyewitnesses. Two fine compilations of past attacks stand out: Scott McMillion's 1998 book, *Mark of the Grizzly*, and a slightly older book by Stephen Herrero, *Bear Attacks*. McMillion skillfully interviews survivors and shares a few tips; Herrero offers analysis and his own interpretations based on his extensive experience with North American bears.

■■ What do grizzlies bring to the wildlife-encounter table? They carry the genetically encoded predisposition of their genome combined with the lessons learned from their mothers and all the other ursine experiences of their lives. That's a lot. The result is a flexible menu of behavior capable of wide-ranging and fast-acting adaptability. Their extensive learning curve never stops climbing. They have an investigative curiosity and are smart animals. They also have distinct individual personalities and can be moody.

The North American grizzly, as previously noted, is innately aggressive. Mitigating this aggressiveness is the individual's desire to survive. Bears need to stay alive to pass on their genes, and a grave injury can prove fatal to an animal who tends to be solitary in its feeding habits.

Before the arrival of Europeans in America, people and grizzlies lived together, often in the same habitats. Armed with bear lore and a belief system that placed them within the natural world, but without the option of European firearms, native people and grizzlies had to share the landscape. The occasional removal of the overbold bear or human was a meager drop in the great sea of evolution. Since 1804, however, grizzlies have been shot on sight. With the repeating rifle, the great bear's fate was sealed; the grizzly was extirpated from some 99 percent of its former range in the lower forty-eight states, and the population plummeted to fewer than a thousand.

Whether 140 years of unnatural selection produced a different bear remains speculative; death is a poor learning experience. Today's grizzly is probably much the same critter who roamed the range ten thousand years ago.

■■ I grew up hearing that "grizzlies have an innate fear of man," and that one should constantly reinforce this intrinsic fear (usually by hunting) or bears will become bold and attack people. On the other hand, there are people like Charlie Russell who maintain, "bears (are) neither naturally fearful nor naturally aggressive toward people." Russell based this opinion on his childhood experiences with the grizzlies of Denali, later reinforced during his experiences with the Kermode black bears on Princess Royal Island and, by extension, with grizzlies in the Khutzeymateen of British Columbia. He then set out to test his hypothesis by living among the Russian brown bears of wild Kamchatka, contending that human fear of bears was the "true obstacle to coexistence."

Leaving aside the issue of human fear, I've always suspected that Russell was on to something about living peacefully with bears. Most of my time has been with the surviving grizzlies of the lower forty-eight states; you can reasonably assume many of the bears you run into in these places have had at least minimal contact with humans. In my experience, these bears ran away more than 95 percent of the times we met up. Once, I encountered a grizzly I felt with certainty (a guess based on her behavior and the geographical location) had never seen a human before; I found her on a diminutive salmon river in remote British Columbia. This small female had three cubs of the year, and I spotted her fishing a shallow riffle around a bend a quarter mile upstream. After some time, the mother grizzly finally made me out; I was a safe four hundred meters away and simply stood there, neither moving nor looking at her. We spent the next four hours fishing together; she went for the pink salmon while I fly-fished for steelhead. The upshot was that this small grizzly fished closer and closer throughout the afternoon, eventually abandoned her salmon run and cubs, and walked over to check me out close up. I detected no sign of alarm or aggression, just curiosity. Finally, she stood just ten meters away on the other side of the stream. Her cubs were quite a ways behind her. At the last minute, I charged across the water, throwing pebbles and shouting for her to get out of there. She complied. I felt bad about running her off, but the place was no sanctuary. Hunting season would open here in six weeks, and a human-friendly grizzly would be taken out.

Nonetheless, engraved somewhere on a grizzly chromosome is probably a cautionary note saying the upright ape is dangerous. Brown bears show tremendous—learned or instinctual—restraint around humans, those puny, murderous, two-legged critters they might justly attack at any minute, but for some reason almost never do.

With rare exceptions, such as the mauling on the Hulahula River, grizzlies don't attack without reason (though such cause may be obscure to the human victim who stumbles mindlessly close to a bear, then wonders how he got there). These infrequent and unfortunate daytime events resulting in physical injury merit some examination. Virtually all involve human blunders.

Getting a grizzly to chomp on you is not an easy accomplishment. You have to surprise the bear at close range, somehow induce the bear to charge, and then behave in such a way that convinces the animal to conclude that charge rather than veer off. Even then, even if contact is made, you have a good chance of not being chewed on.

Here are some tips and comments based on my own experience and the sound guidance of others. The stark and obvious advice is don't stumble upon a bear to begin with. Once the animal spots you, never run. In the unlikely occasion of the grizzly charging you, stand your ground inoffensively; don't try to climb a tree, shout, look directly at the bear, or make any sudden movements. If the grizzly makes contact, hit the ground and play dead. Don't fight back.

The simplicity of these suggestions is almost, but not quite, ridiculous. There are nuances. How do you avoid blundering upon a bear at close range? You need minimal knowledge of where grizzlies might bed, feed, or travel at certain times of the day or year, and you need to be alert. Application of your own senses is the one thing in bear country you have control over. Sweep the trees for potential bedding areas, and look for tracks and digs. The freshness of the sign will tell you if the bear was there last night or last week. Grizzly scat lets you know what the bears are feeding on and—if grass, roots, berries, nuts—you can keep an eye out for where those plants grow. Don't hike robotically down the trail worrying about your stock portfolio. Move or bushwhack like another wild creature; stop and listen every five minutes or so, more often in brushy country. Your rusty senses are better than you think, especially your senses of smell and hearing. Humans can detect an animal carcass a long ways away (and avoid the bear that is probably bedded nearby). Bears can make a lot of noise when they're not bedded or wary of intrusion.

If you prefer to stay on popular hiking trails, you may travel for years in prime grizzly country without encountering a bear. Resident grizzlies generally know where and when humans pass through their habitat and adjust by using backcountry trails only at night or during seasons when few people are around. But there are exceptions: Grizzlies roam widely to seasonal ranges, subadult males may wander to totally new areas, and older boars bluster all over the place during the mating season (mostly late May and June). So you might encounter a nonresident animal traveling on or bedded near a trail you are using. If the bear knows where you are and you are behaving predictably, the grizzly will be looking out for you. If, however, you choose to bushwhack and leave the hiking trails altogether, the practical responsibility for not surprising the bear shifts heavily to the human.

The most dangerous encounter is surprising a mother grizzly with cubs, especially if she is on a day bed. This situation results in the vast majority of daytime bear attacks. About three-quarters of known attacks are by female grizzlies with young. Seventy-five percent is a minimal number, since mauling victims often don't see the cubs the attacking mother is protecting. In my experience, mothers with yearlings can be just as aggressive, at least initially, in defense of their family as a sow with cubs of the year; others think that the females with young cubs are more dangerous. The fact that these ursine mothers charge from day beds is often not recorded as people don't see the bear until she charges and because past field investigations of human mauling sites were not designed to find bear beds. The association of female grizzlies on day beds and human injuries is accordingly a presumption based on frequent reports by people who have been charged or mauled by sows with young: that the grizzly was first sighted up and running, coming out of the brush or other thick places that didn't appear to be feeding areas. The other observation concerns the time of day of the incident; during the heat of the summer season, when the most people visit grizzly country, bears can be expected to bed out the middle of days, often sleeping until the evening shadows fall. The probability that many of these attacking mothers were surprised on day beds may go unreported.

For example, a young man was badly mauled by a grizzly while running on a Forest Service trail up Pacific Creek south of Yellowstone Park. A mutual friend arranged for us to meet in Salt Lake City sometime later (after his wounds had healed) and talk about his encounter. It seemed baffling; the bear came out of nowhere, racing down the trail for a couple of seconds, and then it nailed him. He fought the grizzly fiercely with his fists. He was a religious man and thought that was what God wanted him to do. He was terribly injured. It might have been only a long minute, but he was conscious the entire time. Then a voice told him to play dead, and this worked. He remembers the bear leaving and then returning to stand over him with her paw resting on his back. The grizzly kept looking back into a thicket of willows along a tiny creek, he said, still resting a forepaw on him. He suffered no further injuries. The bear ran off into the willows. The officials from the Forest Service and Wyoming game department never found the responsible bear or any evidence to indicate that it was a mother with young.

Again, this aggressive attack, officially recorded as "unidentified bear," sounds like it could have been by a mother who was surprised by the jogger on her day bed in the willows. If so, his violent resistance no doubt exacerbated the severity of the mauling.

At any rate, it's a good idea to know something about grizzlies on day beds. For openers, grizzlies sleep soundly and can be approached on their day beds to within dangerous proximities. The same adult male grizzly who wouldn't tolerate me three hundred yards away in a high shrub field allowed me to pass by fifty feet from his bed. I would never try this with a mother grizzly; fifty feet is way too close, and the female bear often reflexively charges at any threat to her cubs within this distance. The second observation concerns when they bed; grizzlies tend to be crepuscular in their feeding patterns, out and about during mornings until it begins to heat up and again when the day cools toward evening. They can be expected to be more active on cool days and early in the spring. The presence of abundant food may shorten the duration of their naps. During the fall, after hyperphagia sets in, bears might feed all day long. These generalizations constitute only the broadest of guidelines. See how the day feels and use common sense about when and where grizzlies might be sleeping.

Grizzlies tend to bed in predictable places: next to trees not far from the edges of meadows, near carcasses, or in thick places along creeks, clumps of stunted trees in alpine areas, or willow bottoms up in the Arctic. The idea for the bears is to find a secure, comfortable spot not too far from their particular feeding areas. A cool spot is important in summer, and sometimes they like to be able to see out. Where bears congregate, such as along salmon streams for coastal brown bears, intolerance for other grizzlies (and people) breaks down when food is abundant, and they might bed very close to the creek or streamside pathway. A friend once almost stepped on a sleeping boar sacked out in the middle of the trail.

Grizzlies may use the same day beds for extended periods of time or during the same season year after year. They also may stop by for a single afternoon's sleep on their way to another food source. The amount of bear scat present gives a clue as to how long and when the animal uses the day bed. Grizzlies maintain a separate latrine not unlike pigs. An 1860 report from the San Joaquin Valley of California told of "dens of grizzlies [which . . .] always had a dung pile one to two feet high at one place outside; the animals did not foul their shelters." These "shelters" were most certainly beds, not dens. I have found similar scat piles associated with beds in the high Rockies stacked two feet high against whitebark pine trees in krummholtz zones. This is a lot of bear scat and indicates years of use during early summer (grass scat) and again in fall (pinecones).

You may have to walk through or near a possible bedding site. At these times, I circle widely (at least a couple hundred feet if I can) to the windward of the site and let my scent blow toward the bedded animal. I may cough or click rocks together to alert and elicit movement from a potentially bedded grizzly. I listen for rustling sounds then back off quietly if I hear anything. On two occasions, grizzlies (both times big males) growled at me from day beds fifty and sixty feet away. Each time I froze, and then backed off silently and slowly. These two bears let me go, but I think if I had come any closer and interrupted their nap, I would have paid the price.

Once you have blundered close enough to get a grizzly's attention, your options are indeed limited, and the advice does become simplistic and redundant. If you don't want to get charged, don't run or try to climb a tree; in fact, in those first critical seconds, don't move a muscle. For example, one early May morning in Yellowstone Park at the southern edge of Hayden Valley, I ran into a mother grizzly and her two yearling cubs digging up the seed caches and nests of voles in a meadow, which lay buried under a blanket of spring snow. This was decades ago, and I had been hired to take bear pictures for a fancy magazine. I wasn't alone; I had a lookout, and these were the first grizzlies of the year.

The family hadn't seen me yet. I sat hidden by a tree with a stiff wind blowing in my face, which muted the clicking of the camera shutter. The sow did all the work, digging through two feet of snow, pulling up the nests with her claws, and dumping their grassy contents out on the snow. The little rodents tried to scamper away but were quickly gobbled up by the two yearling bears. I snapped away and then retreated back a couple of hundred feet into the timber to reload the film in the borrowed camera I hadn't taken time to learn about.

Back in the woods, I posted my lookout at the edge of the clearing and picked my way through the trees up a tiny thermal creek to the foot of a medium-size lodgepole pine tree. The bear family was probably two hundred yards away and out of sight. I sat down next to the tree. The pine, I noticed, had a branch about eyeball level; it was a perfect tree for climbing.

I messed with the camera for some time. Off to the right I caught movement: My lookout was leaving the area fast, clearing out with long strides. I looked back down the little creek. Moving directly toward me, perhaps fifty feet away, was the grizzly mother trailed by her two young. A number of deadfalls lay across the drainage, and I probably hoped this might slow her down.

At any rate, I couldn't stay on the ground; they'd walk right over me. I slowly rose and reached for the branch. The bears caught the movement. They froze and looked right at me. Stupidly but instinctually, I pulled at the branch, frantically scraping at the tree with my army surplus rubber boots. The grizzly charged. There was no way I was going to get up that tree. She raced at me, leaping and rolling over deadfalls like water. I stopped moving; with one hand still on the tree, I turned toward the charging bear and started talking, saying, "It's only me, a pathetic human" and other "please-give-me-a-break" platitudes. All this unfolded in three or four seconds. I didn't move a muscle but kept jabbering in conversational tones. The charging grizzly bore down on me. At ten or twelve feet away, the mother bear veered, never breaking stride, and led her yearlings out and away into another clearing. Profoundly shaken but safe, I slumped down against the tree that I could never have climbed in time.

This is an example of doing almost everything wrong. Never trust a lookout, even if you have a reliable one. Because I thought my ass was covered, I lost my vigilance. Once I spotted the bear family walking up on me and then startled them at close range, I precipitated a charge by making a sudden movement. Of course, I was sitting on the ground, which made me feel especially vulnerable. I don't know what I was supposed to do about sitting or standing—it only happened to me one time. But once I was on my feet, I should have frozen and spoken quietly to the grizzly without staring directly at her. If the deadfalls hadn't impeded her progress, the mother bear would have concluded that charge. She couldn't have helped it. I was very lucky.

Over the years, fourteen different grizzlies have charged me about thirty-four times—some were multiple charges, where the bear stopped short and then backed up, and I wasn't keeping count. Most were mothers with cubs. Three were probably subadults. Two solitary adult bears also charged: One was a dominant boar. The subadults and the boar hop-charged (sort of a jump-run toward you that ends with the bear slamming its paws on the ground). These are not a serious risk, though anything that brings a big male close to you is a life-threatening miscalculation. Of the thirty-four charges, only a handful were dangerous, and all of these were by mothers with young. Each time, I stood my ground, usually with my arms out, my head off to the side, and talked softly but audibly to the charging grizzly. I knew that looking directly at a grizzly represents a challenge, and the bear may choose to resolve it with a fight that I would lose. Four bears veered off. The others stopped abruptly, turned, and ran away (one of these first walked up to within five feet of me).

If you end up within a mother bear's critical distance—the area in which she will violently defend her cubs (sometimes as much as one hundred yards, though one hundred feet is more common)—don't shout, make sudden movements, or run. I know of two incidents where a loud shout or a roar from a human induced a mother grizzly to charge; the respective distances were 100 yards and 150 feet. The first case of shouting at the bear resulted in minor injuries. The second involved a large friend of mine who roared at a mother grizzly with two cubs on a well-used Glacier Park trail. The sow charged. The two young women he was hiking with flailed away at nearby trees they couldn't climb. My friend was carrying a small umbrella, which he popped as the grizzly charged. Standing his ground, he hid his large body behind the tiny parasol that was decorated with pink flowers. The mother grizzly slowed to a walk, approached the umbrella, and sniffed it before spinning on her heels and running off. No one was hurt.

Once in the backcountry of the Yellowstone Plateau, I tracked a female grizzly and her single cub and got caught in the open. A stiff wind blew in my face as I approached the tree line at the periphery of a broad meadow. The sow, who I had lost sight of, started coming out of the timber right at me, only thirty-some yards away. There was a solitary skinny dead tree just at the edge of the meadow, and I froze behind it. The mother grizzly hadn't seen me yet; she couldn't smell me because of the wind. But when she got within fifteen yards, she spotted me. She looked directly at me for fifteen or twenty seconds, waving her nose in the air trying to catch a scent. I didn't so much as blink an eye, literally, for all this time. Finally, she turned and herded her bear cub back into the trees. The only overt sign of agitation I saw was right at the end, when she loped off with her young: She made jawing movements with her mouth.

This blunder happened when I was relatively young and inexperienced. I don't know if this grizzly ever made me out as a human or not. The sow never smelled me. She looked right at me from thirty feet for almost half a minute. But I was absolutely still, not moving an inch, and my guess would be that—whatever she thought I was—I wasn't perceived as a threat to her cub. My carelessness was inexcusable and, again, I was very lucky. Had I moved or ran, it would have been another story.

I used to climb trees when I spotted grizzlies headed my way but still a long way off. I mean four hundred or five hundred yards, far enough so you could finish climbing to a safe height before the bear detected your presence. Now I just get out of their way and let them pass. The single biggest cause of grizzly mauling is people running and trying to climb trees after drawing the attention of bears. Fleeing triggers the bear's charge, and frantic climbing induces contact. The precise problem is that it's too late to climb a tree once the bear is aware of you. You can't get safely up there in time. If you doubt this, do a dry run and time yourself.

One of the most competent and experienced bear-persons I have ever known, a ranger in Glacier National Park, spotted a mother grizzly a few hundred feet away in the North Fork country of the Flathead River. He was right next to a climbable tree and tried to go up it. This man was a climber and athlete. The sow charged, pulled him from the tree, and nipped him up a bit. He didn't resist, and the bear family retreated into the forest, leaving him with minor injuries. Weeks later, the ranger went back to the site of the mauling with another friend of mine, and timed himself trying to scramble up the tree. The conclusion: There was no way in hell he could have made it safely up there. The fastest any human can run is 27 mph. A grizzly in Denali was clocked at 41 mph. Grizzlies run well up or down hills. Climbing trees is not an option if the bear knows you are there.

Should the bear make contact with you, the recommendation to play dead is sound: You will minimize your injuries by not resisting or fighting and taking your licks quietly. When you know for sure the bear is going to clobber you rather than bluff-charge, leave your pack on, drop to the ground (wait until the last fraction of a second before doing this), and curl up in a fetal position with your hands locked behind your neck. You may have to stay there quietly for a long time until you are sure the bear has left the scene for good. Do not move. This is tough counsel, but many have avoided further or serious injury by playing dead.

Is there any time in a grizzly attack when you should fight back, as you would in the case of a black bear attack? Much of the conventional literature tells you to fight back aggressively and fiercely if you think the attack is predatory rather than defensive. The problems with this dichotomy have previously been discussed. Though I personally know of no specific instance where a grizzly deliberately intended to kill a human, that doesn't mean it hasn't happened or couldn't. One could imagine an old, infirm, or wounded bear, not unlike the infamous man-eating tigers of India. Or, late in the year, a dominant, hungry, intolerant male grizzly launching a lethal attack. Timothy Treadwell might have run into one of these. Or, perhaps the grizzly that was involved in the Huffman mauling in Alaska or another cantankerous bear who happened to be in a particularly bad mood. And, of course, there are those fearsome stories of grizzlies prowling campsites at night. If you believe a bear will continue the attack no matter what you do, fighting back may be the only option left.

■■ Guns and pepper spray are most frequently mentioned as deterrents to grizzly attacks. In national parks it is illegal to carry firearms, and throughout grizzly country, dedicated zealots peddle bear spray as a panacea to all kinds of bear problems. As a design product, pepper spray is very impressive. Despite near mystical endorsements of capsaicin as bear deterrent, however, there are drawbacks, and most of them occur within the habitat of the human mind. Pepper spray should not be a placebo or a substitute in place of putting on your thinking hat. To the extent that carrying a can of bear spray decreases your sense of personal responsibility for entering bear country or diligence in engaging the land, it's false courage; you need to stay alert so you don't run into bears in the first place.

On the other hand, you may feel more confident walking down the trail with a can of cayenne spray, and in the unlikely case you have a run-in with a grizzly, perhaps you won't be as tempted to panic, run, or try to climb trees. Also, having a can of pepper spray next to you in a tent may help you get a better night's sleep—that and your choice of tent sites. Never camp in a place where bears feed, travel, or bed; this is perhaps the most important safety decision you make in grizzly country. Incidentally, I always set up in a tent regardless of weather. In prime grizzly country, I bushwhack back into the trees or thick brush, away from open areas, carefully checking out an area for any sign of bears—beds, trails, scat, plants grizzlies like. I only set up the tent if I find none. By choosing such a campsite (despite the lack of scenic views), I know that no bear will accidentally stumble upon me. In the highly unlikely and potentially terrifying event a bear comes in to check out the tent, I will be able to hear the animal coming. Night is the only time I expect garbage-corrupted grizzlies to slip into that fearsome predatory personality you read about in magazines. It's rare as hell, but it has happened. It feels good to roll over and see that can of bear spray lying next to the flashlight.

My own experience with pepper spray is limited. Read the literature: This product has been extensively tested. My usual advice is not to use one of these sprays during daytime encounters with grizzlies. It's not that pepper spray doesn't work—it does. I'd never ride subways in New York without it. And, of course, it deters bears most of the time. But, again, daytime encounters with grizzlies are defensive on the part of the bear. Most are mothers defending cubs. These protective grizzlies don't intend to kill or maul the unfortunate human who through his or her own carelessness gets too close to the grizzly. Pepper spray may deter nine out of ten bears, but I think it is possible that one day the tenth grizzly will seriously injure a human for no other reason than the bear was made more aggressive by pepper spray.

All hunters in occupied grizzly habitat should carry capsaicin spray. Most illegal and unwarranted killing of grizzlies results from armed hunters assuming a bear is a threat—when it isn't—and shooting it. Besides, as a deterrent, pepper spray is more efficient than a hasty bullet. The argument that guileless hunters surprise bears because people are silently stalking prey is hogwash. Good hunters are acutely aware of their surroundings. These illegal grizzly kills result from ignorance, incompetence, malice, or a combination of all three. The fact that authorities seldom prosecute these criminals encourages the incessant and senseless "self-defense" shooting of grizzlies. The lack of account-ability is unfortunate because it maligns ethical hunters who look beyond sport and technology for an authentic experience appropriate to the twenty-first century.

I like guns and have lots of them. But a long time ago, I decided not to carry guns in grizzly country. In my life, it became profoundly hypocritical for me to voluntarily invade the last homeland of grizzlies and consider blowing them away whenever events didn't unfold to my advantage. Also, you don't need guns there. In brief, a firearm will get you in more trouble with a bear than it will get you out. Short of shooting the bear that is actively chewing on you, for example, it is never quite clear when to begin shooting. Most of the official bear literature speaks of the necessity of guns for shooting charging grizzlies. Grizzly bears who charge—as noted above—are mostly mothers with cubs who will stop short of you if you inoffensively stand your ground. Shooting a female grizzly either removes a key reproductive bear from the population or, if you don't kill her, creates a more dangerous wounded animal who will either turn on you or become a menace for other people.

■■ If your sole wilderness objective is to avoid bear attack, and you don't want to stay home or get your exercise somewhere other than grizzly country, you could travel with a large pack of other like-minded travelers and make excruciatingly loud noises. That's the standard analysis: Hike in tight herds of a half dozen or more and hoot it up or blow off air horns so you don't surprise a grizzly.

You also probably won't see many bears. If this is your agenda, this human-centered approach works. People don't all go into grizzly country for the same reasons. Some consider the bear a nuisance, an unacceptable risk, at odds with the legitimate goals of recreation such as scenery, hiking, photography, fishing, and hunting. In terms of human safety, not stumbling onto a grizzly at close range makes a lot of sense. And if your argument is that you are protecting wild bears (who might be killed in management reprisals) by not getting mauled, you could be onto something.

In Montana's Glacier Park, the din of shouting and whistle blowing drifts down every major trail—as recommended. Screams and air horns, however, disrupt the life of virtually every animal in grizzly country. This practice is both unfortunate and unnecessary. The more you know about wild grizzlies, the less noise you will feel compelled to make. Experience will make you comfortable in confining the human voice to soft coughing or clicking stones in those situations where thick brush, running water, day beds, or carcasses might be involved. At other times, I prefer to travel quietly. Padding the margin of human safety out there any more than we already have is not worth the trade-off. Grizzlies and wildernesses are risky propositions, as they should be.

What if you want to experience a grizzly bear or see a bear without bothering it? Many commendable and adventurous souls go to the mountains for a "wilderness experience," which traditionally has something to do with respect for other people and animals, restraint, physical courage, a desire for encountering nature on her own terms, and solitude. The one unrelenting piece of advice (and sometimes regulation) is to never travel alone. Analysis of grizzly bear attacks supports this recommendation; the odds of being attacked in tight groups of more than four people are close to zero (indeed, all attacks by grizzly bears on the continent are statistically nonevents, averaging fewer than two a year, with a single person killed every other year). Bureaucracies and agencies also assume that encouraging noisy pods of ecotourists is the best way of not getting sued. Hence this advice persists most everywhere.

There is another point of view: A crowd of hikers is not safer than an alert, experienced solo traveler. Rather, groups are inherently louder and less attentive to the natural world. How do you think pre-Columbian hunters wandered through grizzly country for millennia? Solitude is the deepest well I know, and it is your right to drink from it.

It's been nearly forty years since I first lived seven months a year with the bears. That time in grizzly country has been a privilege, a sustained pleasure. There is nothing in my life that could replace the delicious sensuality of stumbling upon grizzly sign in a wild landscape. The great majority of this time I was alone, solitary, moving solo across the untrammeled topography we call grizzly habitat.

If you want to travel alone in bear country, do so, but with care and deliberation. The advice is, as always, to carry with you a sense of responsibility for entering grizzly country and the humility necessary to deal with it.

Despite all the advice in the world, a trip into griz country remains a crapshoot, an opportunity for the unexpected and the unpredictable. This is not a bad thing; you might even savor it. The overwhelming odds are that nothing will happen out there. But it could. At such heightened moments, your senses are honed with the palpable awareness of the element of risk. In the intimate presence of this animal, you may experience the ancient alchemy of fear concocted with awe and respect, which is a window to the connectedness of all life. The sum is a psychological entity exceeding its parts. This is the gestalt of meeting the bear. Coming out of a grizzly encounter is not a one-way street named survival. The psychic prospect of opening your mind to the bear's world is imbued with the invitation to transform your personal life. On occasion, something is exchanged, like an adventure that crosses a mythic boundary.

NOTES

Introduction
Servheen, Christopher, Stephen Herrero, and Bernard Peyton. "Bears: Status Survey and Conservation Action Plan." I.U.C.N., Gland, Switzerland, 1999.

The Black Grizzly
The Black Grizzly is both the name of an actual bear who Doug Peacock encountered in Glacier National Park and the name given to the fictional composite grizzly Doug has written about in this chapter.

Fear of Bears
Carney, Dan. E-mail to Andrea Peacock. 9/6/05.

Cheek, Roland. *Chocolate Legs: Sweet Mother, Savage Killer?* Columbia Falls, Mont.: Skyline Publishing, 2001.

Connelly, Marty. Telephone interview by Doug Peacock. Tape recording. 7/23/05.

Gilbert, Barrie. "Victims of Fatal Bear Mauling Should Not Be Blamed." *Los Angeles Times* (10/12/2003): M5.

Grigg, Kalin, and Jennifer Stark. Telephone interview by Doug and Andrea Peacock. Tape recording. 9/28/05.

Medred, Craig. "Deadly Ending: Treadwell, Girlfriend May Have Argued About Dangers." *Anchorage Daily News* (3/28/2004): A1.

Treadwell, Timothy. *Grizzly Diaries* (video). Discovery Channel, 1999.

Treadwell, Timothy, and Jewel Palovak. *Among Grizzlies: Living with Wild Bears in Alaska.* New York: Ballantine Books, 1997.

Treadwell, Timothy, to Roland Cheek. Correspondence. 9/14/03.

Van Daele, Larry, to Jeff Hughes. "Kaflia Bay Bear Mauling/Fatality Investigation Results." Memorandum (10/8/03): 5 pages.

Our understanding of the events surrounding Timothy Treadwell and Amie Huegenard's deaths were informed in part by incident reports of various Katmai National Park employees compiled under case number 3–109, as well as by reports of Alaska State Troopers in case number 03–74975.

The Photographers

Animals of Montana, www.animalsofmontana.com, accessed spring 1999 and 6/16/2004.

Associated Press. "Photographer Accused of Habituating Grizzlies." *Daily Inter Lake* [Kalispell, Mont.], www.dailyinterlake.com, 2/16/99.

Cambell, William. Personal interview by Andrea Peacock. Notes. 1999.

———. Personal interview by Andrea Peacock. Tape recording. 4/17/04.

———. www.homefire.com, accessed 5/1/2004.

Christian, Pat. "Monument Valley Photo Safari." http://patchristian .com, accessed 4/30/2004.

Cox, Daniel. "Captive Animal Photography: The Artist's View." www.naturalexposures.com, accessed 4/30/2004.

———. "In Focus: Cat in the Canyon." *Wildlife Conservation Magazine* (September–October 2001): 52–59.

"Daniel J. Cox: The Power and the Beauty." *Nikon Centre: Legend Behind the Lens.* www.NikonNet.com, accessed 4/30/2004.

Hoshino, Michio. "Diary Entry, 1978," from *Coming Home: The Photographs of Michio Hoshino* exhibit at the University of Alaska Museum website, www.auf.edu, accessed 5/2/04.

———. *Grizzly.* San Francisco: Chronicle Books, 1987.

———. "Natural Rhythms." *Alaska Airlines Magazine* (August 1991): 18.

Iseli, Carl. "Capturing the Beauty of a Snowy Day: Daniel Cox, Photographer of the Great Outdoors." www.takegreatpictures.com, accessed 4/30/2004.

Krasemann, Stephen. Personal interview by Andrea Peacock. Notes. Spring 1999.

Mangelsen, Tom. Telephone interview by Andrea Peacock. Tape recording. 6/15/04.

Manley, Tim. Telephone interview by Andrea Peacock. Notes. Winter 1999.

Moore, Shane. Telephone interview by Andrea Peacock. Tape recording. 5/24/04.

Murphy, Tom. Personal interview by Doug and Andrea Peacock. Tape recording. 5/5/04.

"NANPA Truth in Captioning: A Statement and Suggested Wording for Images." North American Nature Photography Association. Undated.

Revenko, Igor. Personal interview by Andrea Peacock. Tape recording. 2/20/05.

Rue, Leonard, Lee III. "Photographing on Game Farms." www.vivid light.com, accessed 5/18/2004.

———. Telephone interview by Andrea Peacock. Tape recording. 5/21/04.

Sartore, Joel. Cover photo for "Grizzly Survival: Their Fate Is in Our Hands." *National Geographic* (July 2001).

Schooler, Lynn. *The Blue Bear: A True Story of Friendship, Tragedy, and Survival in the Alaskan Wilderness.* New York: HarperCollins, 2002.

———. Telephone interview by Andrea Peacock. Tape recording. 5/18/04.

Simpson, Sherry. "A Short, Happy Life." *We Alaskans/Alaska Daily News* (10/13/96). www.adn.com, accessed 5/2/04.

Bear Keepers

Anderson, Casey. E-mail to Andrea Peacock. 1/27/05, 2/7/05.

———. Personal interview by Andrea Peacock. Tape recording. 12/7/04.

Chu, Ted. Telephone interview by Andrea Peacock. Notes. 12/13/04.

Department of Agriculture, Animal and Plant Health Inspection Service. *Code of Federal Regulations.* Title 9, Chapter 1, Parts 1–3 (10/21/2004).

Feldner, Tim. Telephone interview by Andrea Peacock. Notes. 12/14/04.

Hyde, Troy. E-mail to Andrea Peacock. 3/8/05.

———. Personal interview by Andrea Peacock. Tape recording. 12/04.

Idaho, Fish and Game. *Idaho Code*, Title 36, Chapter Seven, Sections 701, 703, 708, 709, 713 (2004).

———."Rules Governing the Importation, Possession, Release, Sale or Salvage of Wildlife." IDAPA.13.01.10.

Montana, Fish and Wildlife. *Montana Code*, Annotated, Title 87, Chapter 4, Part 8 (2003).

Pauli, David. E-mail to Andrea Peacock. 2/1/05.

———. Personal interview by Andrea Peacock. Tape recording. 12/17/04.

Seus, Doug. Personal interview by Doug and Andrea Peacock. Tape recording. 12/28/04.

Seus, Lynne. E-mail to Andrea Peacock. 12/10/05.

"Summary of State Laws Relating to Exhibiting Exotic Animals."
Animal Protection Institute, www.api4animals.org, accessed
12/14/2004.

U.S. Fish and Wildlife Service and National Oceanic and Atmospheric
Administration. "Policy Regarding Controlled Propagation of Species Listed Under the Endangered Species Act." *Federal Register*
65.183 (9/20/00): 56916–56922.

The Politics of Bear Biology

Alberta, Minister of Sustainable Resource Development. *Report on
Alberta Grizzly Bear Assessment of Allocation* (2002): 7.

Bartlein, P. J., C. Whitlock, and S. L. Shafer. "Future Climate in the
Yellowstone National Park Region and its Potential Impact on
Vegetation." *Conservation Biology* 11.3 (1997): 782–92.

Bjornlie, Dan, and Mark A. Haroldson. "Grizzly Bear Use of Insect
Aggregation Sites Documented from Aerial Telemetry and Obser-
vations," in C. C. Schwartz and M. A. Haroldson, eds. *Yellowstone
Grizzly Bear Investigations: Annual Report of the Interagency Grizzly
Bear Study Team, 2001.* Bozeman, Mont.: U.S. Geological Survey,
2002: 33–36.

Boyce, M. S., B. M. Blanchard, R. R. Knight, and C. Servheen.
"Population Viability for Grizzly Bears: A Critical Review." *Inter-
national Association for Bear Research and Management Monograph
Series* Number 4 (2001): 45 pages.

Craighead, John. Personal interview by Andrea Peacock. Tape recording. 6/2/05.

Craighead, John. "Status of the Yellowstone Grizzly Bear Population: Has It Recovered, Should It Be Delisted?" *Ursus* 10 (1998):
597–602.

Eberhardt, L. L., and R. R. Knight. "How Many Grizzlies in Yellowstone?" *Journal of Wildlife Management* 60.2 (1996): 416–21.

Eberhardt, L. L., B. M. Blanchard, and R. R. Knight. "Population
Trend of the Yellowstone Grizzly Bear as Estimated from Reproductive and Survival Rates." *Canadian Journal of Zoology* 72
(1994): 360–63.

Emmerich, John. E-mail to Andrea Peacock. 8/19/05.

Fremont County, Wyoming, Board of Commissioners. *Grizzly Bear Occupancy Management Proposal Deemed Socially Unacceptable.* Resolution 2004–20 (12/14/2004).

Friedman, Paul L. *Order of U.S. District Court for the District of Columbia in The Fund for Animals, et al., v. Bruce Babbitt, et al. 903 F. Supp. 96* (September 29, 1995).

Greater Yellowstone Whitebark Pine Monitoring Working Group. "Interagency Whitebark Pine Health Monitoring Program for the Greater Yellowstone Ecosystem, 2004 Annual Report," in C. C. Schwartz, M. A. Haroldson, and K. West, eds. *Yellowstone Grizzly Bear Investigations: Annual Report of the Interagency Grizzly Bear Study Team, 2004.* Bozeman, Mont.: U.S. Geological Survey, 2005: 92–125.

Greenward, Noah D., and Kiernan F. Suckling. "Progress or Extinction? A Systematic Review of the U.S. Fish and Wildlife Service's Endangered Species Act Listing Program 1974–2004." Tucson: Center for Biological Diversity, May 2005.

Haroldson, Mark. E-mail to Andrea Peacock. 7/14/05, 8/15/05.

Haroldson, Mark, and Kevin Frey. "Grizzly Bear Mortalities," in C. C. Schwartz and M. A. Haroldson, eds. *Yellowstone Grizzly Bear Investigations: Annual Report of the Interagency Grizzly Bear Study Team, 2004.* Bozeman, Mont.: U.S. Geological Survey, 2005: 24–29.

Idaho, Grizzly Bear Delisting Advisory Team. *Yellowstone Grizzly Bear Management Plan* (March 2002).

Idaho, Office of Governor. "Kempthorne Says Idaho Will Go to Court to Stop Feds Grizzly Bear Plan." Press release (11/16/00).

Jonkel, Charles. Personal interview by Andrea Peacock. Tape recording. 6/2/05.

Kaeding, L. R., G. L. Boltz, and D. C. Carty. "Lake Trout Discovered in Yellowstone Lake Threaten Native Cutthroat." *Fisheries* 21.3 (1996): 16–20.

Kaminski, Tim. Telephone interview by Andrea Peacock. Notes. 7/27/05.

Keating, K. A., C. C. Schwartz, M. A. Haroldson, and D. Moody. "Estimating Numbers of Females with Cubs-of-the-Year in the Yellowstone Grizzly Bear Population." *Ursus* 13 (2002): 161–74.

Kendall, Katherine. Personal interview by Andrea Peacock. Tape recording. 5/5/05.

Kendall, Katherine, and Robert E. Keane. "Whitebark Pine Decline: Infection, Mortality, and Population Trends," in D. F. Tomback, Stephen F. Arno, and Robert E. Keane, eds. *Whitebark Pine Communities: Ecology and Restoration.* Washington, D.C.: Island Press, 2001: 221–42.

————. "Whitebark Pine: Ecosystem in Peril," in E. T. La Roe, G. S. Farris, C. E. Puckett, P. D. Doran, and M. J. Mac, eds. *Our Living Resources.* Washington, D.C.: USDI, National Biological Service (1995): 228–30.

Kendall, Katherine, and S. F. Arno. "Whitebark Pine—An Important but Endangered Resource," in W. Schmidt and K. McDonald, eds. *Proceedings—Symposium on Whitebark Pine Ecosystems* (1990): 264–72.

Knight, R. R., B. M. Blanchard, and L. L. Eberhardt. "Mortality Patterns and Population Sinks for Yellowstone Grizzly Bears, 1973–1985." *Wildlife Society Bulletin* 16 (1988): 121–25.

Koteen, L. E. "Climate Change, Whitebark Pine, and Grizzly Bears in the Greater Yellowstone Ecosystem." *American Zoologist* 39.5 (1999): 113–14.

Langer, Jonathan. E-mail to Andrea Peacock. 8/16/05.

Logan, Jesse A., and James A. Powell. "Ecological Consequences of Climate Change Altered Forest Insect Disturbance Regimes," in F. H. Wagner, ed. *Climate Change in Western North America: Evidence and Environmental Effects.* Lawrence, Kans.: Allen Press, in review.

Logan, Jesse A. E-mail to Andrea Peacock. 7/21/05.

————. E-mail to Andrea Peacock. 10/09/08.

Mattson, D. J., and D. P. Reinhart. "Bear Use of Whitebark Pine Seeds in North America," in W. C. Schmidt and F. K. Holtmeier, compilers. *Proceedings of the International Workshop on Subalpine Stone Pines and their Environment: The Status of Our Knowledge.* U.S. Forest Service General Technical Report INT-GTR-309 (1992): 212–20.

Mattson, D. J., and Richard R. Knight. "Effects of Access on Human-Caused Mortality of Yellowstone Grizzly Bears." *USDI National Park Service Interagency Grizzly Bear Study Team Report 1991B* (1991).

Mattson, D. J. E-mail to Andrea Peacock. 7/19/05.

————. "Sustainable Grizzly Bear Mortality Calculated from Counts of Females with Cubs-of-the-Year." *Biological Conservation* 78 (1997): in press version.

Mattson, D. J., Bonnie M. Blanchard, and Richard R. Knight. "Food Habits of Yellowstone Grizzly Bears, 1977–1987." *Canadian Journal of Zoology* 69 (1991): 1619–29.

————. "Yellowstone Grizzly Bear Mortality, Human Habituation, and Whitebark Pine Seed Crops." *Journal of Wildlife Management* 56.3 (1992): 432–42.

McCaughey, Ward. E-mail to Andrea Peacock. 7/20/05.

Miller, C. R., and L. P. Waits, "The History of Effective Population Size and Genetic Diversity in the Yellowstone Grizzly (*Ursus arctos*): Implications for Conservation." *Proceedings of the National Academy of Sciences* 100.7 (4/1/03): 4334–39.

Montana Fish, Wildlife and Parks. "Grizzly Bear Management Plan for Southwestern Montana." *Final Programmatic Environmental Impact Statement* (October 2002).

Reinhart, D. P., M. A. Haroldson, D. J. Mattson, and K. A. Gunther. "Effects of Exotic Species on Yellowstone's Grizzly Bears." *Western North American Naturalist* 61.3 (2001): 277–88.

Robison, Hillary. "The Ecological Relationship Between a Rocky Mountain Threatened Species and a Great Plains Agricultural Pest," in C. C. Schwartz and M. A. Haroldson, eds. *Yellowstone Grizzly Bear Investigations: Annual Report of the Interagency Grizzly Bear Study Team,* 2001. Bozeman, Mont.: U.S. Geological Survey, 2002: 37–40.

Romme, William H., and Monica G. Turner. "Implications of Global Climate Change for Biogeographic Patterns in the Greater Yellowstone Ecosystem." *Conservation Biology* 5.3 (1991): 373–86.

Schwartz, Charles. E-mail to Andrea Peacock. 7/19/05, 8/16/05.

Schwartz, Charles, M. A. Haroldson, G. C. White, R. B. Harris, S. Cherry, K. A. Keating, D. Moody, and C. Servheen. "Temporal, Spatial, and Environmental Influences on the Demographics of Grizzly Bears in the Greater Yellowstone Ecosystem." *Wildlife Monograph* 161 (2005).

Servheen, Chris. Personal interview by Andrea Peacock. Tape recording. 6/2/05.

Sizemore, Dennis. Personal interview by Doug and Andrea Peacock. Notes. 1/12/05.

Tomback, Diana F., Stephen F. Arno, and Robert E. Keane. "The Compelling Case for Management Intervention," in D. F. Tomback, Stephen F. Arno, and Robert E. Keane, eds. *Whitebark Pine Communities: Ecology and Restoration.* Washington, D.C.: Island Press 2001: 3–25.

U.S. Fish and Wildlife Service. *Final Conservation Strategy for the Grizzly Bear in the Greater Yellowstone Area.* March 2003.

———. *Grizzly Bear Recovery Plan.* (1993): 33.

U.S. Forest Service. "Grizzly Bear Conservation for the Greater Yellowstone Area National Forests." *Draft Environmental Impact Statement* (July 2004).

Varley, J .D. and P. Schullery, eds. "The Yellowstone Lake Crisis: Confronting a Lake Trout Invasion." A report to the director of the National Park Service. (1995).

Willcox, Louisa. Personal interview by Doug and Andrea Peacock. Notes. 12/15/04.

———. Personal interview by Andrea Peacock. Tape recording. 8/11/05.

Wyoming Fish and Game. "Grizzly Bear Occupancy Management Proposal Following Delisting as a Threatened Species." (6/13/05).

———. "Wyoming Grizzly Bear Management Plan." February 2002.

Our understanding of how grizzly biology evolved during the years since the grizzly was listed as a threatened species was informed in part by the Interagency Grizzly Bear Study Team's annual reports, published from 1974 through 1993 under the auspices of the National Park Service, and from 1994 through 2004 by the U.S. Geological Survey (and variously titled "Yellowstone Grizzly Bear Investigations: Annual Report of the Interagency Study Team," as well as simply the "Annual Report of the Interagency Study Team").

Hunting Grizzly

Alaska Department of Fish and Game, Division of Wildlife Conservation. *Harvest Summary 2003–2004:* 7 pages.

Atcheson, Keith, and Jack Atcheson. Telephone interview by Andrea Peacock. Tape recording. 8/29/05.

Genovali, Chris. E-mail to Andrea Peacock. 12/30/05.

Lackey, Jebb. Telephone interview by Andrea Peacock. Tape recording. 7/27/05.

Mills, J. A., Simba Chan, and Akiko Ishihara. "The Bear Facts: The East Asian Market for Bear Gall Bladder." *TRAFFIC International* (1995).

Thomas, E. Donnall, Jr. *Longbows in the Far North: An Archer's Adventures in Alaska and Siberia*. Mechanicsburg, Pa.: Stackpole Books, 1993.

———. Personal interview by Doug and Andrea Peacock. Tape recording. 9/19/05.

Living with Grizzlies

Anderson, Sam, and Roseanne Anderson. Personal interview by Andrea Peacock. Tape recording. 8/21/05.

Carney, Dan. Personal interview by Andrea Peacock. Tape recording. 5/5/05.

Hunt, Carrie. Personal interview by Andrea Peacock. Tape recording. 7/26/05.

Interagency Grizzly Bear Committee. *Winter Meeting Minutes* (December 8–10, 2004).

"Not in My Backyard . . ." *60 Minutes.* Narr. Lesley Stahl. CBS (6/5/05).

Russell, Charlie. Personal interview by Andrea Peacock. Tape recording. 2/20/05.

Russell, Charlie, and Maureen Enns. *Grizzly Heart: Living without Fear Among the Brown Bears of Kamchatka.* Toronto: Random House Canada, 2002.

———. Walking with Giants: *The Grizzlies of Siberia* (video). Nature/PBS, WNET/thirteen (1999).

Timpany, Phil. Personal interview by Doug Peacock. Tape recording. 8/10/05, 8/11/05.

SELECTED BIBLIOGRAPHY

Busch, Robert H. *The Grizzly Almanac*. New York: The Lyons Press, 2000.

Craighead, Frank C., Jr. *Track of the Grizzly*. San Francisco: Sierra Club Books, 1979.

Craighead, John, Jay S. Sumner, and John A. Mitchell. *The Grizzly Bears of Yellowstone: Their Ecology in the Yellowstone Ecosystem, 1959–1992*. Washington, D.C.: Island Press, 1995.

Craighead, Lance. *Bears of the World*. Osceola, Wis.: Voyageur Press, 2000.

Herrero, Stephen. *Bear Attacks: Their Causes and Avoidance*. Guilford, Conn.: The Lyons Press, 2002.

McMillion, Scott. *Mark of the Grizzly*. Guilford, Conn.: The Lyons Press, 1998.

McNamee, Thomas. *The Grizzly Bear*. Guilford: Conn.: The Lyons Press, 1997.

Mills, Enos. *The Grizzly*. New York: Ballantine Books, 1919.

Olsen, Jack. *Night of the Grizzlies*. New York: Signet, 1969.

Quammen, David. *Monster of God.* New York: W.W. Norton & Company, Inc., 2003.

Shepard, Paul, and Barry Sanders. *The Sacred Paw: The Bear in Nature, Myth, and Literature.* New York: Arkana, 1985.

Storer, Tracy I., and Lloyd P. Tevis Jr. *California Grizzly.* Lincoln: University of Nebraska Press, 1978.

Wright, William H. *The Grizzly Bear.* Lincoln: University of Nebraska Press, 1977.

INDEX

ACKNOWLEDGMENTS

We greatly appreciate the contributions of everyone who helped in the research and writing of this book, but owe particular thanks to Trent Alvey, Pat Armstrong, Ashley Benning, Paul Bresnick, Jeff and Susan Bridges, John Burbidge, Bill Campbell, Marty Connelly, Lance and April Craighead, Roland Dixon, Lloyd Findley, Barrie Gilbert, Donna Greenberg, Pat and Beth Hagan, Shannon Hatch, Doug Honnold, Brian Horejsi, Mark Howser, Carrie Hunt, Heather Kilpatrick, Jack and Kathie Loeffler, The Lyons Press, Tom Mangelsen, David Mattson, Karen and Ian McAllister, Craig Mielke, Doug Milek, *Outside* magazine, Linda Papworth, Steve and Susan Prescott, David Quammen and Betsy Gaines-Quammen, Derek Reich, Holly Rubino, Charlie Russell, Chris Servheen, Doug and Lynne Seus, Dennis Sizemore, Dan and Carole Sullivan, Ellen Urban, and Louisa Willcox.

ABOUT THE AUTHORS

Doug Peacock is a renowned grizzly bear expert and nature writer. A Vietnam vet and former Green Beret medic, his memoirs, *Grizzly Years* and *Walking it Off*, chronicle the healing of his war-torn soul through his relationship with this quintessential carnivore. He is also the author of *¡Baja!* and served as the "wild grizzly consultant" for the classic 1988 Jean-Jacques Annaud film, *The Bear*. Doug also writes extensively for magazines, including *Audubon*, *Backpacker*, and *Outside*.

Andrea Peacock is the author of the critically acclaimed *Libby, Montana: Asbestos and the Deadly Silence of the American Corporation*. Her articles have also appeared in *Mother Jones* and *High Country News*. She is the former editor of the *Missoula Independent*. Andrea and Doug live in Livingston, Montana.

BOOKS BY DOUG PEACOCK

Grizzly Years: In Search of the American Wilderness
¡Baja!
Walking It Off: A Veteran's Chronicle of War and Wilderness

ALSO BY ANDREA PEACOCK

*Libby, Montana: Asbestos and the Deadly Silence of
an American Corporation*